William S. Phillips has painted most of the major
aircraft against backgrounds that tell an important story.

The detail from the above painting that appears
on the cover of this book is used by courtesy of
The Greenwich Workshop.

Barnstorming . . .

Flying after World War I was a rough and ready business. Landing strips were fields dotted with tree stumps and ditches, wind cocks were the direction cows' tails were pointing, maps were your instincts, and knowing the weather depended on your sense of smell.

But it was a whole world full of sky. You could buy a World War I surplus Curtiss JN-4D for a few hundred dollars, fit it with a temperamental but powerful souped-up Hizzo engine, and fly and fly and fly—always seeking new stunts, new thrills, and new limits. Country fairs and air circuses, stunt flying for movies, rum-running and smuggling—the sky was the kingdom, and flying was the rule of life.

The planes became faster and faster, the circuses and races wilder and wilder, and the pilots quicker and more skilled. Then came World War II. The barnstormers provided a vital nucleus of experienced, able pilots. Many became famous aces, and more than a few went on to become major figures in the development of aviation.

It's a little different now. The days of flying one jump ahead of the sheriff are over. Modern barnstormers run in air races using highly modified, ultra-powerful planes, and in high speed air shows, flying complex, intricate patterns executed with hundredths of a second precision. One thing hasn't changed, though.

The sky is their kingdom. It belongs to them.

THE BANTAM AIR & SPACE SERIES

To Fly Like the Eagles . . .

It took some 1800 years for mankind to win mastery of a challenging and life-threatening environment—the sea. In just under 70 years we have won mastery of an even more hostile environment—the air. In doing so, we have realized a dream as old as man—to be able to fly.

The Bantam AIR & SPACE series consists of books that focus on the skills of piloting—from the days when the Wright brothers made history at Kitty Hawk to the era of barnstorming daredevils of the sky, through the explosion of technology, design, and flyers that occurred in World War II, and finally to the cool daring of men who first broke the sound barrier, walked the Moon and have lived and worked in space stations—always at high risk, always proving the continued need for their presence and skill.

The AIR & SPACE series will be published once a month as mass market books with special illustrations, and with varying lengths and prices. Aviation enthusiasts would be wise to buy each book as it comes out if they are to collect the complete library.

BARNSTORMING

Martin Caidin

BANTAM BOOKS

NEW YORK · TORONTO · LONDON · SYDNEY · AUCKLAND

This edition contains the complete text
of the original hardcover edition.
NOT ONE WORD HAS BEEN OMITTED.

BARNSTORMING

A Bantam Book / published by arrangement with
the author

PRINTING HISTORY

Duell, Sloan and Pierce edition published 1965
Bantam edition / January 1991

ISBN 0-553-28818-0

Published simultaneously in the United States and Canada

PRINTED IN THE UNITED STATES OF AMERICA

OPM   0 9 8 7 6 5 4 3 2 1

In stark memory of that crazy flight
across the Atlantic in 1961
and that very long night in Santa Maria,

this book is for

BILL MASON

Acknowledgments

The author is indebted to Mr. R. C. "Tex" Marshall of Portales, New Mexico, for the loan of personal papers, letters, photographs, and other documents to prepare outstanding cross-country barnstorming material; to Don Dwiggins of California, for the loan of invaluable archives, guides to rare sources, and his superb historical material on Frank Clarke and other stunt men, and for his kind permission to utilize these sources; to Russ Brinkley, former barnstormer and pilot, and one of aviation's great historical sources, and especially for his invaluable assistance in providing hitherto untouched documents and personal reminiscences of the barnstorming era; to Dr. S. H. Kleiser of Lebanon, Pennsylvania, for assistance in locating many survivors of the barnstorming era; to Julian Messner, Inc., publishers, New York, New York, for permission to quote material from *Old Soggy Number One,* by Hart Stilwell and Slats Rodgers, copyright 1954 by Julian Messner, Inc.; and especially to Herbert M. Mason, Jr., without whose long and dedicated assistance, research, and coordination of material this book would not have been possible.

MARTIN CAIDIN

Contents

1

The Way It Was

The rules were simple enough—even if they were loosely applied and even more liberally interpreted. Landing fields were a gift of God and the sweat of a farmer's back, and part of the game was guessing about the low stumps or the ditches that you couldn't see. You played the wind by gosh and by guess, and you looked for cows with their rumps pretty much pointed in one general direction, for there's no better natural wind sock in the business than the tail end of a cow; the stronger the wind the more likely you were to see all those cow-rump wind indicators.

It was flying, said some of the old-timers, the way that God intended man to fly. He had to be a part of his machine, to wear his airplane instead of climbing into it. And the old-timers were hard to argue with. You came to know the sky by instinct and feel and smelling the weather almost as much as you did by studying the clouds and hunting for the signs splashed across the sky. You looked for the wispy signature of coming storms in mare's tails way up in the high blue, and you watched the way the anvils formed atop the looming cumulus. You looked for wind shifts and at night you stared, half out for beauty and the other half for knowledge, at the ring that might form around the moon, for there was a gentle wash of ice crystals in the night heavens that also told you of coming weather. Sometimes you smelled the air as much as you studied your altimeter to watch for pressure changes. And when you talked to the farmer who came warily from his barn to stare at your strange wood-and-fabric contraptions, you tried to draw him into personal conversations, for every

1

farmer with his corns and aching shoulder and his intimacies with the habits of animals was, without knowing it, a superb meteorologist.

As to where you would go in your caravan with the hump-backed dromedaries that bore wings and coughed and snarled behind the big flashing wooden propellers—why, anywhere and any place close enough to roads and a center of population would do. If you could get the wheezing, staggering planes in and out of the field, and entice people to come out to watch you skid and careen on the ground and through the air, and let them know that yes, you and a couple of the others were sure-enough likely to get killed right before their eyes, and if you were smart enough to collect your money *before* your death-defying aerial show—why, you were in the barnstorming business!

You were a member of the aerial circus troupe, a vagabond with wings. Your calling card was your profession itself; the kids were awed about and wild over the very fact that you were a live, real, sure-'nuff *aviator*. The girls, the young girls with wide eyes and long lashes and bodies that were something to see beneath their thin summer cotton dresses, etched clearly in the wind . . . well, they sort of took your mind off flying and led you to think about barns and hayfields beneath the summer moon. But that always had to be for later; for now there were the farmers and their wives and families, and the storekeepers and the local businessmen, and you had to look at them shrewdly and play your crowd smartly.

You learned how to act on the ground with cunning; no matter what you might personally believe, you made friends with the kids and you also made friends with every confounded hound and mixed-breed dog that came loping up to the field. For the country folk would sometimes judge a man as much by the way their dogs reacted as they would through forming their own opinions. And even if you hated the curs, you never showed it. You were first, last and foremost a showman, and if you were good enough and you had the breaks with you—your engines didn't crack or the big props splinter, and you set up your show when there was a high pressure area and clear skies instead of low and scudding black masses directly overhead, and some other smart barnstorming sonofabitch who was a thief and a pirate hadn't come in here first and ruined everything—why, you'd eat well and **sleep comfortably (maybe even in a bed instead of under a** wing), and stash away an extra bottle or two of fine bourbon, and have enough money to pass around to the whole crew and also pay for gas and spare parts. Even the sheriff might not demand his little stipend on the sly before you ever did anything in his territory; once in a while you ran into a decent sort, with the star pinned carelessly to his shirt.

When the breaks went that way, then the whole world had never looked quite so good nor the sun shone so clearly, nor that body etched in the windblown cotton dress beckoned so enticingly.

You were a barnstormer and the sky belonged to you, and you came to earth to please the folks and make them laugh and gasp a little and even shriek when they thought someone was about to be splashed across the ground. You were a showman and you put on the grandest show ever seen anywhere on *or above* the whole world. You had three rings for your performance like none that man could ever build.

Your high-wire act took place hundreds of feet in the sky, and your Big Top changed every day with the height of the fleecy clouds that sparkled in the high blue. You came to live with the problems of an old, many-times repaired engine that might quit at just the wrong moment. An engine failure was *always* at the wrong moment when you had a friend standing on the upper wing, because he might just be standing on his hands or was about to transfer to another plane, sans parachute, or performing some insane stunt that the crowd loved; any sudden acceleration could throw him wildly off balance and if that happened, at just that wrong moment, the crowd might be witness to what they secretly hoped to see—the blood of a man pulped out of his body as it smashed into the unyielding earth.

These facts of life, unpleasant as they were, went along with the good times. It was a kaleidoscopic mixture of both. Subject to the whims of weather, the perils of an empty wallet, the idiosyncrasies of mechanical devices and the unpredictable fancies of the audience, the barnstormer pursued a life of vicarious thrills not calculated to rest, comfort, or longevity.

John Moisant was one of the first airmen to realize that the threat to longevity came from sources other than the fragile and wicked contraptions of the year 1910 that he and his friends flew. It was in the summer of that year, Moisant's lips pressed tight and his anger fair to choking him, that he faced an angry Texas crowd. They were not only angry, but had the means to vent their emotions, as they demonstrated in thunderous fashion by drunkenly firing volleys into the air from ugly-looking Colt .44's.

It was at that moment that Moisant, who led what was probably the first real barnstorming troupe in the world, realized that those who flocked to the impromptu airfields to watch the show were not necessarily air-minded. Their lusty yells and roars, punctuated with a mixture of breaking beer bottles and booming shots into the air, seemed almost to be a response to their smelling the blood they had come to see splashed wetly across the grass.

With this stage setting there began the wild and often frantic era of barnstorming. It was an era ushered onto the American scene along a high-breaking wave of enthusiasm for flying and for things of the sky. It fired the imagination of the entire country, and immediately it was starred with its heroes and its favorites, and conceived of by the public as essentially a spectator sport staged and carried out by wealthy and eccentric daredevils.

Moisant, for example, was a practicing architect until the flying fever shot through his veins. The fascination for the air was to prove his end shortly afterward when, trying to please a screaming and theatening crowd, he lost his life in a crash. Moisant thus provided the ultimate thrill to his audience, the spectators witnessed the gore they had come to see, and Moisant unknowingly—and quite unwillingly—helped to create a precedent that would endure for decades.

Our story of the barnstormers of America is, essentially, that of the flying circus. For this is the other, and perhaps more fitting, name for the barnstormers. Theirs was a circus. Their purpose, their intent was to please, to entertain, to thrill and to excite their audiences, made up of men, women and children of all ages and the inevitable dogs. Their skill was not nearly so important as the manner in which they demonstrated risks and thrills with their aircraft; the drunk act that appeared dangerous, but was not, was far preferred to the superb, and perfect, demonstration of aerobatics which might quickly bore, and thus greatly annoy, the rowdy onlookers.

The greatest wellspring of barnstormer pilots and mechanics proved to be the aerial debris of World War I—debris in the form of dashing young men, trained only for combat flying and the knowledge of blazing death should they lose an aerial duel, filled with the morbid excitement that it engendered, who came with discharges fresh in their hands into the unsettling world of peace. These were the men who had to *keep* flying in order that they might live, for to live was to them to experience life to its utmost. And whatever were the hazards and the perils of barnstorming, it could not, of course, be equated with the finality carried in the twin Spandaus of a Fokker. There was also the matter, somewhat more prosaic but nevertheless demanding, of being able to eat—so the young warriors turned to the air and the promise it held for their living and their livelihood.

Barnstormers, flying mostly Jenny biplanes left over from the scrapheap of 1918, hopped and struggled across the face of America from one pea patch to another, in the process caroming from cloud to cloud, dashing down valleys, and much too often barely evading mountains obscured within cloud and fog. They thrilled millions of people at large fields

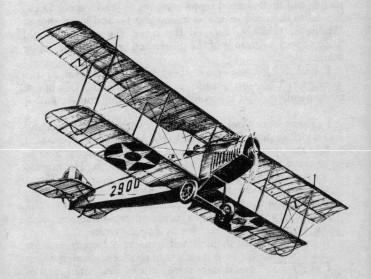

Jenny (Curtiss JN-4)

and isolated pastures with such acts as wing-walking without parachutes, snatching handkerchiefs from the tops of waving weeds, low-level aerobatics that included deliberately scraping wing tips in the dust or "slapping" the ground in wing-tip-to-wing-tip maneuvers, smoke-writing in the sky, spectacular delayed parachute jumps while trailing behind them a white plume of flour from XXX sacks. They jumped from one plane to another, engaged in mock dogfights, made wild takeoffs and landings, clowned around, and effected World War I flying togs. They stood patiently for pictures with local boys and femmes and, whenever they could do so, took up the locals for quick rides, for whatever ready cash it might bring.

Often, these scratch air shows were barely one jump ahead of the sheriff, and only a stagger away from mechanical failure.

And while the barnstormers lived their precarious existence, they introduced aviation to the most distant corners of the country. It was this success in publicity—despite the rash of financial failures—that brought an unexpected respectability and a new meaning to the air circus. The United States Army, faced with the problems of "selling" aviation to the people and their elected representatives in Washington, D.C., turned to the ready-made audience that flocked to air shows. Whenever possible, decreed the brass, the military would utilize every advantage of the glitter and sparkle of the "open house" air show.

Robert S. Johnson remembers what it was like in the summer of 1928, just outside the town of Lawton, Oklahoma; he remembers what it was like to look up into the sky and—

There were three of them. Each with double wings and a whirling propeller flashing in the bright Oklahoma sun. I first saw them as they rolled on their backs, arcing over to inverted flight to begin a plunge to the earth. The ground seemed terrifyingly close to the descending trio. For a moment the sun gleaming off their whirling propellers made three simultaneous flashes of light in the sky. The beautiful winged machines increased rapidly in size, slicing downward from the blue as a single entity.

I did not know it then, and I would not appreciate for years to come the rare spectacle of precision piloting which I observed. I could only stare, utterly fascinated, as the three little pursuits seemed to rush headlong to oblivion, about to dash themselves into the ground.

Then I heard their cry. A shrill and weird sound; the painful whine of the engines, whirling propellers faster and faster as they flung the little planes through the air.

The three pursuits were almost into the ground, when the planes were wrenched from their dives. Three hands, operating as one, gripping control sticks in three different cockpits, flawlessly timed, hauling back. The trio snapped up into the sky. I followed every motion, struck dumb, staring, as the pursuits zoomed up and over, twisted and turned intricately as if a single hand were maneuvering them, then floated mysteriously in an invisible balance of their wings and of gravity.

In later years, I have been able to look back and recognize this scene as *the* moment: the very first time I had ever *seen* an airplane. The fascination of these three snappy pursuits, orange wings bright in the sun, alive, incredibly agile, held for the eight-year-old boy I was then the barest promise that would one day be fulfilled in a way not even the dreams of youth could imagine.

What was it like at one of these air spectaculars, at the circus to which one and all were invited? As Bob Johnson recalled:

I'd seen the airfield many times before, but it was only a big empty space with high and thick buffalo grass covering the field. There were plenty of those in Oklahoma, and Post Field was nothing special. But something was going on; hundreds of people milled around the field. And so many cars! They were parked, it seemed, by the hundreds. Wagons and horses were also on the field, making the whole place look like a county fairground. Clouds of dust boiled up and . . .

There! In the sky! Three tiny airplanes . . .

That military air show with its spectacular three-ship formation flight was the first for Bob Johnson; it was not the last. For the barnstormers were to come through Lawton, and with the fire singing in his veins, the mention of an airplane was enough to bring the youngster and his friends rushing to the local fields. The magic words had been shouted: "The barnstormers!"

Johnson recalled:

On several occasions, barnstormers came to town to put on flying shows. They landed on large open fields near Cameron College, bringing in all different kinds of two-seat and three-seat open-cockpit biplanes. Our entire troop would go out to the fields to help the barnstormer pilots. In addition to their daredevil acts, the pilots took up passengers for rides. We helped people to and from the planes, and aided the barnstorming group in controlling the crowds.

All this for the promise that we would each get a ride in a plane before the day was over. The promise was worth it; especially to me! Not even the hot, dusty, and crowded fields dampened my enthusiasm, or passing the day without food, or carrying water buckets, or dashing about madly to deliver messages. *Anything* was worth it—just so long as I'd get my chance to fly.

But somehow whenever my turn came to fly, the day would be over. The pilot would grin in a friendly way and say, "Sorry, kid. Got a schedule to keep; I've gotta leave. Maybe next time." And away he would go.

I was twelve years old when the Great Day arrived. I should say the Great Night. It couldn't have come as a bigger surprise.

A giant (it was a giant in those days) Ford Tri-Motor transport—corrugated skin, three roaring engines, and blazing with all manner of lights—landed at the municipal airport. That pilot sure knew his business.

The Tri-Motor was lit up like a county fairground. Lights had been fastened to the wings and the fuselage until it looked like a big carnival show floating through the night skies.

Dad took the entire family down to watch the Ford taking off and landing at the airport with passengers, for short flights over Lawton, to let the townspeople see what the place looked like at night. It was an eerie sight, and I think perhaps that pilot had once worked at a circus. As the plane flew over the edge of town the pilot released a string of Roman candles. Immediately the sky blossomed forth with a procession of fireballs, brilliant and multicolored, illuminating the entire valley. This pyrotechnic display, of course, caught the interest of people in the town, who flocked by the hundreds to the airport just to see what was going on.

Ford Tri-Motor

And then, out of the blue, Dad asked *the* question.

"Son, would you like to go up?"

Would I!

I climbed aboard. The interior of the Tri-Motor was dark. The smell of gasoline and oil came to me; I was aware of the feel of the metal. Wonderful sensations all; I drank in every moment.

I was tense and breathless as the pilot hit the switches. The engines ground over slowly and abruptly burst into a shattering roar. The airplane shook and vibrated as it rumbled over the ground, taxiing across the field and swinging into position for takeoff. From the window I could see the wing outlined dimly against the night sky, and an engine with blue exhaust flames ghosting out from it.

The moment arrived. The roar deepened, increased in volume as the pilot fed power to the engines. I felt a sensation of sudden and rapid movement . . . a rumbling as the airplane accelerated in its dash over the ground.

I expected—a sudden upward rush, I suppose, a feeling of soaring. There was none of this. Without prelude, the vibration and the bouncing just stopped. The engines roared sweetly, a new note, a throbbing, in their voice.

I could hardly believe it—I was flying! Nose glued to the window, eyes wide open and hungry, I stared out and down at the lights so far below us. I could see for miles and miles. Far off in the distance lights gleamed through the night. I had a feeling of enormous depth, of a vast and endless plain stretching before me.

All too soon, the motion of the airplane changed. We were returning to earth. Wind whistled past the wings and the engines descended in volume to a friendly sigh. A rumble, ever so slight a jar as the wheels touched. Then the vibration and bouncing on the grass as the pilot taxied back to the operations shack.

We had been aloft for fifteen minutes—the best quarter hour of my life!

Perhaps the reader has recognized the name of Robert S. Johnson. The young boy who saw his first airplanes in the sight of the diving Army pursuits, who made his first flight in the big Tri-Motor of a barnstormer, went on to earn his own wings. And then in World War II, behind the controls of a mighty Thunderbolt fighter, Bob Johnson in eleven months shot down twenty-eight German fighter planes in aerial combat to rank as one of America's greatest fighter aces.

Many of the men who flew the aerial circus troupes as barnstormers later became world famous. Men such as Frank Hawks and Charles Lindbergh began their aviation careers with the gypsy fliers. Others, who flew as much and often for many more hours and with a far wider range of aerial activity, are not so widely known. But their stories—such as that of Tommy Walker, whom we will meet in a full chapter devoted to this unusual cloudbuster—give us thrilling and intimate glimpses of what barnstorming really was like in terms of behind-the-scenes views and personal trials, tribulations, and wild fun—as well as constant brushes with death.

Men like Walker were barnstormers before and after World War II, and they were a very special breed who performed the full gamut of aerial circus antics. They added to the curriculum of the three rings by both flying and performing

Republic "Thunderbolt"

parachute jumps. They accepted immeasurable risks by deliberately smashing airplanes into houses, cars, trains and special obstructions. They leaped from cars to planes, from planes to cars, and jumped back and forth from planes to boats—to say nothing of switching planes in flight.

Out of World War II came a rash of new barnstorming pilots, jumpers and stuntmen. For a while the sport, as now it had come to be considered, faltered and seemed committed to the musty pages of history. There were a few aerial shows that toured the nation, but they were bereft of finances, weary of overdue bills, and afflicted with the rash of a postwar America. The rash was suffered in a plague of high-density areas within which flying was strictly controlled and new regulations rushed into being which were enough to snarl any pilot and his airplane in ground-chaining frustration. And what could the old circus troupe do with the people of a nation who were overwhelmed with supersonic jets, hydrogen bombs, rockets to the moon, and the other glittering paraphernalia of this new and frightening world?

And then, something seemed to happen. Despite the nuclear mushrooms that stalked into the high heavens, despite the fiery ignition of wars across the globe, despite even the dazzling impact of men rushing into space, there began anew the fascination for "things with wings that fly."

Barnstorming today is experiencing a tremendous, vital resurgence. The patched-pants jumpers have been replaced with flashy skydivers, the new planes are superb, the organization is getting smart. But the drunk act is still with us, and showmanship is more important than it ever was before. The pilots are sensational, their aerobatics flown with razor-sharp precision. But the crowd still demands the element of thrill, the smell of danger, the chance that death will spring, full-blooded and hot, into the rings of flight.

Every now and then the crowd is rewarded, and there is the ghostly background of the roar of the Roman Colosseum when the stretcher bearers carry away into a shiny new ambulance the lifeless form of one who didn't make it, who paid the crowd in the coin they had secretly coveted.

That's the way it was a long time ago. It's the way it is today and—fervently hope the barnstormers—the way it will always be.

To live . . . is to live life to its utmost. These men wouldn't change it for the world.

②

"A Pack of Jackals"

Ernest Hemingway once commented that "nobody lives their life all the way up, except maybe bullfighters." In this reckoning, Papa Hemingway neglected the likes of men like Lincoln Beachey, whose challenge was in the high blue, not in the sand, and who faced an opponent reeking with oil and gasoline that was infinitely more treacherous and lethal than the earthbound half-ton of hide, horn and gristle.

There were times when it appeared that the Fates leaned over backward, perhaps to the point of strain, in order to accommodate Lincoln Beachey. The Good Lord knows that at every opportunity possible Beachey flaunted all the laws of and odds against survival; he shouted into the winds for the gods of survival to do him their very worst: If, as many of his contemporaries swore, Beachey manifested such utter contempt for death, it was because he had such a passionate desire for living.

Throughout a life we can only mourn as depressingly brief, Beachey enjoyed popularity with neither his close associates nor any chance acquaintances who stumbled upon his fiery temperament. This man, who gained the awe of millions, was surly, ill-tempered and gruff, and totally impervious to insult and kudos alike.

Like all truly dedicated enthusiasts with a grim single-mindedness for their chosen pursuits, Lincoln Beachey lived his twenty-four hours of every day only for himself and his cherished obsession: the breathtaking new element of the sky.

* * *

In 1905 Beachey was eighteen years old and well possessed of the personal traits which were to bring him both curses and cries of praise. Schooling lay behind him; Beachey considered himself a man among men and ready, if not eager, to grapple with the mysteries and the intricacies of flight. Less than eighteen months had passed since those epochal moments on the windswept sand dunes of Kitty Hawk, when the Wright brothers electrified—not the world, certainly—a few men of vision with the awesome possibilities inherent in the mating of the internal combustion engine with a brace of wings and awkward control surfaces. Beachey was one of the younger men, one of the very few, whose imagination flamed with the possibilities of flight.

But Wright airplanes in those days were distressingly few and, to a young man of limited financial means, terrifyingly expensive. Faced with this problem, which he considered temporary, Beachey turned his back on the Wright airplanes and contemplated his personal construction of a balloon.

It proved enormously helpful to his ego and his exuberance that Beachey was a grimly determined individual. The youthful would-be aeronaut constructed a clumsy, elongated gas bag which, with a touch of reality, he contemptuously christened the *Rubber Cow*. With only a bare minimum of instruction and the sketchiest understanding of how, or even why, the monstrosity was able to fly, Beachey prepared to invade the skies. In the fashion for which he was to become famous, he flung into a canvas bag spare socks, one shirt, one pair of suspenders, assorted crude tools, and patching materials, and set out to storm the country.

No one would dare to hazard the odds for Beachey's surviving the first dozen miles, the first strong winds and turbulence, even his own crude workmanship—but the youth prevailed and his ugly machine continued to sustain itself and its pilot through whatever the elements and the odds had to offer against him. Beachey's *Cow* became a familiar sight to many thousands of people who gathered at exhibition grounds, pea patches, roadsides, untended fields, or even in the midst of real-life cows, wherever the irascible "balloonatic" took it upon himself (or the whims of his cantankerous machine) to descend.

But if the farmers expressed great delight with the misshapen balloon, Beachey failed to share their wide grins. Although no one could argue that the *Cow* was unpredictable, the swollen gas bag offered little in the way of thrills. It did not take long for Beachey to build up deep anger at the manner in which he was forced to puff and wheeze his way over the countryside, his *Cow* trembling and quivering like a sick animal in the summer heat, while other men drank deeply of the heady wine of true flight in real airplanes. Beachey was as much fed up with the screaming crowds of children and the inevitable barking dogs who greeted his unpredictable descents as he was with the groaning passage of his contraption. He wanted to *fly*.

Reprieve came in 1910, several years after Beachey embarked on his misadventures with the *Cow*. After several attempts to join the Glenn H. Curtiss Exhibition Company, Beachey succeeded in convincing Curtiss of his merits as an airman. Curtiss, one of the better and well-known pilots of the time, was determined to build a new industry on his own. To build, one must sell, and Curtiss was acutely aware that to sell, he must convince a torpid public and the nation at large that his flying machines were the finest made and that they had an almost limitless variety of thrills to offer (the state of flying being what it was in 1910, this claim rang with authenticity). To pursue his goals with success, Curtiss assembled in one group the best pilots available. Impressing upon them the need for the desired impression with the public, he sent his men and airplanes off to barnstorm the circuits where there seemed the most likely prospects for airplane customers. Curtiss was convinced that what advertising could never do, the actual thing would accomplish: he hoped to separate the customer from his cash with the sight of the mighty biplanes streaking by at the breathless speed of forty-five miles per hour.

With his summons to Curtiss crammed into a pocket, Beachey disposed of the sagging and hated *Cow*, and set out at once for Buffalo. Shortly after his arrival, in the midst of the experienced pilots working for Glenn Curtiss, Beachey climbed arrogantly into the seat of a spanking new Curtiss Pusher. He was eager to fly the new machine, and unquestionably far more eager to "show up" the others by demonstrating to the watching Curtiss that he had made the best possible decision in hiring what was undoubtedly the greatest pilot in the world. That pilot being, of course, none other than Lincoln Beachey.

Several of the older and more experienced pilots, in open

friendship, offered Beachey their own hard-earned sugges-
tions on how best to control the tricky pusher. Beachey
snorted in open contempt and waved them off. He was not in
need, he sneered, of advice on how to fly an airplane. The
others looked at each other, shrugged in resignation, and
walked across the grass field to stand alongside Curtiss, who
had fastened a critical eye on the new pilot.

Beachey strapped himself to the seat, grasped the wheel,
shoved full power to the machine, and immediately began
weaving an erratic path down the field. Ever impatient,
Beachey cursed the slow acceleration of the airplane; his
impatience took over common sense and Beachey sought to
get up in the air where he felt more at home than this
bumpy, ragged crawl across the ground.

He did not ease back on the long control column; not
Beachey. Instead he hauled back suddenly and the airplane
lurched upward at a steep angle in response to the control
movement. The Curtiss shot into the air, but lacked enough
speed and lift to remain there. For a moment it sagged in the
air. Then the wings gave up trying altogether, the nose
dropped sickeningly and the airplane dropped down at a
steep angle to crunch into the grassy earth.

The watching pilots sighed at this demonstration of the
inevitable, then dashed across the field to pull the unharmed
Beachey from the wreckage.

Curtiss gave Beachey a withering look, and suggested that
he confine his skill in the future to balloons. Before the
hot-tempered Beachey could retort—and thus probably ruin
his chances forever with Curtiss—another pilot stepped in
between the two men. He recognized from the cut of Beachey's
jib that despite the crude demonstration, here was a natural
pilot; he interceded and prevailed upon Curtiss to give Beachey
another chance.

It was not very long afterward when a second Curtiss
biplane lay in splinters and crumpled fabric on the field,
while Beachey truculently refused to offer any defense for his
latest demonstration of how to wreck a new airplane. Beachey
clamped his lips shut, stuck out his jaw and glowered, waiting
for Curtiss to bring down the axe. But the man who would
become one of the giants of the aircraft industry had already
decided that such brashness might well be turned to good
account. He kept Beachey on the Curtiss payroll, hoping that
the young man would find his way by himself before manage-

ment's patience and the stock of available biplanes were exhausted.

Immediately after the two crashes, things "fell neatly into place" for Beachey. He caught the feel of powered flight with a smoothness that delighted Curtiss and amazed his companions, and in quick order Beachey emerged as the most daring pilot on the team.

In those early days of flight, most men who braved the air considered that getting from Point A to Point B in what was relatively a straight line was enough for any flier. Not Beachey; still glowering at the world, he was jealous of the eagle's ceiling and the agility of the hawk. These he sought to imitate.

In 1911, within a year of his joining Curtiss, Beachey set his sights on the altitude record. The extent of his determination is found in the fact that he swallowed his pride and went to Curtiss' engineers to seek advice on how he, Beachey, might become the highest-flying pilot in the world. The engineers quickly pulled from their desks fuel consumption tables, spread out their papers, and began plotting curves. Dryly, they explained that the cutoff point in fuel consumption lay far below the established record, and that the only wise course for Beachey to follow was to forget the whole thing.

Undaunted, Beachey retired to his room to mull over the problems he had just heard explained to him as insurmountable. He was convinced that somewhere, somehow, the engineers had committed an error. And then it dawned on Beachey that the cutoff point predicted by the engineers was predicated on the fuel supply needed to power the airplane to its desired altitude *and then back down again.* Later that day Beachey grimaced (the nearest he had ever come to a smile, said his associates) his thanks to the engineers, but without word of explanation, and sauntered away. He had the key he wanted.

When Beachey announced soon afterward that he was ready for the record attempt, the Curtiss engineers gathered in a flock to watch the fruitless preparations; they reiterated again and again the inexorable laws that govern powered flight, and demanded to know why Beachey was so determined to attempt what was obviously impossible. Beachey snarled and barked out that engineers' imaginations ended when the index ran off their slide rules. Just watch, he snapped, and perhaps they might even learn something about flying.

Beachey personally studied the filling of his fuel tank, and allowed the cap to be screwed down tightly only after the gasoline began to run down the sides of the filler hole. He capped the tank, carefully wiped off the excess fuel, clamped his cap down to his ears, lowered his goggles and bellowed: "STAND BACK!"

The others scattered, and Beachey fired up his engine. He listened carefully to its coughing rumble, revved it up and down a few times, and then immediately rolled down the field. As quickly as the airplane reached flying speed Beachey was airborne, pulling heavily from the grass.

Beachey's "key" was simplicity itself; he intended to climb steadily until he exhausted the fuel within the tank. At this point the airplane would fall off into a glide. Beachey would return to the earth in a powerless descent and accomplish a deadstick landing, a normal procedure for the day.

For what seemed like hours watchers on the field craned their necks to watch the pusher biplane diminish steadily in size, until it was no more than a pinpoint, the faintest dot, that seemed to be swallowed up by the sky. The men on the ground strained their eyes and squinted through binoculars. They watched the little craft seem to hang suspended in space. Then perceptibly it grew larger in size as Beachey sailed it down through scattered clouds.

"He never made it," muttered an engineer with dripping sarcasm. "Complete waste of fuel."

If Beachey had not "made it," then he must have found *something* up there to raise his spirits, for the biplane came to earth as a falling, whirling dervish. Beachey stunted in wild abandon as he slipped and slid earthward. When the pusher came close enough to the ground for its engine to be heard, the onlookers gasped—that mad, insane pilot had lost his engine! There was no reassuring, clattering sound so familiar to these men . . . only the sighing of the wind as it sped through the bracing wires.

Beachey flung his machine about until the earth loomed up to snare him in his antics; quickly he leveled the wings and sighed down from the air to a near-perfect landing. As he climbed awkwardly from the seat he furiously swung a varnished wooden box—the barograph.

Incredulously, while Beachey heaped abuse upon them, the engineers studied the line on the graph. There could be no mistake, and there wasn't any. Lincoln Beachey had shattered the altitude record! He had dragged his frail machine to the unprecedented height of 11,600 feet, risking his life in a two-mile fall through the sky in a powerless airplane. As he stalked away from the scene, the men watching him depart knew that from this moment on, nothing could or would hold back Lincoln Beachey.

Before the year was over, Beachey stood the aviation world on its ear by challenging the awesome might of Niagara Falls. On a day that would have grounded a sensible duck, Beachey shot into the air and then roared down, below the thundering cascade of water and spray.

Thousands of fascinated onlookers lined the cliffs and gasped as Beachey dropped lower and lower. Spray lashed his flimsy airplane, and as the machine rocked and tossed in the turbulent air he all but disappeared in the perpetual mist of the Falls. Beachey's three-wheeled gear was a scant twenty feet above the churning water when the audience saw the airplane dip down still lower. It was an act of madness, yet Beachey had no choice; he had to skim the foaming water in order that he might clear the nether span of the great Niagara bridge. He pounded on through the bridge, burst through the span and clawed upward through the mist with superb timing.

Afterward, Beachey expressed his contempt for his audience. They had come not to see history made, he snorted, but hopefully to see a damned fool get killed.

Beachey did his level best to fascinate and to please the morbid—or so it seemed. He made a laughing mockery of caution, scorning the safety of altitude as a warrior in the midst of battle flings away his shield. In a thousand different and breathless ways he courted the finality of death. His Curtiss hugged the contours of the earth with all the clutching grasp of an impassioned lover, breaking away only to avoid crashing headlong into trees or telephone poles.

One of his observers was spellbound at Beachey's antics. It was none other than Orville Wright, after witnessing a reckless display of skill by Beachey, who stammered out for all to hear, "why, he's the most wonderful flier I ever saw—he's the greatest aviator of all!"

From no less a man than Orville Wright, the fiery Beachey accepted this compliment with what might just have passed for grace. But on another occasion Beachey openly insulted

the Governor of California, a man Beachey scorned as un-
qualified to pass judgment on real "birdmen."

Following a wild, on-the-deck exhibition of suicidal flying,
Beachey slid to the earth and was met by the Governor who
came to greet him with outstretched hand. Astounding the
by-standers, Beachey swept his eyes up and down the length
of the state's highest official much as though he were eyeing a
serpent, then turned his back on the man and strode off,
leaving the hand of welcome thrust foolishly outward in thin
air. The Governor, cut off by Beachey's conduct directly in
the midst of a flow of praise, slowly retrieved the spurned
hand and watched Beachey clamber back into his airplane.

Once again Beachey dragged the pusher into the air, and
the crowd stirred among itself, wondering just what this
insolent pilot might have in store for them. They quickly
found out, for Beachey had built himself into anger and then
whipped it to white heat, for what reason no one seemed able
to fathom. At low altitude Beachey clattered over the bleachers and the colorful banners flapping in the breeze.

Something fell from the airplane to flutter down to the
ground. A man ran out to retrieve the object, and held aloft a
coat. People stared at one another blankly.

The Curtiss pushed rapidly across the field, banked steeply
into the wind, and roared back in a wide circle toward the
bleachers. There was a flash of white and a second object
fluttered away from the airplane, floating lazily to the ground.
And then a third object detached itself from the machine and
followed the same flip-flopping descent.

Then it was clear enough to them all. The pilot was slowly
stripping himself in flight!

The bizarre performance continued as the airplane circled,
until it was more than apparent that Beachey, in the sky,
must be reduced to no more than his shorts and his socks. In
the stands the ladies began to blush furiously, while the men
about them pounded their knees and guffawed. The bright
splash of red on the face of the Governor, however, had
nothing to do with embarrassment; it was a clear signature of
pure rage.

Beachey landed near his hangar, taxied up smoothly to his
parking place, cut the switch and leaped nimble to the grass.
Standing almost nude in the sunshine, he held his pose for a
moment, a gesture of brazen defiance to one and all. He
lifted a corner of his mouth and growled to his mechanic:

"*Now* I'd like to hear what that damned stuffed shirt has to say about Lincoln Beachey!"

So saying, Aviation's Angry Young Man marched barefooted, head held high, into the hangar to borrow some clothes.

There existed no challenge of the sky that Lincoln Beachey considered beneath his talents to refuse. The immortal Barney Oldfield, king of the automobile racers, once flung the speed gauntlet to Beachey; the angry young flier flew immediately into a rage and responded in a fashion that terrified both the hard-bitten Oldfield and the thousands of spectators who rushed to watch the event. Oldfield would race on the ground and Beachey was to beat him—or attempt to do so—with his airplane.

The car roared out onto a long track, trailing smoke and roaring with the unmuffled blast of its racing engine. Beachey let Oldfield select the pace—full throttle, as it turned out—and then calmly played piggyback with the startled automobile driver as he raced around and around the track. The gaping onlookers could see Oldfield hunched within the cockpit of his open car, his neck jammed well down between his shoulders. It seemed an unnatural position for the great Oldfield, but it proved more necessary than comfortable—for Beachey was apparently doing his very best to sink his wheels into the seat alongside Oldfield.

Even on the turns, where the slightest miscalculation would have meant a flaming death for them both, Beachey handled the airplane with unbelievable skill, rocking lightly in the air bouncing from the car and over the ground. From a distance the embattled pair resembled a contest between a hawk and a jackrabbit, the winged hunter toying with a prey that could run only in a counter-clockwise direction.

When the hair-raising duel with its splattering roars ended, Barney Oldfield admitted readily that his admiration for Beachey's reflexes and depth perception while at high speed knew no bounds. But to race again with that madman? Ah, that he would have to consider *most* carefully!

At the great San Francisco Exposition, Beachey flirted openly with death by slamming his B-model Curtiss Pusher through the narrow confines of Machinery Hall. Fly? There wasn't a shred of doubt but that Lincoln Beachey could *fly*. But what else could he do?

He could *land,* that's what!

San Franciscans, ordinarily an urbane, blasé lot, were jolted rudely from their aplomb when the irrepressible Beachey began to forsake landing fields—and took to setting down his clattering contraption on the tops of the Bay City's biggest office buildings. Even Glenn Curtiss had to admit that Beachey had far exceeded his wildest notions of what could be done with one of his airplanes.

The city's feminine population in particular afforded Beachey a tremendous reception; his Viking jaw and sneering, go-to-hell attitude worked wonders with the opposite sex, and he was a hero to his smitten audience. Secretaries shattered their office routines as they shrieked with girlish glee at the sight of the quickly familiar biplane buzzing through the city at dangerously low altitudes, rocking and buffeting in the thermals and wind currents that tumbled among the buildings. But the alto squeaks turned quickly to screams of fear when the clattering Curtiss plunged toward the windows, pulling up sharply at the ultimate moment of imminent disaster to bump down on the graveled roof over their heads!

On September 1, 1913, there occurred in distant France an event that sent Beachey into a monumental rage: Adolphe Pégoud became the first man in the world successfully to fly an aircraft upside down. If this weren't insult enough in the eyes of Beachey, the crafty-looking, mustachioed little Frenchman had added insult to injury by looping his Blériot in full view of incredulous witnesses. The press notices of Pégoud were fabulous, and Beachey was stunned and mortified.

Why hadn't *he* done it first? Why hadn't he even *thought* of being the first man to fly in such a manner! Beachey's supreme ego and pride simply could not accept the fact that there were, after all, other aviators in the world who were possessed of both skill and daring. Those who knew him best of all would agree that Lincoln Beachey felt, deep within his innermost thoughts, that other aviators should be banned from the skies, and he be left unbothered and unmolested to astound the world.

Galled to action by his own seared ego, Beachey flogged the Curtiss workmen with threats and, astounding the workmen, even with pleas to rush through a special design which was capable of being looped. Lashed on by his acid tongue and purple vocabulary the workmen rigged a ninety-horsepower

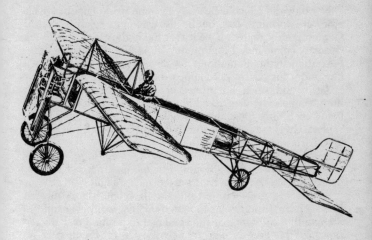

Blériot

engine to a new aircraft that suited the impatient Beachey in
every respect.

Thus it was that, only a few weeks after Pégoud had
astounded the aeronautic world and become a candidate for
the history books with his feat, Lincoln Beachey flew his
Curtiss in inverted flight. On Thanksgiving Day, while his
friends seated themselves before sumptuous tables, Beachey
was in the air. He took the Curtiss to eight hundred feet,
checked his straps, and pushed the nose of the airplane
down. With the engine thumping away merrily the airplane
swiftly built up speed. Beachey hauled back on the controls,
holding full power with the throttle. The Curtiss rushed
higher and higher until the nose was vertical; then it began to
come back, continuing until the airplane was completely in
inverted flight. Pulling back even more on the column, Beachey
brought the nose down and as the earth rushed back into
view to replace the sky, he chopped power. Seconds later the
airplane rushed out of what was a perfect loop.

Looping now became a passion with Beachey. Within the
twelve months after his first loop, he took the new Curtiss

through additional loops *more than one thousand times*—and all from the suicidal low altitude of eight hundred feet!

Not only did Lincoln Beachey become world famous for his epic barnstorming feats, but he also came into relative wealth. Contemporary reports have it that the high-priced, low-flying Beachey commanded a minimum of $1,500 per special demonstration flight. Sometimes he flew two and three times a day under his contracts to appear before massed audiences.

Again and again he proved that his arrogance knew no limit. Somebody once asked him how he dared to risk his life flying such flimsy machines. Beachey snorted and snapped in reply: "Hell, man, if you can find somebody to fit an engine on a barn door, I'll fly *that!*"

And he meant it. Had the opportunity been there, Beachey would have made the attempt. But his luck ran out on him before he had the occasion to make such a flight.

Always the great crowed-pleaser, Beachey was requested to star in the program for the air show that would kick off the mammoth San Francisco International Exposition of 1915. To Beachey the crowds were a necessary evil. Frequently he swore at the public, damning them for their bloodlust, and comparing them to "a pack of jackals, eager to be in on the kill."

But it was the jackals who paid for the freight, and Beachey knew it. This didn't stop him, however, from bleeding the jackals for as much as the freight could get. Quoting an outrageous fee, to which his customers agreed quickly, Beachey told the Exposition officials that he would give their sensation-seekers the kind of thrill they would not easily forget.

It was a prophecy that proved to be tragically accurate.

That day in March was washed with brilliant sunshine, from a shining blue sky unmarred with a single cloud. Only vestiges of brisk winter winds remained to whip the bay waters into harmless whitecaps. Thousands of people were on hand to witness the aerial extravaganza promised them, and the atmosphere gained the excitement of the circus by the brassy cannonading of the band on one side of the grass field where the airplanes were ranked.

Shortly before noon Beachey climbed with his now-famous confidence onto the narrow seat of his Curtiss. He tightened the wide strap across his abdomen, placed his feet on the stirrup-like rests that jutted out from the axle of the nose wheel, moved the clumsy controls back and forth several times, and then signaled for the engine at his back to be fired up. With all eight cylinders settled down to a satisfying roar, Beachey pronounced himself ready for flight. Mechanics yanked away the chocks, and the biplane began to move down the field to the swelling cheers of the crowd.

Beachey proved from the start that he was going to make this the star performance of all his many demonstration flights. He pulled the Curtiss off the ground in a steep climbing turn that pushed the lifting capability of the wings and the engine to their maximum, hanging on the edge of a stall as he clawed around to a different direction from takeoff.

With only a minimum of altitude beneath him, Beachey flung his machine through the air as though making clear his contempt for the vast throng below—as well as for the engineers who had assembled the airplane with all due regard for the stress limitations inherent in the design. Abruptly, Beachey leveled off and headed for the Bay.

He climbed smoothly to what was for him a relatively high altitude—about one thousand feet—and then pushed forward on the control wheel. The Curtiss dropped its nose and arrowed straight for the glittering water below. The howl of the engine mixed with the growing shriek of the wind blasting past the airplane, until there issued from the sky a single cry of speed. Faster and faster plummeted the fragile machine . . .

The horrified onlookers saw disaster strike even before they heard the sound. First they witnessed the lazy motion of the wings coming free from their mounts and folding back in a slow-motion scene. Then they heard, seconds later, the distant cracking sounds as the wings tore themselves free of their bracing struts and wires.

In clear view of the thousands of people, the tiny figure in the sky struggled madly with the wheel in what was a desperate but futile effort to wrest the machine from its screaming dive. The actions were pure reflex, the motions of the skilled artist moving by instinct, for Lincoln Beachey had no control surfaces left with which to change the direction or the speed of his last moments of flight.

There was one ultimate sound to be heard; the sickening *smack* as the scanty remains of the airframe struck the water. The massive bulk of the engine and radiator smashed into the back and head of the helpless pilot, and the flotsam of machine and man disappeared quickly beneath the surface of the Bay.

Later, bits and pieces of the craft floated to the top of the water and bobbed with the choppy waves. But Lincoln Beachey lay dead many feet below.

At only twenty-eight years of age, Beachey's anger and the bright, wonderful spark of life that made this man finally was extinguished. Yet, as he had promised, he had given the hated "pack of jackals" something they would remember all the rest of their lives.

The Gallic Crew

The study of crowd psychology—or the actions of a mob repeated in no other way in human behavior—is a myriad subject unto itself. But from this chaos of behavior, there can be no doubt of the truth of Beachey's judgment of the crowd at air shows: many of the paid admissions to the aerial circuses came with the secret hopes of seeing one of the pilots come a cropper. There is nothing that matches the ultimate end.

To state unequivocally that many of the onlookers wished, even subconsciously, to see men *killed* would be an unpardonable simplification. The fact remains, however, that most crashes in the early days of flight were fatal. To desire the accident could hardly be other than to covet the invariably grisly fatality that ensued from the crunching of metal, wood and fabric against the softer and yielding substance of the human pilot. An appreciation of the piloting skill involved in and demanded by these air shows was not something grasped by the audience; such understanding lay beyond their shadowy knowledge of flight.

Another famous American barnstormer, John B. Moisant, who led a heterogeneous collection of fliers, had this point driven home to him in rather spectacular fashion.

Moisant was a forty-year-old architect who enjoyed his profession at the drawing boards by virtue of his being able to abandon the surplus of straight lines at any time he desired; this freedom was guaranteed by a fortune Moisant had made in mining. A further disturbance to his career came in 1908, when Moisant stared spellbound at the Wright brothers' performance on the outskirts of Paris, France. Moisant was bitten deeply with the flying bug and could hardly wait to fling his well-financed energies into the realm of the air. A handsome and debonair sports enthusiast, Moisant immediately enrolled in the Blériot school of aeronautical instruction. Quickly he demonstrated skill and competence, and shortly thereafter was rewarded with his certificate as a *pilote-aviateur* from the *Fédération Aéronautique Internationale* (FAI).

With the barest minimum of flight time penned in his logbook, Moisant quickly established an aviation "first." On August 16, 1910, he carried a frightened passenger all the way from Paris to Dover, happily braving the multiple hazards of the cross-channel flight in a machine that would have been risky just to circle the local airport. The airplane bounced, rocked, swayed and sailed up and down in the strong air currents so prevalent over the English Channel, but Moisant and his rickety craft persevered and arrived safely in England.

On his return to the Continent Moisant conceived the idea of forming an aerial circus that would go on an extended tour to amaze, confound, and excite many thousands of gaping onlookers. And what better way to do this than to travel across the vastness of his native land? With its huge size and growing population, the United States beckoned to the ideas of Moisant. The new pilot carefully selected four of the most noted pilots in France, promising a breadth of adventure, much flying, and financial reward. Pilots and planes were carried aboard an ocean liner, and on their westward voyage the members of the aerial troupe planned great things for their immediate future.

It was while touring the sprawling southwestern United States that Moisant learned, in the bluntest fashion one might imagine, that instead of merely braving the risks and hazards of the new era of flight, he and his pilot companions were also clay pigeons in a spectator sport, to which the spectators responded with alarming enthusiasm.

Moisant and his Gallic crew—Edmond Audmars, René Simon, René Barrier and a man who was to become almost immortal, Roland Garros—came to know at firsthand the many characteristics of the American southwest. They rolled on jouncing railbeds from hamlet to village, from cowtown to bustling new city, from water stop to whistle stop, carried along a special train that was jammed with dismantled airplanes, a mass of spare parts, collapsible hangars, portable bunks, personal clothing and gear, emergency rations, secret caches of fine French wine, and the human flotsam that were to assist the pilots.

"We were veritable Bohemians," Garros explained, and then added with a touch of sadness, "and we were no different from high-wire walkers or weight-lifters."

Moisant's rough-and-ready crew one late afternoon wheezed into the outskirts of a small Texas town near Houston. The winds blew, strong and blustery, but a show had been scheduled for the following morning, and all hands worked hard and late into the night to set up the hangars and aircraft for the coming performance. That night the men lay exhausted on their cots, bodies caked with dust and sweat, and listened with growing apprehension to the keening of the wind that swept noisily across the flatland. Moisant was the last to pass into slumber, his mind assailed with doubts: Would the winds abate? Could they fly the show tomorrow? And if they didn't fly, how would the crowd—ah, the mob—react in their disappointment? What if . . . ?

Perhaps Moisant slept finally after shaking free of the thoughts that spun in his mind. After all, if the winds were so high that flying was patently impossible, it would be as obvious to the spectators as it was to the pilots. That conclusion proved to be a classic error.

The first sign of daylight brought all Moisant's fears rushing back to him. He struggled up from his cot with a background of banshees and moved quickly outside his tent. The first thing that happened was enough to wreck his day: the wind snatched his hat from his head and sent it tumbling across the field like a thing alive. The tent flaps of the canvas hangars seemed to have gone mad with rippling movement, and they cracked steadily like the sound of rifle shots. The wind was so strong that Moisant was forced to narrow his eyes to slits to avoid the stinging particles of sand that whipped furiously through the air.

The men collected together to share their dismal thoughts. Dust clouds boiled along the ground, and sent haze floating up above the horizon. Perhaps as the day went along . . . ? But no; by noon the wind was still at almost the same strength with which it had howled at daybreak. The men ate lightly of their lunch and collected in an unhappy knot, fidgeting near the hangars, while the mechanics remained gratefully within the canvas, away from the wind.

Alfred Moisant, the pilot's brother and business manager of

the aerial troupe, shouted out a question—which everyone had asked himself the entire morning—that had all the overtones of a plea: "Can we go ahead with the show?" He flung an arm around to take in the periphery of the sprawling field where several thousand people had gathered almost unnoticed by the pilots, in their shared misery at the weather. Alfred Moisant had done his advance work too well, it seemed, for the audience was much larger than anyone had expected. The faint hopes that the stormy winds might keep the crowds at home vanished; apparently the Texans were accustomed to this infernal shrieking of air.

John Moisant studied the sky, bracing himself against another fresh onslaught of wind. "No!" he shouted in reply. "It would be suicide to send up men in winds like this!"

His brother brooded over the words, then shrugged in resignation. "All right, John," he said, "you know best. I will see what I can do with this crowd." His shoulders slumped as he walked across the grass to approach a cluster of red-necks; then he began his explanations of why there could be no flying that day.

The pilots looked on with growing feelings of apprehension. From the violent gestures and head-shaking of the cowhands it was obvious they were not accepting gracefully the explanations of Alfred Moisant. Indeed, the words of the manager were met with roars of outrage, a stream of blasphemy, and shouted threats. Moisant did his best to placate the Texans; he offered to refund any money paid out by the purchasers of tickets.

The Texans proved singularly unresponsive to all his explanations and his pleas for understanding. With his continued words the bellows of anger grew louder, the gestures more violent, the cursing more colorful and then, as if to punctuate their arguments with a final word, there came the sudden and unexpected thunder of .44 caliber revolvers being discharged freely into the sky.

Money? To hell with their blasted money! This crowd didn't want their money back; they wanted action. And, by God, if Moisant and his lily-livered fancy pants couldn't provide action with their airplanes, then action would be found through the hefty revolvers and, just perhaps, a little spilling of blood.

In between the smacking of lips against open-necked bottles there came drawling cries and shouts of "Cheats!"

"Thieves!" "Damned dirty furriners!" More Colts were unholstered and a fusillade of lead erupted with explosive thunder from the milling spectators. Narrowed looks and gestures in the direction of the pilots brought Moisant's flying crew to make their decision in a hurry.

Recalled Garros: "It was a matter of choosing between death by revolvers of large caliber or death by an airplane. *Alors,* we preferred the airplane, a device with which we were far more familiar."

While the crowd cheered the signs of activity on the part of the pilots—cheers which sounded like good-natured but meaningful threats to *keep* things going—Garros took to the air. As his airplane started to roll the mob roared out with the thunder of massed voices and volleys of shots from their Colts. The takeoff was one long moment of fright to Garros, as the brutal winds cracked hard against the machine, and flung his fragile *Demoiselle* into and out of control with heart-stopping impacts of blustery air.

The takeoff, to his watching friends, was not so much a matter of how well the skillful Garros could handle the featherlight monoplane, but whether he could keep himself from being dashed into a tumbling pile of wreckage.

Severe blows shuddered through the airplane's framework as Garros struggled above the ground. Then he swung into two wide circuits of the field, his upwind passage a labored crawl, and his downwind move a blur of speed created by the high winds. As he banked around the field, remaining as low as possible to please the crowd, his wingtip barely scraping over the dusty soil, his associates feared for his life. A single error and the end would be at hand.

Finally Garros slammed the *Demoiselle* back onto the earth, fighting desperately to keep control of his flighty steed. He sat immobile in his seat, white and drained of energy, as the mechanics dashed out to clutch his flimsy craft and prevent the winds from hurling it through the air and onto its back.

The crowd rewarded Garros for his masterful flying with bellowed cries of "Coward!" and a fresh thundering volley of lead. In open disgust of his audience, Garros turned his back and stalked away.

René Simon next took to the air and held the other pilots spellbound with a five-minute exhibition of low-level aerobatics that by every law of flight should have ended in a splintering fatal crash. Instead, Simon flew through the gusty winds with the grace of an angel, and ended his performance in a flawless upwind landing, touching down like a feather to terminate the show. The crowd responded with a chorus of boos and curses. Then, with a final ragged volley of lead, the crowd melted away.

They were still disappearing over the horizon, trailing their windblown plumes of dust, while the Moisant pilots were hurriedly packing their gear and making their own tracks away from Texas.

As they gratefully left the scene of the near-debacle behind them, the pilots pleaded with Moisant to return to Europe. There, they stressed, flying was looked upon as a gentleman's sport, and not held in the obvious drunken contempt displayed by the Texas barbarians. Why, they cried with eloquence to the silent Moisant, should men such as they be required to fulfill the role of Christians in an arena filled with filthy lions?

Moisant smiled and at last replied. People were slow to learn, he would admit, but even the Americans eventually would come to see flight for what truly it was: a new challenge that one day might serve its purpose as a stepping-stone even to the stars.

There was never to be either appreciation or fulfillment of the dream for this man who peered so far into the future. Moisant's lifetime, despite his confidence in the long tomorrow, proved to be tragically brief. On December 31, 1910, John Moisant plunged to his death while trying to please still another shouting, gesticulating mob in New Orleans. After they buried his mortal remains, the citizens named their municipal airport in his honor.

The heavy (even ultimate) price paid by the early barnstormers in their bids to thrill the crowds did not escape the attention of the public. Aviators came to be universally regarded as "flying fools" who had replaced common sense with their own brand of madness. Aviation, most people agreed, could never rise above the level of the sandlot carnival—and this meant to remain at about the lowest position in society. Certainly this madness of flitting about the sky, with all the danger of tumbling lifelessly over the ground, could never achieve the status of a national pastime. To the majority of Americans, in those formative years of flight, aviation was all too often equated with an early death.

One of the earliest, and the greatest, spokesmen for aviation was Glenn H. Curtiss. In a vain effort to educate the general public to the true meaning and purpose of man's taking to the skies, Curtiss stated in a widely distributed publication that:

All improvements are accepted slowly and with protest by man. New inventions always meet with opposition, advanced ideas with adverse comment. Nevertheless, nothing worth while ever fails to triumph, finally, when its worth is actually proved and recognized by the world.

It is said that the first baby carriage brought with it a storm of protest and scorn. Some even went so far as to predict the death of its occupant and the ultimate destruction of the home as a result of its adoption and use.

It is a fact, too, that laws were passed limiting the speed of the first railway trains to eight miles per hour.

The automobile was believed by some to be only a mechanical means to suicide. Yet how quickly have all these natural but strangely perverse prejudices been dissolved by the ever brightening light of knowledge and progress.

Only a short time ago a man made his will, bid his family a tearful farewell and went aloft with a feeling akin to that supposed to exist in the heart of a soldier going into battle. . . .

True, there are accidents, occasionally, but seldom are these due to flying alone. Stunts in the air, as on the ground, often result in fatalities, but even these are less frequent than those occurring with other forms of transportation, as can be easily shown by reference to comparative records. Flying is not a hazardous occupation, rather it is a safe one. A few daring pioneers have conquered the air. It is now yours to possess and enjoy.

It was not long after he wrote these words that the Fates made a cruel mockery of Curtiss and his message; the sky became anything but a place to "possess and enjoy."

Man was just truly spreading his wings when the sky became a lethal battleground.

(4)

Fledglings of Death

It was in the year 1910 that the *Commandant* of the French Staff College made a significant remark that was not destined to be remembered with favor. *Le Commandant* declared with all the pomposity of an old-guard brass hat that "the aeroplane is all very well for sport, but for the army it is useless." It was to take only four years until these became very bitter words indeed.

In the first onrush of exultant German military forces smashing their way toward Paris that tragic fall of 1914, it was the aeroplane—one solitary machine—that saved the capital of France and perhaps the nation itself.

The Germans under von Kluck had plotted a maneuver that, executed with great precision and timing, would have smashed with irresistible force against the battered French Army, and rolled it like a worn-out rug up against the wall of the Swiss Alps, there either to surrender or be decimated by the steel of Germany. The maneuver required, above all else, concealment from the French. It was in regard to the latter aspect that there appeared the breach in the German master plan; a lonely pilot in a slow-moving parody of an airplane crossed over the moving German forces, stared with wide eyes at what lay spread before him, and rushed as quickly as his clattering engine would take him back to his base. The aerial reconnaissance of this fragile winged machine stirred the French into frenzied action and enabled a scratch force of poilus—hastened to the Front in a wildly careening fleet of taxicabs—to crunch into the German flank and bring to a grinding halt the stampede.

There could have been no more dramatic demonstration that the airplane was anything but useless for the military, and the combatants of World War I were quick to seize upon this new device as a welcome replacement for cavalry. Horses had proved to be terribly vulnerable to the German machine guns and, across the vast European battlefront, their reconnaissance value was far outweighed by their vulnerability as targets for the German soldiers. Thus aircraft were rushed in increasing numbers to the front to serve as the high-flying and far-ranging new eyes of the army. Those commanders who had only a short time before regaled their dinner companions with their scoffing at the clumsy machines now were begging frantically for everything with wings on it. The situation was clear enough—without eyes carried to great heights the terrible guns chained to the earth were blind, and their massed firepower ineffective.

Within a few short weeks after the opening of the grisly holocaust that was to sap the strength of nations for four years, the aviator leaped from obscurity to unexpected prominence. Those who flew became the darlings of the combat arena; their exploits, no matter how trivial in the face of the staggering calamity that ground under the lifeblood of a continent, were ready grist for the propaganda mill and an idolizing press. An entire battalion of infantry might be wiped out in a few futile, savage minutes of horrifying bombardment and attack—a scattering of these men to die in protracted agony on barbed wire, where they hung for another day or two until death released them—but the communiqués (and hence the newspapers) would report laconically that "nothing of significance occurred today along the Western Front." A hundred fine young men might be spitted on bayonets and only their friends within the trenches would know of their final sacrifice.

But the single aviator who engaged in an aerial duel with the enemy and shot down his opponent could easily find his picture and exaggerated details of his adventure spread across the front pages of the papers of six nations.

Crouching in a hole where the smell of putrefaction thickened the air and choked the lungs, a French sergeant named Jubert observed just such a singular aerial combat above the heights of ravaged Verdun. Commented Jubert: "For these happy pilots, triumph or defeat gains equally the cheers of those who die beyond glory of any sort. They are the only ones in this war who have the life or death of which one dreams. . . ."

These early combat pilots whose exploits brought them lavish mention in the mass-circulation dailies of Paris found themselves besieged in yet another fashion denied the hapless soldier trapped in the muck of the trenches. The airmen were the romantic heroes of the land, and they were bombarded with an increasing quantity of fan letters, most of which seemed to be penned in a delicate hand upon perfumed stationery. Those who survived the first year or two of the war were wont to rise to yet new heights; by virtue of skill and the roll of the dice of war most of them were now aces, or even aces two or three times over. Their length of duty enable them every now and then to return to civilization, and they discovered in their mail invitations from famed actresses of the day to hurry back to Paris, where they might pass their precious hours of leave in what can only honorably be described as captivating circumstances.

The aviators of World War I wore uniforms of distinction; often designed by themselves, they were a tribute to imagination and what might best attract the femme, as well as representing their sneers to the ever-present shadow of flaming death. Live, live well, and as much as possible in as short a time as possible, was their code. Circumstances aided them in this pursuit; in the French Air Service the airmen's pay, by infantry standards, was astronomical. Why, a sergeant-pilot earned the magnificent sum of thirty cents a day!

Not a few of the reconnaissance and fighter pilots of the early war days were well known to the public before donning their uniforms. Many of them, in fact, had already started to claim a starring role in aerial exhibitions. These were the men who had received their F.A.I. pilot certificates before the war, and they found fast company in well-known racing car drivers and sportsmen of other types. They were all of a distinctive breed and wherever possible they tended to come together in their own lofty cliques—in which death was always the invisible participant in the "ultimate sport" of combat high above the earth. Many of these men were well educated, and experienced in the ways of the world. Among their ranks were men of considerable wealth; some were millionaires.

With this mixture of personal ingredients, it is not difficult to understand why they were looked upon with a broad spectrum of emotions, encompassing the more obvious ones of wonder, awe, admiration, respect and, above all, envy.

This last element of the regard in which they were held—envy—would have been tempered radically had the grimy foot soldiers spent a week or two living the life of the aviator and, especially, had the soldiers been able to engage in the cold hell of combat in the highest arena of all.

While many of the stories of the pilots' adventures, on the ground and away from their airfields, were true, they applied only to a few of these men, and then portrayed but a fraction of their wartime lives. The day-in, day-out living conditions for most of the frontline pilots were far from the idyllic repose imagined by the infantryman. During the winter of 1916–17, the coldest ever recorded in France at the time, one group of pilots changed their duty sectors and discovered with a shock that there were neither sleeping quarters nor mess facilities waiting for them. In fact, they had become the common military casualty—people for whom no preparations had been made, and for whom no one very much seemed to give a damn. Their status as pilots availed them not at all in securing quarters, and provided even less aid in warding off the savage cold.

The men had no choice but to find some place—*any* place—which would provide them with protection from freezing to death. Cursing all military organizations in general they clambered into underground bomb shelters, which had all the warmth of freezers, and slept on the icy floors, breathing knife-sharp air that seemed to burn the lungs, until flimsy barracks were erected. Pneumonia, inflammatory rheumatism and premature arthritis—hardly the afflictions one connects with dashing young aviators!—cut down the pilot strength of many squadrons during the winter more than did the heaviest barrage of enemy bullets.

In between the roaring hell of ground offensives, the greatest enemy of the poilu or the Tommy was an appalling boredom; there was nothing to do except to follow inane military requirements, and this consistent blankness of life was made all the more maddening by living conditions that most hogs would have spurned. Impersonal shelling took its toll, but even this sporadic harassment was considered by the ground slogger to be bearable, and most of the veterans accepted it with the stoic fatalism of men who have long been in the front lines and old companions with unexpected death.

There can be no contest but that the World War I frontline infantryman led the most inhuman of existences—yet he was spared that special agony reserved solely for his contemporary in the air, the nervous strain brought on by the certain knowledge that he was going to meet an armed, vengeful and skilled enemy face-to-face every day that weather permitted. Added to this certainty was the special nature of aerial combat: falling to one's death from many thousands of feet, or burning alive, because there were no parachutes to be had, and also because very few men of the many who were shot down ever lived to talk about their escape.

An American from Arkansas, flying SE-5 fighters with the British, recorded in his diary:

> More rumors of more battles. We were told there is going to be a big push shortly. Push? What's a push to us? That's for the Poor Bloody Infantry to worry over. We push twice a day, seven days a week. We go over the top between each meal. Oh, yes, the flying corps is the safe place for little Willy—that is, as long as he doesn't have to go near the front!

SE-5 Fighter

. . .I can't write much these days. I'm too nervous. I can hardly hold a pen. I'm all right in the air, as calm as a cucumber, but on the ground I'm a wreck and I get panicky. Nobody in the squadron can get a glass to his mouth after one of these decoy patrols except Cal and he's got no nerve—he's made of cheese. But some nights we both have nightmares at the same time and Mac has to get up and find his teeth and quiet us. We don't sleep much at night. But we get tired and sleep all afternoon when there's nothing to do.

. . . It's only a question of time until we all get it. I'm all shot to pieces. I only hope I can stick it. I don't want to quit. My nerves are gone and I can't stop. I've lived beyond my time already.

It's not the fear of death that's done it. I'm still not afraid to die. It's this eternal flinching from death that's doing it and made a coward out of me. Few men live to know what real fear is. It's something that grows on you, day by day, that eats into your constitution and undermines your sanity. . . . I've lost all interest in life beyond the next patrol. . . . I haven't a chance, I know, and it's this eternal waiting around that's killing me. . . . Last week I actually got frightened in the air and lost my head. Then I found ten Huns and took them all on and got one down out of control. . . . It takes a brave man to even experience real fear—a coward couldn't last long enough at the job to get to that stage. What price salvation now?

Not long afterward the writer penned his last entry in his diary. He was shot down and killed. He was twenty-four years old.

The infantryman not only envied the airman his "cozy" life on the ground but, as we have noted, coveted his manner of fighting and dying. The apparently harmless maneuvering in the blue sky (as it might be seen from eight thousand feet below, that is) . . . the faraway and faint *tac-tac-tac* of machine guns . . . the sudden sliding through the air . . . a spectacular spin with the wind-whipped whine of death through the broken machine . . . and it was all over. Ahh, but *that* was the way to go! The foot soldier stirred his feet in the mud and thought of the pilots high above, the pilots who might die but were free of lice, who were clean-shaven, who were attired in immaculate fashion. To the rifleman or the machine gunner, this was "the clean death."

Perhaps. Perhaps this is the way it seemed to the men in the mud, but it was death nonetheless and it came with terrifying suddenness—if the man was fortunate. A youngster in the very prime of life might actually finish a decent meal of scrounged eggs and coffee (not common in the pilot messes), place his napkin beside his plate, walk out to the tarmac and climb into the cockpit of his airplane. All this while he would be the perfect specimen of manhood, filled with life and plans for that same afternoon and evening. And he would take off, arrowing into the blue and crisp air, and twenty minutes later he would be nothing more than a charred corpse buried five feet underneath the wreckage of his machine in Flanders mud.

And then there was the most dreaded hell of all. *Fire.* Few men liked to talk about it, or would permit its discussion in their immediate presence, but the ugly specter of being burned alive for long minutes rode the shoulders of every pilot every time his wheels left the ground to begin a patrol.

The horror of falling several miles while embraced with the savage caress of flames fed by raw gasoline and whipped into frenzied, roaring sheets beggars description. Nothing ever written by any man has the remotest chance of transferring to the reader the mixture of hell compounded by falling, burning, and being forced to sustain horror until the merciful earth smashed the pilot into eternal peace. The chance tracer bullet striking the fuel tank, raw fuel surging against the red-hot whirling cylinders of a rotary engine; it took only this instantly to transform a pilot's smoothly operating machine into a shrieking pyre.

The helpless victims either rode the blazing hearse to earth or flung themselves into empty space when the flames became unbearable. A few, a very few, carried service revolvers hidden within their flying suits against the contingency of fire; and no one can ever know how many men splashed out their brains once that relentless yellow-orange horror curled toward them.

Nor were gunshot wounds any less painful or lethal because they were inflicted at altitude instead of on the ground. A man struck at fifteen thousand feet by a machine-gun bullet in the thigh felt as though he had been kicked by an angry mule, or pounded with a red-hot sledgehammer. Stunned, blind with pain, unable to give himself even the crudest of first aid, gasping for breath in the thin cruel air, the pilot had to fight madly to keep from collapsing in unconsciousness before he had run the gauntlet of continuing enemy fire in the desperate effort to reach the air over his own lines.

Wounded pilots were prime prey in the high arena. The enemy set upon them with eagerness and a frenzy for the kill; the wounded man was less of an adversary and would make an easier victory. And the man who was wounded and permitted to escape was certain to return at some future date, much the wiser and more experienced, and hard after revenge. Many of the men who suffered wounds simply died of shock or loss of blood before they could return to earth. Many still alive who slumped unconscious sealed their doom, for their machines were left uncontrolled to scream with terrible speed and lethal impact into the ground.

There just wasn't anywhere to hide in the sky.

Despite the tragically brief lifespan of the average neophyte in the air over the Western Front—where the rate of attrition was nearly as great as it was on the mangled earth below—the aura of glamor and the unique qualities that cloaked the air service proved irresistible to almost all comers. Recruiters for this knightly form of warfare were besieged with hordes of eager volunteers who sought this newest challenge to their imagination and their skill.

A surprisingly low percentage of the prewar barnstormers made the grade. Many of them were too old. Others were unable to pass the physical requirements, although they could fly rings around many of the combat pilots actually at the front. And too many of them had already been killed stunting before one crowd or another.

However, there was one man of the Moisant Gallic Crew of 1910 who *did* survive the perils of his barnstorming days and who went on to write his own indelible chapter of the First Air War.

The outbreak of war caught Roland Garros still in the barnstorming business—but this time he was touring Germany. He managed to rush from the enemy's camp and returned immediately to Paris. Soon afterward his faithful chauffeur-mechanic, Jules Hue, drove him to the *Service Aéronautique* camp at Chalais-Meudon. Garros arrived at the camp gates in a cloud of dust kicked up by his powerful

Bugatti, and completed his noisy entrance by being sworn in as a member of a Morane-Saulnier reconnaissance squadron.

Two weeks later the gentle Garros, an avowed hater of violence in any form, droned steadily over a German artillery emplacement, calmly marking on his map the coordinates of the enemy target. He would then drop the map to waiting French artillerymen so that the enemy batteries might be decimated by the big guns of the French.

German resentment at these pestilential little machines clattering their way through the air grew in leaps and bounds. The maddening flight of the observation planes, with their studious pilots, was almost always followed with a screaming hell of accurate artillery barrages from the French. Thus the resentment of the Germans was made quite clear to the Frenchmen when furious machine-gunning from the ground forced the planes higher and higher into the air. The practical limit of such vertical retreat was reached on the appearance of German two-seater aircraft; in the rear cockpit brooded gunners armed with two deadly machine guns, the primary function of which was to blow the Frenchmen out of the sky.

During the heated contest as to who would fly and who would fall, none of the combatants could do much more than to fly alongside one another and blaze away in furious and inefficient battle. The opposing aircraft remained without a threat from the front; the whirling blades of the propellers precluded firing along the axis of flight. It boded little good for a man to get in a shot at his adversary, only to smash his own propeller into splinters while doing so. The observation planes, depending upon their performance in lifting payloads, thus were armed with a startling variety of weapons including bricks, hand grenades, pistols, Winchesters and a sprinkling of types of machine guns. Pilots and observers fired at one another with gusto, but generally it was a sloppy way to fight a war.

Then, in November of 1914, Garros took leave of his squadron and rushed to a secret meeting, where he huddled behind locked doors with Raymond Saulnier, the great French aeronautical designer. There were many consultations, many tests and, alas, as many failures in the secret experiments. The cycle kept repeating itself until, at long last, Garros returned to his companions at the front, equipped with a new concept in armament. Quickly he demonstrated its effectiveness.

On April 1, 1915, Garros cruised across the front lines, a lone man deliberately seeking out trouble. He smiled as his search was rewarded over Oudecapelle in Flanders; the smile faded as he swung his airplane over, wings flashing in the sun, and then plummeted straight for an enemy biplane. He did not go unnoticed, but the German pilot never wavered in his course. Why bother? At first the German pilot and his observer must have been puzzled at the unorthodox flying of the Frenchman; obviously, he was coming down to engage in a duel. But why should the madman be coming at them from the *front?* The Germans flew steadily on, for there was safety any time they had the nose of the French airplane pointing at them. The flashing propeller blades protected all the participants in any air fight.

Disillusionment, and then terror, swept away the confidence of the Germans. The first sign that the world seemed to have gone crazy came with the sight of the French monoplane, when its nose sparkled brilliantly with fire. The fool! But wait . . . *no!* It was impossible! The frenchman was firing *through* his spinning propeller!

With desperate movements the German pilot skidded, a frantic maneuver to throw the tracer stream of the enemy away from his own vulnerable machine. The German recovered from his slewing flight, tramped rudder, and with his observer stared after the French plane, expecting to see it wobbling earthward with a shattered prop.

Their eyes widened. The blades of the French fighter gleamed brightly in the sun, still pulling the Frenchman through the air.

At this point the German gave way to the alarm rising in him. He began a series of evasive maneuvers, skidding and slipping wildly, hoping to give his observer an unobstructed burst at the maddening monoplane that buzzed about them, intent on the kill.

Garros with deceptive skill easily evaded the German fire, and rushed head-on once more at the Albatros. Again his single Hotchkiss gun began its chattering cry and this time a hail of lead ripped the length of the German fuselage. And again the German frantically avoided the death blow by maneuvering out of the way. For ten long minutes the one-sided battle whirled across the sky. In the end the Garros magic prevailed; the fuel tank of the big German plane erupted with a tremendous *whoosh!* of flame and the stricken craft hurled itself to the ground three thousand feet below in a fiery plume of sparks, thick smoke and fluttering debris.

The Garros "magic" proved simplicity itself. Two steel triangles bolted to either side of the propeller boss deflected the bullets that failed to pass between the whirling blades (about one in every four slugs), and protected Garros from shattering his own propeller. Unquestionably the device was crude, and just as unquestionably it worked; the funereal pyre of Garros' enemy testified to that. Soon afterward Garros rocked the Germans on their heels with a spectacular double kill; he took on two of the enemy and sent both of them crashing to earth. Within eighteen days Garros shot down four opponents, causing the Germans sleepless nights and a growing fear about the "secret weapon" of the French.

Not content with his electrifying success, the former barnstormer who had braved the Colts of drunken Texans planned to wage still more warfare against the Germans. Why, Garros inquired, should the eccentric parabola of flight across the enemy's lines be confined to dueling with German aircraft alone? Intrigued by the possibilities of extending his own personal air war against the Hun, Garros planned to change concept to reality.

Garros and his mechanic, Hue, worked completely through a night to install primitive bomb racks beneath the fuselage of his Morane fighter. The next day Garros disappeared over the horizon on a solo mission across German-occupied Belgium; from a height of six hundred feet he unloaded his bombs on the railroad terminal at Ostende. The Germans on the ground seemed to go wild with fury at this impudent invader from the skies; Garros flew home through a storm of machine-gun fire reaching up for him from the earth. With a smile on his face he landed at his home field on the last drops of fuel in his tanks.

Shortly after his solo raid against Ostende, Garros was again deep within German lines; this time good fortune looked the other way when a chance shot from the enemy ground his engine to a stop while he was only two hundred feet up, near Courtrai. With his usual skill he dead-sticked his airplane to a safe landing in an open field and, as a platoon of German soldiers rushed toward him, quickly set fire to his "magic" Morane. Unfortunately, the airplane burned less quickly than Garros believed.

Even as the Germans hustled Garros away to the north and

a prison camp, their engineers were methodically examining the partially burned wreckage of his Morane. Leading the German group was the brilliant young Dutch designer, Tony Fokker. The Dutchman shook his head in wonder at the crude manner in which Garros had rigged his propeller, and accurately informed his attentive audience of German air service officers that no propeller could long withstand the continuing shock of being struck by machine-gun bullets. Fokker left the scene quickly to disappear into his workshop where he rushed through a new mechanism that was to change the pattern of war itself.

Three days later a German fighter plane went through special tests before wildly excited officials, who foresaw a tremendous sudden advantage to the German air service. The airplane appeared unchanged from any other model, but it mounted a 7.92 mm Maxim gun that was synchronized with the engine to fire *between* the blades of the spinning propeller. Three weeks after the secret tests, the great Oswald Boelcke shot down a French airplane with the new synchronization device. From that moment on the war in the air assumed chilling proportions of destruction and death.

And what of Garros? For nearly three long years the war passed by the brilliant and courageous pilot, who remained in captivity. But the spirit of certain men remains unquenchable; in January of 1918, Garros and another French pilot, named Marchal, walked nonchalantly out of a prison camp disguised as German guards. Their careless stroll through the camp gates began the perilous foot-and-rail journey that eventually brought the two men back to France.

Despite the violent objections of his superiors, Garros returned to the front and to battle. High French officials stormed against this move; they were convinced that the Germans would deal severely with Garros should he fall again into their hands. While the arguments raged in Paris, eventually the man who put wings truly into war was posted to a Spad fighter squadron operating just below the Argonne.

By now Garros was relatively old and decidedly weary in spirit; his determination, which had brought him through years of captivity, now seemed to ebb away from him. He encountered rising difficulties in keeping up with the new, younger pilots, all of whom looked upon Garros with deep affection—as though he were some special beloved antique. It took time for Garros to regain what he once had been; it

Fokker D-VII

took time for him to master the powerful, strong Spad. But once he was again in his element, instinct took over and he demonstrated that he could be outflown by no man. On October 2, 1918, he tore into a seven-ship formation of the new Fokker D-VII fighters and shot one to pieces. He was now an ace, with five confirmed kills, for whatever that might have meant to him; but the ace status brought to him a new adulation and even greater respect from his fellows.

Three days later Garros stretched his chances again. He plunged into a flight of five more D-VII's, racking the Spad madly about in a swirling fight. This time, however, the magic touch of Garros could not overcome both the odds of long combat and the numerically superior odds of the battle. His companions last saw his Spad spinning wildly to disappear into a cloud.

Seven days later a German pilot flew across the French lines to glide past the airfield from which Garros had taken off. A note fluttered to the earth. It was a message in which the Germans praised a gallant enemy who had fallen to his death, and the assurance that Roland Garros had received a decent burial with full honors.

* * *

The sudden entry of the United States into the high arena over France proved to carry mixed blessings. For nearly four years the French and the British had been fighting a brutal, enervating war in which they were being bled white in manpower and materiel. Not unnaturally these beleaguered combatants turned eagerly to the United States for a flood of war materiel to aid their cause.

Had not the Americans waxed enthusiastic over their awesome industrial might? Had not the United States boasted freely of its vast and myriad technological and engineering skills, its reservoir of scientific talent? Immediately upon the outbreak of fighting between the United States and Germany, Premier Ribot of France dispatched an urgent letter to President Woodrow Wilson in which Ribot requested that America provide as quickly as was possible at least 4,500 new combat aircraft and the trained crews to man these machines.

The enthusiasm of the French Premier, unfortunately, was not matched by his knowledge of the American aircraft industry. Had the truth about this industry been known, Premier Ribot would never have sent his letter and might instead have buried his head in his hands and wept. In 1914, the United States stood fourteenth among the world nations as an airpower force; after years of war in Europe, the United States, by April 1917, had scarcely elevated its unhappy status. Indeed, the official evaluation of the airpower force of the country was that the American aerial armada consisted of "fifty-five planes, all worthless for combat." Notwithstanding these facts of life, well concealed behind the smokescreen of bombastic claims of massive capability by the United States Government, the optimistic Ribot further requested that the Americans organize their industry to produce two thousand aircraft and four thousand engines *every month* to achieve mastery of the air over Europe.

In response to the open conflict with Germany, the Congress quickly flung $640 million into the airpower stew, and the War Department whipped itself into a frenzy of choosing possibly every wrong type of airplane needed for the European war. As the catastrophe of official ignorance threw thousands of engineers into a panic of industrial preparation, there began the confused program of selecting the men who would fly the still-phantom aerial armada.

Overnight the Aviation Section of the Signal Corps, United States Army, became the most glamorous branch of American arms since Jeb Stuart's cavalry. A veritable avalanche of humanity, in the form of store clerks, farm boys, college students, adventurers and men from every conceivable walk of life, descended upon the recruiting offices. They came from everywhere and anywhere, at first delighting and then dismaying the Army by their sheer weight of numbers.

For while there were recruits coming through the woodwork and bursting the Army camps at their seams, training facilities were virtually nonexistent. The first 210 Yankee aspirants for their military wings were quickly hustled aboard Cunard ocean liners and sped on their way to England. There the hard-pressed Royal Flying Corps accepted the human sky fodder with a willingness that should have frightened the recruits but apparently did not, processed them through training, and fed them piecemeal into British squadrons at the front. Not until the summer of 1918 did these American airmen see action under their own colors.

They were not the first Americans to fly, fight and die over the European battlefields. Since the spring of 1916 other Americans had flown combat operations with the French *Service Aéronautique* as members of the Lafayette Flying Corps (there were nearly two hundred of these men). Although by 1918 the renamed United States Air Service was able to provide stateside primary training in such aircraft as the crotchety Curtiss JN-4 ("Jenny"), it remained for the French to provide the finishing touches in gunnery and aerobatic skills. What rankled the French, and brought them to look with a jaundiced eye on that thrashing but ineffectual "massive" American aircraft industry, was the need for the French to outfit entire United States squadrons with French-built fighters, bombers, and reconnaissance machines.

Thus there came about the ludicrous situation in which America failed to flood its European allies with aircraft and airmen, and we were forced to bleed the already slender resources of these nations to provide the wherewithal for us—the mightiest industrial nation on earth, *if* we could get organized—to fight the enemy!

Yet no one would deny the value of certain commodities that the Americans brought to Europe with them, assets that the exhausted English and French hadn't seen for years: enthusiasm for the new warfare in the skies and a boundless confidence in smashing onward to a sure, quick victory. And, above all, a sheer zest for the challenge of flight and for fighting in the air.

One American wrote to his father:

> As I have said before, the sensations in an aeroplane are not in proportion to the danger involved, which you realize only intellectually. It doesn't come to you with a noise; the roar of your engine drowns everything, and that becomes like silence after a few minutes. You don't see the danger until it is on you and the machine guns start popping. Our job is to keep the Boche photo, artillery and reconnaissance planes on their own side of the lines.
>
> As we learn the game, there are all kinds of things to do if a man wants to, especially during attacks. One can drop bombs, attack sausage balloons, shoot up the trenches or organize small expeditions into Germany looking for trouble.
>
> I am expecting to have the time of my life, and am happy as a lark to be in it. I hope the feeling lasts.

The American pilots so newly arrived in France—when not being shot at and shot up by the murderous new Fokker D-VII's of Germany—had every reason to exult in their status. Not only were they looked upon by the majority of the French as outright saviors of the nation, but they were feted as part of the knightly breed of warriors. The treatment accorded them was often little short of slavish (and distressing to the old-time veterans who knew better). Consider the example of one lieutenant whose engine failed—from mechanical difficulties, not enemy action—while he flew patrol . . .

He nursed his Spad fighter down to a rough landing in No Man's Land and very nearly died in the process of just trying to get down in one piece. His head was slammed forward against the cockpit coaming when the lower wings snagged in rusting strands of barbed wire. The impact tore away the wings and sent the fuselage flipping over wildly in a grinding spume of dirt and airplane debris. The groggy pilot recovered his senses while hanging suspended, head downward, in a trench. Before his startled eyes, heaving in and out of focus, were the upside-down faces of wide-eyed soldiers, grimy and covered with dirty helmets. The pilot's heart sank in dismay; surely those fierce faces were German, and just as surely he was doomed to while away the rest of the war chewing on stale black bread in some dismal prison camp.

But no! One hairy face spewed out a joyous greeting in French, and soon rough but helpful poilu hands were busy unstrapping the pilot, who was now nearly delirious with joy. The French infantrymen lowered the American tenderly to the bottom of the trench. He was quickly given a shot of cognac and led along the duckboards to a dugout.

Here the greeting went to the extreme, as two French generals leaped to their feet and advanced with happy cries. The generals planted lusty kisses on his cheeks and then thumped him mightily on the back. Friendship was bursting out in every direction. The generals gestured grandly to a decrepit wooden chair before a decrepit small table—their finest—and then in painful English bade the American aviator to be seated and join with his rescuers in lunch. The crude structure of the dugout belied the enthusiasm of the French cook, no doubt spurred on by cries from the generals. The astonished pilot stuffed himself with hors d'oeuvres, roast chicken and creamed vegetables, while his hosts shouted for him to eat more. Near to bursting from the generosity of the French, the pilot was then plied with liqueurs, brandy and a fine cigar. Afterward, with bellowed praises still ringing in his dazed ears, he was escorted back from the lines through a communications trench. With more gestures of undying friendship he was shown to the rear seat of the generals' limousine, and sent in kingly comfort on the long ride back to his airdrome.

To the average American pilot of the First World War, life during the frantic few months or weeks he spent in combat was a sharp wedge driven deeply between his past and his future. If he had enlisted while still a college student, he emerged from a cocoon and was hurled with a minimum of delay from his scholastic world into the desperate scramble of survival; there did not exist the protective interim period in which one might become accustomed to the realities of life beyond the cloistered seclusion of university classrooms. The sense of normal values, of orderly progression into a life of growing responsibilities, received a severe jolt. Men were denied the period in which they might mature slowly, age gracefully and perhaps die in peace; with the impartiality of war they were cut down in the flower of youth and cast out of life. Pilots learned quickly that there was little romance in certain aspects of their new winged career; the man who sat down next to you at breakfast might not be there for lunch. And he might never again be seen.

Youths of nineteen became men at twenty. Those who lived through the savage period of becoming veterans instead of green replacements developed physical symptoms and the mental outlook of men twice that age. The first time in the thin air that death reached out gropingly with its blind fingers to stab into a man's flesh, or when a man realized he might become a blazing and shrieking animal beset with fire within a few seconds' time . . . something changed within him. The remnants of memories of a developing youth were lost forever, shattered into whirling fragments which might never again be assembled into the person-that-was.

The first time that a pilot watched a close friend burn to death, whatever emotions existed before were transformed into an intellectual porridge of anger, hate, frustration and creeping fear. Through every man there ran the alchemy of realization that life truly is not forever and that war, no matter how noble the cause or high the new arena of contest, is supremely and senselessly wasteful of the finest of a nation's youth, leaving the residue at home.

A constant exposure to combat in the sky proved to be, like alcohol, both a stimulant and a depressant. When finally the carnage spent itself in its quicksand of blood and pulped flesh, there were 650 American pilots who had experienced in one degree or another the narcotic of combat in the air. A great number of these young-old men were weary, and mildly astonished, to count themselves still among the living.

The embryonic American aircraft industry had grown, if not to maturity, at least to adolescence. Scattered throughout the land was the debris of this hurried industrial sputum—thousands of new and unused training planes, observation machines, and even long-range bombers. The men on the one hand, and the machines on the other, posed a dilemma.

What, asked the pilots of experience and skill, shall we do with the rest of our lives?

And what, queried a bewildered government that had produced too many airplanes much too late, shall we do with all these machines?

The dilemma was to be solved in unprecedented fashion. The combination of some of these men and some of these machines gave birth to this nation's wildest, perhaps slightly mad, period of aviation history. It was the era of the barnstormers.

5

"The Circus! The Circus!"

It happened exactly at the eleventh hour of the eleventh day of the eleventh month of the year 1918. The lethal thunder of the great guns along the three hundred and fifty miles of the Western Front was vented for the last time. Silence crept across the battlefields and through the trenches like a life-giving fog. There were brief sputters of violation: an isolated rifleman or a cursing artillery crew who damned surrender and wanted only decisive victory or defeat hammered out a defiant snarl with their weapons. But the fog rolled on and the ghastly slaughter faded into a history of horror, no more to claim its victims.

Unbelieving of the silence, the doughboys, poilus, the Tommies and the *Sturmtruppen* rose slowly from their trenches to stare hollow-eyed at one another across the tortured waste of No Man's Land. The miracle had come to pass; a man could stand and not be ripped to bloody shreds . . .

High above, the sky was empty. The winds stirred the air in peace; there were no angry splotches of flak, or greasy streamers of smoke, or a twitching body amidst crumpled wreckage. The airmen who had strained to kill one another only hours before were now, like their tired and oil-spattered machines, grounded by the Armistice.

The infantryman and the airman shared between them the same sense of overwhelming relief; no longer were they the targets of so many forms of death, no longer would the thick shells or the copper-jacketed needles seek them out. God willing, now they might look forward to a world in which each man shared his chances of living out his normal lifespan.

Yet there were disturbances that rippled across this new sea of peace. To many airmen this new life had suddenly, and strangely, lost some of its savor. Senseless death could never be coveted, yet the vague stirrings also could not be denied. These were men who had tasted the incomparable thrill of flight, of plunging through misty whiteness of cloud, of watching their wings shimmer and gleam in golden sunlight. They had sailed amidst cloud mountains, tasted a new freshness of life and of challenge brought to them in the high blue, and this was a heady wine of life not so easily dismissed.

What awaited them at home? Universities paled to a leaden memory, jobs were things of the past, close ties and professional careers were gone.

Back in the States, with the discharge and the medals framed against the wall, the proud uniform hanging in the darkness of the closet, the world seemed smaller, stifling. Not a few of the men who had soared in the Spad and the Bréguet, the Salmson and the Nieuport, the Camel and the De Havilland could keep their eyes from turning upward, seeking in the sky what they had lost.

De Havilland DH-4

Somehow, in some manner, they must return to their adopted element.

The veterans were not alone in their search for solace above and amidst the clouds; the Armistice had caught hundreds of cadets just days short of winning their wings and their commissions. How could these men, of which only a few had passed twenty years of life, satisfy their gnawing desire for flight? And the younger ones still? Lads in their early teens had had aviation drummed and hammered into their heads since 1914. The new hero was not the man with the wide-brimmed hat and the brace of six-shooters hanging loosely at his sides—he was a man dressed in leather, with a fur collar, and with a white silk scarf fluttering from a leather helmet, facing the world through goggles, clenching his teeth from behind a brace of Vickers machine guns. Rickenbacker, Luke, Lufbery . . . Spad, Fokker, Nieuport, Bristol, Albatros, Camel . . . Courtrai, Colombey-les-Belles, St. Mihiel . . . these were now the magic names of youth!

But the war was done, and even magic may go up in smoke. There appeared in the newspapers of early 1919 a single photograph that told the story all too well; somewhere behind the former lines of battle, a mountainous heap of new American-built warplanes had been drenched with aviation fuel and then set aflame. A million dollars worth of unflown airplanes went up in a blazing pyre in one day alone.

Who needed them? Wars, the people were told, were now a thing of the past. German militarism had been forever crushed. Against this entrenched conviction the newborn American air arm was mercilessly whittled down to a sliver of its former self. Throughout the United States there stood factory-fresh training airplanes in useless ranks across abandoned airfields. No bonfires had yet been made of these machines on this side of the Atlantic; the cries of outrage from the taxpayers could easily have sent too many political careers up in smoke as well.

But what to do with all these winged craft? Why, sell them, of course! So it came to be that anybody with three hundred dollars in his hand could haul away a Curtiss JN-4D and take it upon his own life and limb to learn to fly the thing.

Veteran fliers claimed that the Jenny was like a well-bred woman. She was basically stable and even forgiving of mistakes, but if you manhandled or mistreated her she would spin like a dervish. Powered with her original OX-5 V-8 engine, the Jenny would clatter along in calm air at 75 miles per hour, and if the pilot knew what he was doing, he could slide her out of the sky for a neat landing at only 45 per. The rate of climb was less than phenomenal; Jenny demanded fully five minutes to climb to a thousand feet, and she just refused to pick up her skirts and run. It took a brilliant mechanic and then a patient pilot to set up Jenny so that she might be dragged laboriously to a height of eleven thousand feet—several thousand feet lower was her normal ceiling. The top wing, considerably longer than the lower, spanned just over 43 feet. When empty, the squarish-bodied and ungainly machine balanced the scales at a little over 1,400 pounds. With the fuel tank topped off to its limit of twenty-one gallons, Jenny could rumble along for two and a quarter hours. But this was the fuel limit and not one of practicality, for it was seldom that the airplane managed to stay airborne for so long a period; the engines had the nasty habit of acting up at all the wrong times, making it imperative for the pilot to return to earth while he could still do so safely and in some comfort.

Although it was possible in 1920 to purchase spare OX-5 engines for the piddling sum of only twenty-five dollars, most pilots preferred to switch over to the more powerful Hispano-Suiza engines that ranged from 150 to 300 horsepower. The Hissos were wonderful engines with a lot of "git" to them; they made many a pilot unhappy, however, because they would quickly become traitorous in a rapidly shifting temperature range. The exhaust valves proved overly sensitive to cold air, and they warped viciously when hit by the frigid blasts while the Jenny thumped its way in for a landing. Then there was nothing for it except to remove the engine and laboriously regrind each valve. It was time-consuming and irritating, but most pilots considered this problem, plus the added engine weight, well worth the trouble, and they remained faithful to the Hisso and its power.

Although there were an estimated 1,500 Jennies on hand at war's end, not all of these machines were assembled and ready for flight when the future cloudbusters shambled up to the government agents with the necessary cash. Recalled one pilot: "The ship was usually in pieces when you got it, and sometimes it was in pieces at the end of the runway when you fastened it together and poured on the coal with the idea of flying. What it took to fly was gas and guts. . . ."

Guts was one thing that young Douglas Davis, of Griffin, Georgia, never lacked. As soon as he was of age, Davis left the red clay country of his native hearth and joined up with the U.S. Air Service in Atlanta. Sent to Kelly Field near San Antonio, Texas, Davis immediately established himself as the least-promising student ever to be fed through that grinding mill of future lieutenants. One after the other his ground instructors threw up their hands in despair. Davis seemed completely inept in being able to grasp even the most basic theories, and from one hour to the next could not remember the most rudimentary facts of flight, or even some of the terms which were used to describe them. With hope almost but not completely abandoned, the ground instructors finally turned Davis loose on the flight line where he was delivered to the tender mercies of badly overworked pilots. Having heard of Davis' performance in the classroom, these worthies regarded his coming with all the joy a man feels when sinking into quicksand.

To Davis the controls of an airplane were alien and hostile creatures to be regarded suspiciously as enemies, and it was only his fierce determination to conquer his inner fears of flight that enabled him to stay with his student class—right at the very bottom.

Again and again his harried flight instructor beseeched Davis to give it all up. Another instructor went so far as to suggest strongly that Davis would make a far better living by selling fish than he ever would as an aviator. Others pleaded for Davis to quit so that they—the instructors—might have some hopes of surviving the perilous moments in the air with him. But through it all Davis gritted his teeth, lurched through the air and banged on and off the ground, and ignored the moans of his teachers. He stuck it out to the end of the line, had his wings and commission thrust upon him with a chorus of relieved sighs, and was rushed off to France where, it was felt, the Germans were better prepared to deal with his peculiar flying talents.

But the war ended before the Germans could come to grips with Davis, and he continued on his perilous path of winged survival. He returned to the States with but one thought in mind: to earn his livelihood as a flier. He spent his last dime to purchase a well-worn, clipped-wing Jenny and promptly set himself up in business as one of the first barnstormers ever to rock his wings in Georgia.

Davis hangared his precious machine in a patched-up canvas shed pegged down in the center of the old Chandler racetrack, eight miles east of Atlanta. Davis discovered very quickly that the enthusiasm he felt for flying was not shared financially by the rare customers who came to Chandler to gawk at the maniac with the old airplane. Undaunted, Davis clattered his way into the hinterlands to seek paying customers; it did not take long for his zest to give way to reality. There were few paying customers, and there was a staggering lack of interest in flying. Echoing the prophesies of his wartime instructors, Davis commented bitterly that his efforts at providing airshows earned him barely enough to keep him fed, and with cheap soda crackers, at that.

At the point where Davis was reduced literally to crumbs for his meals, and when even his hopes for the future of aviation sagged hopelessly, a miracle appeared in the form of unwanted and obnoxious competition. A second barnstormer by the name of Beller Blevins wheezed his way into Chandler one afternoon, pegged down his own tent, and clumped his way over to where Davis stood gaping.

Pulling a wet cigar from his face, Blevins rasped: "Sonny, we're going to start divvying up the pie." His pronouncement over, Blevins jammed the sopping stogie back between his teeth and clumped back to his airplane. He began carefully to wipe down and polish his Jenny, anticipating his first stolen customer.

It was not without some alarm that Davis fretted away the rest of the afternoon, wondering how he might stave off this latest threat to his economic survival. He mused unhappily that there weren't enough interested clients for riding in airplanes for one barnstormer, much less two hungry men. Then inspiration clutched at Davis; he smirked and made up his mind not to wait for the customers to come to Chandler where they would be enticed by the much-waxed airplane and shiny boots of Blevins. Instead, Davis would do the Mohammed act. *He* would go to the mountain.

At sunup the next morning the Hisso thumped mightily as Davis roared away from Chandler. During the day he slammed down onto a dozen pastures, literally chasing customers in their own backyards with an enthusiasm that amazed even himself. Fortune had blessed Davis with a fresh face and a winning smile, and Davis kept his teeth flashing brightly in the direction of his customers while he went into his spiel. He counted shrewdly on the farmers' constant desire to get something for nothing, and Davis offered the farmers "two rides, suh, foah the price of one!" Success warmed to him and Davis began to gather customers handily. But there was a string attached to the offer: the farmer could have his first ride right there in his own backyard, but the second flight must be made at Chandler.

His competitor might have a shinier airplane and boots, Davis reasoned, but he—Davis—had personality to spare, and once the natives had the opportunity to compare the two barnstormers, why, he figured to place first in the hearts of his "two foah the price of one!" customers. Davis' reasoning proved correct, and he chortled happily as the business rolled in and the look on Blevins' face became sour and dour.

Davis secretly had cause to thank Blevins, since it had been the awful threat of competition that spurred Davis on to an astonishing flow of customers. Business mounted so rapidly that Davis found himself the employer of several pilots hired to keep the incoming customers flying and willing to separate with their cash. He scrimped on expenses, collected every cent available and rushed off to buy more surplus airplanes. With the giddy feeling of success, several airplanes and pilots about him, he proclaimed himself as the head of the Doug Davis Flying Circus.

Among the men who joined his rapidly growing gypsy band of barnstormers was George Sheally, who set some sort of aviation record. Sheally soloed on a Thursday, and the following Saturday—two days later—clanked his way cross-country with cash customers in the airplane. There did not yet exist the Federal monster in the form of cloying regulations and rules to interfere with such operations. Also working for Davis was Johnny Kytle, another graduate of the Brooks and Kelly training fields of the war. Zest and daring came in the form of Vivian Jones, a one-time trapeze artist from the circus world. Davis' younger brother, Paul, ignoring the warnings of gloom concerning Douglas, joined up with him. Completing the cast was the comic of the group, Frank Ward.

In the spring of 1924 the Doug Davis Flying Circus began

its real full-scale operations. Atlanta was the home base, and the Circus began to work over every small town on the Georgia map, and some that were even too miniscule to earn a drop of the cartographer's ink. Shrewdness seemed to have been implanted solidly within Davis, and he refrained from bleeding his circus of its profits; instead, he plowed back the early profits into newer airplanes and newer engines, in this fashion always managing to keep more and better aircraft in the air than could his competitors.

By the summer of 1924 Davis was flying high as a businessman. He nosed his roaring fleet across the state line and invaded Opalika, Alabama. The Circus put on a show so dazzling that it left the townspeople rocking for weeks afterward. In the meantime Davis also separated the crowd from the lordly sum of $1,400 for a single performance, a feat that had his retinue in awe. The truth was that money proved to be the magic elixir that worked wonders for Davis. He became cockier by the minute and the more cash that he stuffed into the little tin box, the wilder became his shows. His was a circus in every respect of the word.

"You give the public what they pay to see," he commented in grave business tones (very unlike Davis the pilot) "and you will receive more cash in return." No one could argue with the one-time nemesis of the military flying school. Davis closed the year 1924 with his books in the black, fuel in the tanks, and his team in the pink. As far as the southland was concerned, Doug Davis was the undisputed King of the Barnstormers. The blatting thunder of his airplanes became known and respected wherever he appeared, and the clamoring for the Circus promised the happy tinkling of cash registers. Davis was immensely pleased. His future soared on bright clouds. Or so he thought . . .

Early the next year the receipts of the Doug Davis Flying Circus inexplicably took a nose dive. No one could understand what had happened. The planes were better and the performances glossier, but along with this improvement of the Circus went thinner crowds and an unexpected sneering enthusiasm. The alarmed Davis lost no time in sniffing out the source of his woes; when he returned to his waiting associates, it was with a look of chagrin stamped across his face.

Cherchez la femme, so say the detectives of the French *sûreté,* and that is exactly what Davis found: a woman who was slowly but steadily stealing away his customers and crimping his receipts.

Her name was Mabel Cody, and she was hell both in skirts and on wings. She seemed to have sprung from nowhere, an enigma blossoming into a heroine; overnight it seemed that she had captured the imagination and the heart of every man, woman and child in Alabama. People talked of Mabel Cody with awe in their voices; children adored her, women shook their heads about her, and men went through a variety of emotions calculated to bring them back again and again into the paying stands to see Mabel Cody.

Davis caught her act as a paying customer and it took only minutes to realize how she so effectively and swiftly had rounded up *his* cash customers. Mabel Cody was, first of all, a *woman*. She was pert and energetic, endowed with a figure that would have attracted covetous glances anywhere, and she carried within her a torch of living that almost radiated outward from her presence.

In addition to these characteristics—more than enough to bring the swooning swains of the farm country stumbling over their own feet to throw their cash on the line—Mabel Cody was a woman of spectacular skill. And with that skill went courage and steely nerves of a nature not even Davis had ever seen, known, or even heard about. Miss Cody had teamed up with a lackluster group of gypsy fliers in Birmingham, Alabama, and in short order had every man startled with her presence. Not from her looks (that alone was enough to cause dissension within the ranks) but because of her spectacular performance in the air.

And, they noted, an absolute lack of fear. Men in her presence felt like timid children.

Wearing tight-fitting white coveralls—that distracted her pilot—Mabel Cody rode the top wings of Jennies and Standards with a grace and sure-footedness that was nothing less than astounding. Sailing through the air she seemed oblivious of height, turbulence, howling wind and other factors, and cavorted with all the unleashed joy of a starving monkey that has just stumbled into a treasure grove of ripe bananas.

She walked the wings of airplanes in flight as though she were blithely skipping rope on a sidewalk. While her pilots gnawed their fingernails in fear for her life and observers on the ground turned white with fear, Mabel Cody laughed at the world and temptingly tickled Fate. When her act grew boring—to *her*, not to any other human soul—she undid the safety harness that kept her safely on the top wing of her airplane, and then slithered down the side of the airplane's fuselage.

That was too much, even for the hardened veterans of the game! Flying at slow speed, the Jenny or the Standard, with its forward movement and great whirling propeller, still kicked up a tremendous blast of wind, into which Mabel had to stand and to perform. At low altitudes on warm days the air, which looks smooth and inviting to the ground observer, is usually filled with all manner of rocks, bumps and pitfalls. Thermals rising from the ground, eddies of wind, invisible currents . . . all these contribute to many different motions of an airplane. It rises and falls, the nose slues to the right while the tail answers by going to the left. The wings rock and the machine sways. It is not so bad if you are high enough and wearing a parachute, but when you are without that silken angel strapped tightly to your body, cavorting about an airplane is an experience that, the writer swears from first-hand experience, may be described as terrifying.

Just clambering out to the lower wing and clinging for dear life to the struts and wires is bad enough. Making the mistake of looking down and thinking about what happens if you let go is guaranteed to turn the legs of the average man to quivering jelly and possess him with a screaming urge to climb back into the cockpit.

Having the courage to direct your shaking limbs to bring you climbing atop the fuselage and onto the upper wing— where the flashing meat grinder of the propeller can bring an inarticulate cry bubbling from the lips—guarantees you first place on the line for hero medals. Then—*shudder*—to stand up in the teeth of that howling wind, and to gaily wave your arms and sway your body, to laugh at the wind and flash smiles at the crowd, while the engine roars and the horizon tilts and bangs about in sickening fashion . . . It is more than sufficient to make a healthy and brave man crawl weakly into bed and lie there quaking for a week.

All this Mabel Cody did with deceptive ease and absolute confidence in herself. And then she got bored, released her safety harness, and slithered down the side of the fuselage. Fighting the wind and the rocking motions of the airplane, and staring into the slashing blur of the propeller, she reached down to grasp the spreader bar—and hung by only her manicured fingers fifty feet from the ground.

The first time that Doug Davis saw her act, not even his many years of flirting with death and disaster could keep him from gasping aloud. Mabel crouched in the rear seat of an open automobile that sped at breakneck speed down a road. The wind flattened her clothes against her body, but she seemed as oblivious of the wind as she did of the rocking motion of the vehicle. And then there was a great shadow overhead and a louder roar as a Jenny eased its way down the sky to slide just ahead of the racing car, and hold its position there. A rope ladder trailed stiffly in the wind.

Davis had sense enough to note that the entire crowd about him was on its feet, breath sucked in, jaws agape, as the beautiful girl suddenly stretched upward. In a single, blurred, lithe motion Mabel grasped the bottom rung of the ladder. Davis could almost feel the pilot easing back on the stick, for in the next instant Mabel was snatched from the car and carried higher and higher into the sky, still hanging on to that bottom rung of the ladder.

And then the Jenny faltered. Davis caught himself grinning as he realized that the crowd had gasped at a beautiful illusion. Mabel Cody was scrambling up the ladder while the airplane held a steady altitude, but it *seemed* as though she were dragging the Jenny back to the ground and that a disastrous crash was about to ensue.

Davis' admiration for the girl soared even as his economic outlook blackened. Mabel Cody was spectacular in a way he could never have imagined. Any one of her acts would have been enough to fill the stands. The fact that they were performed by a girl, and a lovely girl, was even more of a crowd pleaser, and pure honey to the yokels who flocked in with mouths agape. The fact that she performed a series of stunts each time left Davis weak with awe, and with a slow shaking of his head.

On the same day, Davis watched Mabel Cody repeat her act of scrambling up a rope ladder into an airplane—but this time she went through her routine by balancing herself on the deck of a speeding motorboat racing across a lake!

Mabel capped her day's performance by leaping away from a high-flying airplane, and dropping earthward in a free fall of such length that numerous women in the audience collapsed in the stands. Ever working, the shrewd mind of Davis noticed that more than one man left his female companion in a crumpled heap by his feet while he kept gaping into the sky, waiting while the few remaining seconds of safety flashed by and, finally, the white silk of the opening canopy flashed into view.

The understatement of the year, Davis mused, would be that he had nothing like Mabel Cody in *his* act. He mulled over the facts in his mind, and again drew the conclusion (accurately) that the crowd not only loved the dangerous stunts, but was uproariously enthusiastic about them because they were executed by a mere slip of a girl.

Some time afterward Davis' concern slipped into deep gloom. He received word that Mabel Cody had decided to go into business on her own. She invited the best pilots in the southland to work for her, and the word spread that Mabel was going to knock the competition right into a cocked hat.

One of the first pilots to join Mabel Cody's new organization was Bonnie Rowe, who began his career as a smokestack painter, and went on to become an observer in a hydrogen-filled balloon during the war. Within a few years of his return to the States Rowe was known from coast to coast as one of the most incredible daredevils ever to leave the ground. He was one of the first men ever to leap from one plane to another in flight—but Bonnie Rowe did it with one hand tied behind his back. Another of his stunts that set off the crowds to roaring their approval was to hang *by his toes* from a trapeze swinging fifteen feet beneath an airplane.

Like many other stuntmen, however, Rose had learned bitterly that he and his breed had to ride the surges of popularity and income, and that just as often as not he would be flat broke and hungry. An expert parachutist, Rowe on more occasions than he liked to remember had to pawn his parachute to keep from starving to death. And it was just this problem that gave him his greatest—and fully deserved—claim to fame.

There had been a badly needed show for the stuntman; he needed cash desperately, and thanked the good fortune that had set him up for a show the following morning. But it proved to be a Greek gift—his parachute was in hock and neither Rowe nor his friends, with all their change combined, could retrieve the precious chute. Cursing the twist of fate, Rowe suddenly had an inspiration. He and several close friends locked the door of Rowe's hotel room to hide the fact that they had filled the room with stolen bedsheets. The men stayed awake all night patiently sewing together the sheets to form a canopy!

Early the next day, blind with fatigue, the incredible Bonnie Rowe threw his body away from a Jenny. The makeshift parachute uncrinkled its way from its package and, miracle of miracles, opened to form a canopy that let him down safely. The extent of the miracle was realized fully when Rowe was ten feet above the ground. Suddenly the seams of the crude canopy split wide open, dumping the chutist to the ground, shaken, but alive.

Miss Cody, with all the acumen of an especially shrewd businesswoman, was fully aware that barnstorming essentially was an outdoor form of entertainment for the masses. Making anything else of the aerial performances was simply avoiding reality. Unlike many of her contemporaries, she did not suffer the delusion that these outdoor circus acts were advancing the cause of aviation.

Whether performed beneath the big top of canvas or the sky itself, a circus was a circus, no more and no less, and it needed good, solid ballyhoo to assure its success. These conclusions led Mabel Cody to hire one Curly Burns, described by an associate as "the only one of his kind—and thank God for *that*." The full meaning of this remark may be obscure, but the results obtained by Burns's loud-mouthed oratorical approach and his grasp of fleecing the suckers left no room for argument. Just as Mabel Cody was perfection herself in the air, so Curly Burns was the Gabriel who spectacularly blew the horn that attracted the crowds. Within a despairingly short period of time Doug Davis watched many of his fans disappearing in the distance—rushing to spend their money to see the spectacular airshows put on by Mabel Cody and so effectively ballyhooed by Curly Burns.

Burns knew the masses; he had an empathy with crowds that seemed to be compounded of a mixture of pure instinct and trained avarice. He always queried the pilots to see if any of them had ever flown in the military, and that worthy was promptly reinstated in rank as lieutenant, captain, or major, Burns didn't care which. And if none of the troupe had ever held military rank, that didn't bother Burns at all. He pointed a finger at a selected pilot and informed the man that from that moment on he was an ex-military pilot and would so be addressed.

"The suckers," explained Burns with a smirk, "go big for that officer stuff."

Burns ordered that one pilot among the group, during any one show, must always perform more stunts and receive more adulation than any other man of the troupe. He didn't care who the pilot might be, just so long as one man received attention. And to assure this attention, Burns had the man dress in snappy fashion, with gleaming buttons and leather straps, boots and a uniform—anything to make him stand out among the rest. This pilot always flew lower than anyone else, waved harder and grinned wider, and received more accolades than his fellows.

The natural result of this carefully planned idolatry was to create a hero in the mind of the crowd. Curly Burns topped off his scheme by printing this pilot's name larger than any others on the handbills and posters, and the hammering away at the name preconditioned the crowd to the hero status.

When the daredevil show reached its conclusion and the crowd gasped to catch its breath, it was also in a perfectly receptive frame of mind. Immediately a space was cleared and the pilot-hero was on hand, basking in the spotlight, and always on demand as a flying chauffeur to take the farmers on a circuit of the field, usually at the rate of a penny-per-pound. Back on the turf, the debonair pilot with a grand flourish handed the awestruck rustic a signed scroll testifying to the effect that so-and-so had, indeed, assaulted the heavens. And he had done so in an aerobatic stunt plane of the barnstormers! The possession of the scroll by the one farmer had his neighbors shuffling in line, just itching to get into the air so that they, too, could return in triumph to the hearth, immediately to hammer the evidence of their prowess onto the nearest wall.

Burns never lacked for the income-producing tricks which, his associates swore, he always kept tucked carefully up his sleeve.

While the aircraft carrying the parachute jumpers labored their way to jumping altitude, Burns berated the crowd in gruff good humor. Over the loudspeakers he bellowed that those with courage and imagination could not only go aloft for a ride with the daredevils of the air, but that they could actually be right there on the spot to watch the brave jumpers as they hurled themselves out into space. Actually be right there, close enough to touch the man, as he flung his body into that awful gamble with his own life! The customers stampeded to the planes and, spilling over with enthusiasm, scarcely noticed that they were shelling out double the usual rate for a brief flight.

In order that the Cody troupe be assured of good business in a new area, Burns planned the arrival of the circus with all the cunning of a master bank robber. It was his conviction that the local citizens should have the living bejesus scared out of them right from the very start. The Burns's invasion went something like this:

It's a Saturday morning in the small town of Demopolis, Alabama. The town square is filled with idlers wearing faded denim overalls, and with shoppers scurrying through the dusty streets carrying baskets laden with corn pone, collard greens and fresh-cut slices of sow belly. Dogs with a thousand different ancestors lie asprawl in whatever shade they can find. And there are always the kids, either busy with their own pursuits or jealously watching the older boys. People wave casually to one another. About the loudest sound that can be heard is the accumulated noise of blades from Case knives being scraped randomly against willow sticks; whittling is almost always the favored activity in the small Southern towns. It's pleasant enough, a bit sleepy, and quiet.

Then all hell breaks loose.

The sky fills with a growing avalanche of thunder almost at the same moment that shadows blot the sun from view. People look up in alarm and stare wide-eyed at one another. "What in the blamed hell is . . ." The thunder spills down from the sky and tumbles in ragged waves of painful sound along the main street; the roar spills into sidestreets and dashes through alleys and slaps playfully at glass windows and brings horses' ears straight up. The shadows flash by the sun and blur across the dusty ground and—

"There! There they are! Whoee, just looka them!"

The "them" is the massed formation of the Cody Flying Circus coming to town—but like no other circus these people have ever seen before or even dreamed of. For the circus thunders overhead at a scant one hundred feet above the courthouse spire, and the wings loom hugely in the sky and the sound becomes a clattering rattle of thunder, like a locomotive rolling over and over down a hill.

It's only the Cody Flying Circus, but the impact is tremendous and the natives react as if a flock of pterodactyls had suddenly been loosed among them from the ever-watchful north. Whittling freezes in mid-stroke, merchants dash outdoors and even the dogs spring dustily to their feet as the armada crashes by overhead.

Then the planes split apart in all directions, wheeling sharply in the air. Several of them climb and bank steeply, but one in particular drops down even lower, to second-story height, and pounds his way noisily down Main Street in a beautiful buzzing job. Overhead the other pilots are wheeling and dealing, jazzing their overworked OX-5 and Hisso engines to produce a mighty racket.

The pilots watch carefully until they see the little knots of people gathered in the streets and on the sidewalks, and they see the gesticulating hands, and when they notice that just about every face in town is staring directly upward, they play their trump.

A body suddenly tumbles crazily from the cockpit of one plane. It flops wildly through the air as it rushes earthward, its arms and legs whirling.

"Gawdamighty, somebody's done fell out!"

Startled yells and shouts.

"Sweet Jesus but he is gonna' be killed!"

Here and there a shrill scream.

Whump!

There is a frenzied scramble to the middle of the parched grass that surrounds the courthouse. Voices merge into a subdued babble, and feet shuffle to bring gawking faces closer to the dead flier.

"Funny," someone muses aloud, "how them dead 'uns look just like a heap o' rags . . ."

The townspeople were at first stunned, and then chagrined, to discover that the body of the dead pilot was, indeed, a heap of rags. It was a dummy, and with handbills stuck over it from head to foot that urged the people to "Come on out this afternoon and see some *real* flying!" It was this type of preparation, carefully planned and beautifully executed by the pilots, that practically guaranteed the Cody Circus a full house. Mabel Cody was soon free of financial concern, and Curly Burns never had to worry about a free hand in his advance promotion.

By the spring of 1926, Mabel's hard-working and hard-flying troupe had managed to pull up even with the Davis outfit. This was no mean accomplishment, since Doug Davis had been doing much more than bemoaning his fate. Davis had gotten to the top through shrewd work and excellent flying, and he wasn't the type to take competition lightly. Despite Mabel Cody's magnificent airshow, her own spectacular performance, and the medicine-man promotion of Curly Burns, her outfit managed to equal but not surpass Doug Davis in cornering the financial market for the flying circus.

Doug Davis thought long and hard over the fact that he and Mabel were splitting the available pot right down the middle. Davis was an honest man—most of all with himself—and he admitted freely that the girl's aerial show was unquestionably flashier and more pleasing to the crowd than his own. What kept him in the front-running was the fact that he flew better equipment than did the Cody pilots, and that he was more efficiently organized. As things stood, however, Davis would be beating out his brains for the next several years to try to claw his way back to the top of the barnstorming ladder in his part of the country, but would not be able to get more than half the potential take of the customers, with Mabel still raking in the other half.

One day Davis made a long-delayed decision and flew into the enemy camp. He met with Mabel Cody and offered his competitor a proposition: combine the two air shows into a true flying bonanza, sweep aside the rest of the acts, and really clean up.

Mabel smiled derisively at him. "What's the matter, Doug?" she asked with all the sweetness of a viper, "are you scared of a little girl like me?" She turned him down flat.

In this, Mabel made a serious mistake. She believed that Davis was being hurt, as people are often regarded when they suggest a merger. But Davis was simply trying to be sensible; rebuffed by the woman, Davis stormed away, determined to wreck the Cody Circus. His jaw set grimly, he was about to pursue a variation of an old cliché. "If you can't join 'em," he growled, "then whip 'em!"

Davis began his campaign by trying to steal Mabel's best pilots and her stunt men right out from under her nose. Having known the pangs of hunger within his own stomach, Davis knew that every barnstormer had to try and salt away some cash for the lean times that were inevitable. So his

opening attack was simple: he offered cash fees far in excess
of what the men received from Mabel.

That's where Davis suffered his first setback. Ordinarily
the pilots remained loyal to the highest bidder. This time,
however, the personality and courage of Mabel Cody won
out. The gruff pilots turned down Davis' offer; they admired
the "spunky little gal" so much they stuck with her.

Frustration turned into raw anger and Davis declared open
war on his rival.

He began by maintaining careful records of every movement made by the Cody outfit. As soon as he learned where
they were next scheduled to fly, Davis booked his own circus
in the closest neighboring town and made certain that his
men started flying their show about two hours earlier than
the opening flight of the Cody Circus. He went all-out in his
promotion and, knowing his farmers well, cut his prices below that of the competition.

Mabel Cody was astounded to find her troupe playing to
empty fields.

But this was one female who didn't quit, and she determined to do Doug Davis one better. She studied Davis'
tactics as closely as he had learned hers.

She was well aware that Davis had always appreciated, and
exploited, the value of saturation in advertising his forthcoming appearances. With the open war between the two troupes,
Davis was now plastering his air circus notices on every
available wall, fence, pole and vehicle in the hamlets where
he intended to fly.

Mabel Cody noted the dates of the appearances, and moved
in her circus one day before Davis' scheduled appearance.
She not only capitalized on Davis' advertising, she stole his
crowds, and it didn't cost her a nickel in publicity.

The fierce heat of the rivalry opened wide the eyes of
every onlooker, and brought astonished comments from pilots everywhere. For the competition had become blistering,
and each of the two troupes gained in quality as they sought
to outdo the other. The pilots and stunt men stayed up into
the long hours of the night to devise crowd-pleasing stunts
that would out-perform the competition.

When the no-holds-barred struggle reached its pinnacle,
the actions of the pilots and stunt men would have made the
most callous observer blanch with fear. Both Mabel and
Doug threw away what little sense of safety they had retained

ever since getting into the barnstorming business. The air shows that resulted were more spectacular than ever—and so were the casualties.

Caution became a dirty word, longevity, an object of sneering, impossible, a target for profanity. The pilots scraped the ground with wing tips in wild maneuvers right on the deck. Parachutists delayed their chute openings until there was a question of whether the jumper was a stunt man or a suicide victim. Maneuvers in aerobatics became wilder; spin recoveries were made closer and closer to the ground; loops bellied out almost—and sometimes actually—in the trees.

Mabel's pilots were superb and they were able to stand the gaff, but her planes just couldn't take the beating. And this is where the long-range planning of Doug Davis finally paid its greatest reward. His machinery was the best available; his cash investment in new airplanes and engines sustained his troupe through the wild beating of the violent competition.

In the end, Mabel Cody became the victim of attrition, and faced the stark reality of financial ruin. It's impossible to fly airplanes with weakened wings and engines that won't turn over. She had to cancel acts, and then sometimes the entire show, because her crews were working desperately to patch up the battered machines. And while she was grounded, Davis' men were in the air and reaping the money.

Her coffers empty, her people unpaid, and her airplanes sagging with fatigue, Mabel finally threw in the towel. What happened next was reported—rather quaintly—in the language of the times:

> Doug now had her in his power. She had the choice of either joining him or dropping show business for good. This true daughter of the South loved adventure, thrills and excitement. Aviation lived in her very heart and soul. She fought the battle to the very end, gamely, with honest courage, always keeping in mind the ideals of sportsmanship. Her desire for this colorful life was so strong that she could not resist joining Doug. Her entire troupe joined with her, and it was not long until she and Doug became the best of friends. . . .

Always the sharp businessman, Davis made certain that he also captured the loud-mouthed talents of Curly Burns, who was given free rein in spearheading the combined forces.

Moving swiftly, Burns made the biggest deal of his career when he signed up the big circus with the Curtis Candy Company. From that time on, Doug and Mabel flew under a new banner that read: The Doug Davis Baby Ruth Flying Circus.

The perfect end to this story, of course, would be that Doug and Mabel fell in love, married, and lived in a white cottage somewhere in the West, where they could raise their children away from the stink of exhaust fumes and the blatting roar of Hissos.

But it wasn't meant to be.

In 1934, at the Cleveland Air Races, Doug Davis missed a pylon turn and his racer plowed into the hard and unyielding earth.

They pulled a very dead man from the wreckage.

6

A Guy Named Rodgers

It isn't hard to figure that some of the first men to thumb their noses at the law of gravity might also tend to be somewhat careless about the man-made laws of the land. That this axiom is true is proved in the saga of a lean and hawk-nosed Texan named Slats Rodgers. Slats thumbed his nose at natural, artificial and other laws—among them the laws of adversity. Which is why, against all reasoning and monumental odds, he became the first man in the state of Texas ever to build and fly his own airplane.

That was in the fledgling days of 1912, and in the decade that followed the launching of Slats' creaking, warped and dangerous homebuilt plane this man managed to cram more into life than most men do during their entire lifetime. During the process Slats also accumulated enough brief stays in the pokey to shame a Chicago torpedo always being sprung by a shyster lawyer—and enough air time to command pilot's wings, with cluster and a Bronx raspberry thrown in, had he only bothered to keep a logbook, which he didn't.

Although Slats Rodgers was so unusual that he can't truly be described as typical of the average American barnstormer, even at his wildest, the Yo-Yo life pursued by Slats gives us a decided clue as to just how far a man could go in the days before the Big Brother of the government—the Federal Aviation Agency—began getting in the hair of men who lived freely and to the full.

Slats Rodgers grew up—or rather, fought his way up—on a farm in Dark Hollow, Mississippi, one of those dreary small towns that have been left in the backwash of progress. Dark Hollow crawled with ignorance and superstition, with small town hates and fierce prejudices, and where the chief values for a man were the muscles across his shoulders and his willing readiness to settle any argument with bare knuckles. The boy who was Slats worked from before sunrise to the coming of the moon, laboring over every stinking and dirty chore that a rundown, backwater farm has to offer. It was a dreary life of limited horizons, and there were only two kinds of people in Dark Hollow—those who melted into the nothingness of the local country and stayed there forever, and those grimly determined to get out.

Slats hewed to the second choice and he grew up tough in body, tough in mind, and cussedly independent. When he reached his eighteenth birthday he felt ready for the world. He hitched up his pants, married a fifteen-year-old farm girl, quit his job and signed up to work for the railroad.

Youth and ignorance conspired to keep Slats constantly in and out of trouble, and only his dogged will and strong back enabled him to slug his way out of the bottom of the heap and start climbing upward. Within two years he was a fully qualified locomotive engineer and had earned the respect of the men about him. As things were going, Slats Rodgers might even have ended up as president of the Santa Fe, but he suffered from a malady that left him aching and frustrated.

Slats dearly wanted to fly . . .

In 1912 he started to bring his resolution to the point of reality. From a St. Louis firm he brought home a six-cylinder, 100-horsepower engine that cost him the lordly sum of $750. Then he ordered a wagonload of spruce from Oregon, while a shipment of turnbuckles was on its way to him from France. His neighbors in Cleburne, Texas asked Slats just what in the name of hell he was going to do with all that stuff. Slat's reply, given in a matter-of-fact tone, was direct. He was going to build an airplane.

By himself?

Naturally.

But what did he know of building airplanes?

Nothing.

The news spread through town with a mixture of derisive hoots and low whistles of admiration. Slats snarled at the hooters and rented a vacant store on Main Street, where he hurled himself into his chosen labor.

Several months later, the self-designed, home-built flying machine rolled out of its store-factory-birthsite. At once Slats proclaimed himself a pilot. He had never flown, knew virtually nothing about flying or how to handle an airplane, but there was no one present to argue with him, and so everybody accepted the statement at face value.

Except Slats, who *knew* he didn't know how to fly. Yet. Slats towed his machine to a pasture three miles outside Cleburne, and one fine morning he strapped himself in and fired up the clattering engine. The engine shook and roared, the machine rocked and bounced where it stood; wood groaned and metal cables twanged in sympathetic vibration.

"It was," Slats recalls, "like driving a blind hog to water. It wouldn't go any place I wanted it to, and that crowd that had gathered was raising hell and running around getting in the way and laughing their guts out. Laugh, you silly bastards—I'll dive it at you some day and freeze those giggles."

Again and again Slats attempted to take the shaking creature into the air, and again and again the airplane whirled about crazily as it spun into ground loop after ground loop. Even Slats had to admit that he was smashing wheels and landing gear struts at an alarming rate. But grim doggedness will persevere, and Slats did manage to get the thing off the ground—where he promptly discovered that he was sitting neatly in the lap of an indifferent catastrophe. He learned that through some fault in design and in rigging, the right wing now had the discomforting propensity to slip downwards, and at a dangerous angle. Hell, *any* angle was dangerous at this time to Slats. He staggered back to earth with a bone-jarring crunch and climbed out of his machine. Patience was strained to the breaking as, again and again, Slats rebuilt the right wing.

Patience ran out and was willingly exchanged for a sodden, sopping drunk. Alcoholically angered even beyond his own fiery temper, Slats vowed that he "would fly her, or tear her apart!" Immediately after his self-sworn oath Slats tore raggedly down the open field and hauled the cantankerous machine from the earth. This time he was ready; when the right wing slipped down, Slats leaned hurriedly far to the left. He was astonished to see that the wing warped visibly—and the airplane righted itself back to level flight!

In full flight, twenty feet from the ground, Slats had accidentally learned how to control his airplane. It was a tremendous breakthrough for a man who knew virtually nothing of flight until that moment, but there was a long way to go, and not until many harrowing attempts and flights did Slats tumble onto the secret of being able to turn in the air. Until that dazzling moment of accidental comprehension he was forced to land while flying straight ahead—a moment over which he exercised no control, since it was determined by exhaustion of fuel or a failing motor.

Slats went professional just as soon as he could convince people that they had a use for his flying services. He earned his first cash as a pilot by flying over the county courthouse while a politician standing on the courthouse steps held forth with fiery eloquence, using Slats overhead to dramatically emphasize his points. Slats gave the politician more than was bargained for, because his airplane barely missed smashing into a flagpole and providing an unexpected demonstration of Slats Rodgers and airplane plunging into the ground. Almost crash or not, Slats collected a whopping fee of four hundred dollars, cash.

Six months and some fifty flights later, the indomitable Slats received another offer of four hundred dollars, this time for a flight over a lodge picnic at San Antonio. Alas, the money went uncollected. On a test hop before the big demonstration flight, the troublesome right wing began its perverse sliding motion. Confident of his ability, Slats nosed over to gain additional speed to control the wing. The airplane quickly went into a dive from which, unfortunately, it failed to recover, and Slats with an astounded look on his face smashed into the ground. The plane came apart in a hundred places, and hot water gushed explosively from the cracked engine radiator, burning Slats severely. Half scalded, stunned by the impact and cursing the pain of cracked vertebra, he was hustled off to the nearest hospital for two months' recuperation.

When he finally left the hospital, he returned to cast a jaundiced eye on *Old Soggy*—the name of the winged creature that had flung him into his hospital bed. Grimly determined to conquer the beast, he rebuilt the airplane from the ground up, while his neighbors shook their heads in a combination of wonder and dismay.

Slats never again flew the cantankerous machine. Carpetbaggers from the North descended on the area, flying Curtiss and Wright Pushers greatly superior to his home contraption, and they swept up whatever flying business there was in Texas.

Slats recalls: "One dark and stormy night I went out and hitched a team of mules to *Old Soggy* and hauled her along the road to my Dad's place and left her there beside the barn. I tied her down.

"She died there."

World War I served as a boon to Slats's aspirations as a competent pilot. With his experience in the air, valiantly fighting the attempts of *Old Soggy* to kill him, he had indeed become competent, and was snatched up as a civilian instructor. Steady flying with different students molded his natural talent and brought to him a smooth skill that was to distinguish his future in the air and to serve him well in the harebrained schemes which he would happily hatch.

The close of the war brought a reflective pause to Slats, who concluded that there awaited a bonanza in cold cash for any man smart enough to haul hard liquor into the States from Mexico. Slats laid no claims to fancy education, but he had a tremendous reservoir of common sense and the shrewdness of the ex-farmer. So he began to execute a plan conceived after careful thinking; he set out deliberately to establish his reputation as an honest, hard-working barnstormer. Then, later, when he figured to become one of the country's premier airborne bootleggers, the cops wouldn't even take notice of the Jenny flown by the industrious, honest barnstormer known everywhere as Slats Rodgers. Thus he would be able to make frequent but unscheduled and furtive cross-country flights south of the border.

"It was all straight flying then," Slats points out. "Easy on the takeoff, easy on the landing, no stunting. The rough stuff came later. But in 1919 just getting off the ground in a ship was mighty exciting to most people, and a lot of them made you promise you wouldn't do any trick stuff before you got in. I flew them careful."

Careful, yes; wise, no.

Slats was foolish enough to make his first passenger-carrying flight with a passenger who didn't pay before the wheels left the ground—and then refused to pay after they were back down. Slats didn't make that mistake again; from then on it was cash on the barrelhead before takeoff.

During a low-level flight across the plains, Slat's Jenny rumbled past an open roadster carrying two young men and a girl. They signaled for Slats to land alongside them, and Slats, curious, wheeled around to touch the earth gently. The youths offered him one hundred dollars cash for a fifteen-minute ride. Astonished, Slats agreed quickly. But there was a catch—they all wanted to go up at the same time.

Slats looked at the cockpit-built-for-one just behind the wing, and waved his hand at the forward enclosure. He still found it hard to believe when three pairs of hips managed to wriggle and jam themselves together onto the worn seat cushion. (How the Federal Aviation Agency of today would have loved to catch someone like Slats Rodgers!)

Whenever Slats flew that day from a different landing site, a crowd followed almost immediately. Usually curiosity of the airplane in the remote areas overcame fear. At the end of the day Slats discovered to his astonishment that such curiosity in the form of paying passengers had netted him a cool seven hundred dollars in cash, and all of it, as he says, "made the honest way, the way I loved to make it—flying."

Slats reminisced about the past:

It was funny as hell watching the people go up for the first time. Here would come some middle-aged wife traipsing behind her middle-aged husband, and they would fight anyone who wanted to horn in ahead of them, but they were scared to death all the time.

About the time it was their turn, the man would want to back out. But the woman would argue him into it. Almost every time it was that way—the man was the one that had to be talked into going up, the woman did the talking.

I was getting a big kick out of it all. I was really giving them their money's worth. Some seedy old geezer would get in and say, "Fly me out over that there little yellow house where the one-eyed mule's staked by the barn so's I can wave to my sister, Minnie," and I'd fly him out and circle and let him wave to sister Minnie.

Or maybe some young buck would say, "Dive at that brown house over by them trees. I want to give my girl a thrill." And I'd dive at the house and he'd wave, and maybe some cute little gal would wave back.

I didn't have to do any traveling at first to get customers. I got them right there in Wichita, and the money poured in. Some of the early barnstormers charged twenty-five dollars a head, but by the time I got to hauling passengers in 1919, why, most were charging fifteen dollars, which is what I charged.

Like I said, my ship was built to haul two passengers at the most, but lots of times when I first started flying them I'd give them a little extra time. Later, when it wasn't much fun to me, just business, I'd whittle down on their time. But by then they started getting cagey and they'd check.

At first I could stop that foolishness by going for a loop. They wanted to come down right away then. But that didn't last either. Pretty soon they got to wanting loops and other stunts. Finally, lots of them wouldn't go up if you *didn't* stunt them.

It suited the hell out of me.

I might have just stayed with flying, I mean hauling passengers, if it had stayed the way it was. I was making money fast. But here came the gypsy barnstormers from other parts of the country, horning in. It was easy to see that kind of money wasn't going to be around for many years. People would pay to go up once, twice—then they wouldn't pay any more. Before long you ran out of customers.

So I kept in mind that I was hauling passengers mainly to build up the right kind of reputation for my ship. I wanted her to be a lady, above suspicion.

Slats soon was flying both the Jenny and a second plane, a Standard. But as he had predicted, the local passenger flights ebbed away to inactivity, and he went into the business for which he had so carefully prepared. He used his "lady" to haul everything from illicit booze to Chinese migrants across the border from Mexico into Texas. The peculiar evils of prohibition and the sudden influx of wealth in the form of wildcatters who had hit it rich in the boom towns, combined to create a fabulous ready market for Slat's ferrying service. A fifth of gut-rotting whiskey brought as much as fifty dollars a bottle, and Slats bought all he could in Mexico at a cost of twenty dollars a case.

It wasn't all ferrying and collecting high stakes. More than once irate lawmen along the border sprayed 30-30 slugs into the air in an attempt to blow Slats out of the sky. After holes began to appear in the airplane and the shrill whine of slugs began to be heard uncomfortably close, Slats got smart and

Standard

started flying at night. To mark out his landing field, he had his Mexican cohorts line a stretch of level ground with beer bottles filled with kerosene. They burned swiftly to mark out the landing path and, for safety's sake, could be extinguished just as quickly with sand.

No one could say that Slats was narrow-minded in his business arrangements; soon he graduated from booze and Chinese to smuggling contraband watches. And he devised a delivery system just one step short of genius. He ordered a saddle maker to fashion a heavy bedroll out of thick sheepskin, an item in his airplane above suspicion, since pilots often slept beneath the wings of their planes. But the saddle maker sewed tiny pockets the length of the roll. With the roll packed with watches and carefully bound, Slats roared off across the Rio Grande.

Then, over a barren spot of Texas ground where a confederate waited, Slats chopped the throttle and dumped the precious bedroll through a trapdoor. The bundle bounded to earth in a cloud of flying dust, but the delivery system proved perfection itself—not once was a watch smashed. And the system had built-in protection, since Slats didn't need to land, and would never be caught with any incriminating evidence on him.

But what finally made him decide to abandon the Chinese to other border-crossing devices was the law. At his pickup point one day—which he wisely dragged to study the scene before landing—he noticed the stolid-looking Chinese standing together and wearing handcuffs. Slats looked more carefully; sure enough, there was the law, hiding clumsily in ambush behind a mesquite tree. Slats thumbed his nose at the trap and flew off to safety.

Not even the skill, stubbornness, planning or the good luck of Slats could hold out forever, and the Federals finally caught Slat landing at a remote field with fifty gallons of precious booze stashed neatly into the front cockpit. In triumph the Feds carted Slats off to Dallas and slapped him in jail.

This episode was perhaps the proudest in the long and varied career of one Slats Rodgers. Certainly it established beyond any doubt his cunning and his quick mind, enabling him to turn adversity into profit. While in the Dallas jail, Slats acted the role of a model prisoner and was soon made a trusty. With the gods smiling down on him, Slats lifted a key to the storage room. Quietly and with great expertise, he spirited away all the evidence against him (forcing the government to drop its case)—by selling the booze on the outside at a handsome profit!

Once he was again a free man, Slats had some hard thinking to do. He had made a small fortune prostituting his border-hopping biplane, but now he turned his back on this kind of flying and returned instead to his first love: barnstorming. Dallas suited him well, and he decided to use Love Field as his headquarters.

Recalls Slats:

They called us a lot of different names: Birdmen, Sky Pilots, Boomers, Barnstormers, Gypsy Barnstormers and the Lunatics of Love Field. We tried to live up to that last name. Maybe I overdid the business of wild flying. For instance, Pop Moore, who later ran the tower at Love Field, said that I flew with the stick in one hand and a quart of whiskey in the other. "Hell," Pop said, "it wasn't even safe in the hangar with you flying!" Maybe he was right.

Love Field was jammed with Jennies and Canucks—

JN-4C's. What we called the clip-wing Canuck was a pretty hot ship. So far as I know, I was the first pilot to try it. What I did was to take off the top wing, which had a three-foot overhang, and put on a bottom wing in its place. That cut six feet off the length of the top wing. The boys swore it wouldn't fly. It did, and you sure could do stunts with it.

The few types of airplanes based at Love Field included an almost infinite variety of submodels and modifications. With the original Curtiss OX-5 engines the pilots could barely scrape up a top speed of eighty-five miles per hour. To get more speed and better performance, pilots installed different engines in their planes.

There were, for example, plenty of Standards around, but it was a ship with a bitchy reputation. It had a gawky appearance that belied its stability and its ease of control in the air. Originally it was powered with a six-cylinder Hall Scott engine rated at one hundred horsepower. What seemed to be an airplane gentle enough to handle obscured its past history. Hundreds had been produced during the war as military trainers—which were quickly condemned and discarded by the Army because the airplane had a nasty tendency to catch fire. You can lose a lot of airplanes and pilots that way . . .

Slats bought two Standards and modified the airplanes at once by taking out the Hall Scott engines and replacing them with 180-horsepower Hissos. Despite the extra power and the improved performance, the Standard couldn't be used for the more vigorous maneuvers of air-show barnstorming. Slats, and most of the other pilots, bet their money on the clipped-wing Canucks.

He recalls:

Lots of times we ran out of gas, and sometimes a flier ran out of guts, but mostly they ran out of time and folded their wings forever. Not many of those early barnstormers who stuck to it are alive today. But I stuck to it to the end—long after the Department of Commerce, Aviation Division, said I had to reform. I stuck with it even when they canceled my license. They couldn't make me stop, for I was earning my living when they started making those rules.

When passengers didn't show up fast enough, why,

we'd stunt a little just to draw a crowd; then we began stunting just for the hell of it. We made a game of it, seeing which one could come closest to getting the engine shoved in his face without really getting it there.

Most of the stunt fliers were young fellows, men not too long away from the war. I was around thirty then, and they considered me an old man. But I held my own with them. I figured what the crowd loved was noise and low flying, and that's what I gave 'em. I learned to come down onto the field, touch the ground with the wheels and go on up into a loop, a stunt most of the younger men wouldn't even try. One reason was that they were flying Jennies and Canucks, while I pulled it off in a Travelair that I had latched onto. I did a lot of checking first at altitude, to be sure I wasn't losing altitude. The first time I tried it, it worked, but I got a lot of gravel in my face from my own propwash. I ran the crowd off the field sometimes, and they loved it! All the time I was in the air they were waiting for me to crack up, and I kept making them think I was going to. Now and then, I did, which kept them coming back for more. When I rolled a ship into a ball, the crowd would really get excited and the newspaper guys would run a big story, complete with pictures. This always meant I'd have a bigger crowd whooping it up longer the next time, yelling for me to come on in and crack 'er up again. But I loved it all, I wallowed around in it like a ship without a rudder.

Love Field wasn't the large, modern expanse with which we associate modern airports. It was, literally, just a field, an ordinary cow pasture which had been prepared as an airfield by the planting of Bermuda grass instead of native growth. Runways were nonexistent and the pilots couldn't have cared less, for they didn't require any. Just point the nose into the wind and slap open the throttle and let her take her head . . . flying was swift and unquestioned in those days.

An airfield like that had its advantages, and one of them was the profusion of rabbits. (You can still see them at many fields today; like birds, they congregate in the open areas.) The pilots often spent their night hours using the bright headlights of cars to illuminate their quarry, tearing around the field wildly and blasting away as if they were in the middle of a war. But it was worth it. "We got all the rabbit stew a man could ask for," recalls Slats.

The Government had named Love Field in honor of Lieutenant Moss Lee Love, an air cadet killed in training in 1913. To commemorate the dead flier the government erected a large tombstone at the north corner of the field and then, in the strange manner of governments, promptly put up a wire fence to keep away the people who came to see the tombstone. Slats Rodgers took a different attitude about the fence; he was convinced it had been placed there to keep him from crashing into the tombstone.

Slats remembers:

I guess we were a strange lot, those of us who flew those old traps every Sunday at the field. Maybe we were sort of a mixture of the cowhand of the Old West, the hotrod driver of today, and the real gypsy. We thought we were as free as the birds when we got into the air, just as the old-time cowboy thought he was as free as the coyote. We deliberately missed death by inches, and we played the suckers wherever we could find them, which meant roaming the face of the earth like a gypsy.

That was only forty-odd years ago. But you go back to Love Field now . . .

I was up there not long ago, standing watching the big airliners land and take off just as fast as the tower could clear them. . . . Now and then a little ship, one with wings of cloth, would take off. But it acted businesslike, just like the pilots of the liners, even a little snooty, I thought. It took off and headed someplace, flying to get from one spot to another, not just for the hell of flying.

It was hard to believe a man like me, still flying a little, was called Pop way back there in the days when flying was still new and people would drive half a day just to see a ship take off—or just to see it hit the ground. There were millions of people in 1920 who had never seen an airplane, and millions of others who were dead certain the things would never fly.

That was a different day, almost a different world.

And we were the ones who were changing it, those of us who were doing the wild flying just as much as those who didn't fly wild. That was my day, and I belonged to it. The trouble is, I still belong to it, and it's gone. To me flying is still a game—it was a game when I made my living out of it, honest or dishonest. . . .

But you've got to play the game by the rules now.

7

How to Beat City Hall

Sometimes we find good fortune in trying to re-create the fond moments of the past. In Slats Rodgers we have such a find—one of the few from that time who is still here, still able to reach into history and pass it on to us. And in this chapter, with the help and able hand of Hart Stilwell, we can share with Slats Rodgers one of his more memorable times of the glorious days of barnstorming . . .

The air shows we put on in those days weren't all alike. We kept trying to think up new stunts. Usually there was an advance man who booked the show on a percentage basis, ten percent gross plus advertising, and we all gambled for our money on spot landings, racing, dead-stick landings, and maybe a pants race.

The pants race always gave the crowd a kick. They would line up four or five ships side by side, and close to each ship they would mark a circle, about eight feet in diameter, with lime. Then, when the pilots got their motors going, the flagmen would give them the signal and off they would go. They didn't go far, for the idea was to get back to that circle as fast as you could once you were in the air.

When you got back, you had to jump out of the ship, take off your pants, leave them inside the circle, then get back in the ship and take off again. Then back you came and jumped out and put your pants back on.

Zippers sure would have helped in those races. But most of us were smart enough not to have anything buttoned when we started.

The winner of the race would get maybe seventy-five bucks. The take in cash wasn't always so good at the gate because so many people figured they could stay outside and see it free, which they could.

I did pretty good in the pants races, mainly because I could get out of the ship and get my pants off and get back in the ship so fast. I didn't do so good in acrobatics, but I sure gave the crowd a show on low flying, and before long I began getting jobs hauling the stunt men who would walk wings and all that sort of thing. The wing-walkers and other stunt men I knew liked to have me fly them even if I did fly wild because they figured I never got excited. . . .

I think the best air show we ever staged was at Wichita Falls back around 1923. Clint Foster and I were both flying Canucks at the time, and we had a lot of fun playing around, diving at each other, and doing a lot of other stunts. By that time I had learned the trick of touching the wheels on the ground and going for a loop, and the crowd really liked that.

Well, we sent word up, through our advance man, that we were going to really put on a show at Wichita. And about ten days beforehand Clint and I decided we'd fly up there and look things over. We were flying along somewhere near Bowie when he pulled up beside me, on my left. He was grinning like a jackass and his bald head was shining in the sun. Clint wasn't an old man—just wore his hair off early pushing against the wind.

Each ship had about a five-foot overhang on the top wing, with struts about two feet long and guy wires to hold the overhang. Clint spurred my ship with his wing and stuck the struts through my wing. The wires caught on the broken ribs.

There we were, hung together in the air.

Clint kept laughing all the time. But I hadn't had a drink, and I couldn't see much to laugh at just then. There was nothing to do but go on to Wichita and try to land. There were no radios in ships then, so we couldn't send word ahead to have the ambulance and fire truck out at the field.

We went in over the town and circled. Clint should have flown the lead, since he was on the left. But he didn't seem to want to, so I took charge. He stuck with me all right while we eased on into the field and landed. The ships jerked apart when we hit the ground.

Some soft-headed bird came up to us and said, "You all sure can fly tight formation."

"Thank you, friend," I said.

I picked up my marbles and limped back to Dallas. I had enough for the time. I traded the ship in on a 180-horsepower Hisso Jenny and got ready for the show.

The people at Wichita were expecting plenty, for they'd heard a lot about the Lunatics of Love Field, and all the Dallas crowd was going up. The big secret was that I was going to throw out a dummy. No one knew that except one ambulance driver who was to beat all the other ambulance drivers to the dummy when it hit, and a couple of fellows helping rig things for the stunt.

We got a man in Dallas to make up the dummy, and he did a fine job. That dummy was a good-looking son of a bitch. Once in a while I'd catch myself talking to the thing. He had on polished boots and wore a helmet and goggles—all decked out. Lot better looking than some of the Chinese I hauled.

Well, when the time came to take off for Wichita, I was ready and thought that I had a freshly rebuilt ship with plenty of power and in good shape. An old man was standing there watching me get ready, and he said, "I'd like to ride up there with you if nobody else is going along. I've never had a ride in an airplane and I want to see the air show."

I stopped tinkering with the plane and looked at him.

"You know what you're saying?" I asked him.

"Sure."

"All right. Be ready pretty damn soon. I'll be shoving off in half an hour."

Along came Major Bill Long, a friend of mine who was in the airplane business at Love Field, and said, "Slats, I've got something to help out with the show."

"Let's have it."

"I've got a wind-driven siren. Let's put it on your landing gear and give them some noise up there."

"Put on a monkey and a hand organ if you want to," I said.

They fastened that siren on and put on a brake so I could start it and stop it from the cockpit. Then we thought we were ready. But we weren't exactly—when they were rebuilding the ship I had told the mechanic to put a piece of tubing on for a throttle rod because I had trouble with the piano wire breaking. When I looked I saw it was piano wire, not tubing. And the wire had been brazed to the hand throttle.

There was no time to start making changes at that late hour, so I told the little man who was going with me to climb in. He was in the music business there in Dallas. I don't remember his name.

I yelled at the helper to turn the prop a couple of times to load her with gas. "Switch is off," I said.

That's what I thought. When he gave that prop a twist the motor started. Dangerous business—men have got their heads sliced in half that way. I called the mechanic out and told him the ignition switch wouldn't cut off. He said he was taking off for Wichita himself, and he'd fix it up there.

To cut off the gas supply from the carburetor I had to get out on the ground, take a pair of pliers, and turn the valve. Couldn't cut it off from the cockpit. But what the hell—me and the music man shoved off.

It was a pretty day for flying, and when we got somewhere around Bowie, a place where a lot of things were happening to me, I decided it was too quiet, so I turned on the siren. Sure made a big racket. Me and the music man were half deaf in no time at all, so I decided to cut the thing off. I squeezed the handle put on there to cut it off. It kept going. I couldn't cut the damn thing off at all. The brake contraption they rigged wouldn't work.

On we went, raising the dead for miles around.

A little farther along I saw that the motor was turning too fast. I pulled back on the throttle. Nothing happened that time, either. I pulled all the way back. No good. The piano wire had broken in the conduit.

You read a lot about us barnstormers of those days not giving a damn what shape our ship was in and giving aviation a bad name by cracking up through carelessness. A whole lot of that cracking up was just the kind of thing that was happening to me—jobs messed up by men on the ground, the mechanics.

There I was, siren wide open, throttle wide open, engine roaring to beat hell, about to fly apart any minute, and

I couldn't cut off anything. I knew that motor might never hold together—I kept expecting to see connecting rods and pistons go flying all over the place. Of course that knothead of a musician thought it was all just dandy—he would turn around and grin at me once in a while. Having fun.

There was only one thing to do—go on in and fly over the field until I ran out of gas. If the engine didn't fly apart everything might come out all right. But it sure was roaring away, and I knew no motor was going to stand that long.

But that old Hisso was a sweet motor. She held together for an hour and ten minutes while I circled the field, siren going all the time, everybody in the country coming to see what was wrong. When she finally popped out of gas I started down.

Just as the wheels touched the ground and I set the tail end down for a landing, more gas ran into the carburetor and the motor roared again, wide open. Off we went, siren screaming, motor roaring, people on the ground scattering to beat hell.

I knew she wouldn't run far, so I made a tight turn. When I got about halfway around she popped out of gas again. If that damn foolishness kept up much longer I was sure to crack up.

I headed her back in and as soon as she hit the ground I jumped out and grabbed the left wing. More gas seeped into the carburetor and the motor began running fast again. I hung on. Round and round we went, me digging up dirt with my heels, the motor roaring, the music man trying to get out. I yelled at the damn fool to stay where he was, but he'd had enough of that business. He wanted to feel the ground under his feet.

The men around the field were afraid to come out. They didn't know which way the ship was going next. When they finally did get to the ship I was all out of breath, but I was still hanging on and the motor was just sputtering.

"What's the matter?" some monkey asked. Same old question.

"You think of something that ain't the matter," I said.

Around two-thirty in the afternoon we got the show going. I was to fly Gene Brewer, the trick man, on the wings. The crowds that always showed up for that stunt just knew some day I'd throw Gene off and he'd bust wide open like a watermelon when he hit the ground. He didn't wear a parachute—so if he ever let go that was it.

Well, that time we rigged it so we could give the crowd what it wanted. We were going to bust Gene Brewer wide open for them. I took Gene up and he went all over the wings and back to the tail section—gave the crowd a big thrill, and he gave me a thrill, too. The way that man could crawl around on a ship made the skin on your back crawl.

That was just a preview, though.

The main event was to take place later, around five-thirty. I was to take Brewer up again, and he was to climb out of the cockpit onto the wings while I was looping. That's when we were going to flash the dummy on them.

We had put the dummy in the turtleback of Slim Madison's car. Slim was one of the boys who helped me with the show. I taxied down to the north end of the field to pick up the dummy. The fellow with Slim was supposed to go up with me and throw the dummy out when I got upside down. But when I got there the guy said, "Hell, no. You fellows are too damn crazy for me."

"I thought you were a four-flusher from the start," I said.

I got in the ship, strapped myself in, and told Slim to give me the dummy. I hauled it in and put it in my lap. With that dummy in the cockpit I could barely move the stick, but I shoved off. The crowd wanted a show—I'd give them one.

I got up to about 1,500 feet, went for a loop, and at the top of the loop, when I was upside down, I let the dummy go off on his own. Worked just fine. He went twisting and whirling down and fell right in the center of the field.

Our ambulance man who was on the inside had a good start by the time the dummy was on the way down, and he got to the dummy about the time the other ambulances got started.

There were around sixteen thousand people out for that show, and the whole mob of them started swarming toward the spot where the dummy hit. But before they could get there our ambulance man had the dummy in his car and was headed for the Elm Street Hospital. The cops were clearing the way. They sure were nice to that dummy—had their sirens wide open rushing him to a doctor.

When they got to the hospital and opened the door and dragged out the dummy, one of the cops slammed his cap down on the ground and jumped on it. "I'll have that goddamned Slats Rodgers in jail in fifteen minutes," he said.

I was still up there where things were quiet, except for the motor. I was looping and spinning, just relaxing and enjoying myself, wondering how the dummy was getting along. Finally I landed, taxied up close to the hangar, and sat there, waiting to see what would happen next.

A little kid came running up to me and yelled, "Slats, they're after you."

I saw them, a bunch of cops heading my way. I gunned it—blew enough sand to slow down the cops, and got away. The cops arrested some of the fellows in on the dummy deal and sat around waiting for me. Finally I came on in.

"What'd you run away for?" one cop asked me.

"I went for a ride," I said.

"We want you."

"I don't think it's any city cop's business what happens here," I said. "We're out in the country."

"We'll see," the cop said. "You endangered the lives of hundreds of people doing those tricks."

Those were new cops, put in after the change in city administration—not the old gang who were friends of mine.

"Partner," I said, "the people came out here to see somebody get killed. I made them think somebody got killed. They had a fine time."

They took me to the city hall. They already had the promoters of the show and some others there—five or six in all. One of the officers asked us if we could make bond. I asked him what for, disturbing the peace?

About that time the mayor came in.

"You don't have anything on these fellows," he said. "They were outside the city limits."

One of the cops, the one who jumped on his own cap, still hated to give up. He wanted mainly to see me stuck. So he called the sheriff's office and said, "I've got Slats Rodgers here."

"That's fine," the sheriff said. "What am I supposed to do?"

"Don't you want him?"

"Hell, no. Give him a pat on the back for me. Fine show he put on."

We all had a big time that night. I furnished the liquor for everybody except the cops. They had to buy their own.

8

The Saga of Tex Marshall

Being the Experiences of a Barnstormer and His Pal, in the Days of Iron Pilots and Wooden Ships, Before the Invention of Landing Fields—and the Use of Common Sense, and Government in Aviation.

On May 10, 1920, two hoboes with cloth wings departed from the beach community of Sea Breeze, Florida, on an adventure —it could not properly be called a flight—that they hoped would terminate successfully at Findlay, Ohio. The adventure was nothing more than their fervent desire to get from Point A to Point B, a task to be fulfilled on the wings of one Jenny and one Canuck. In one airplane was Tex Marshall and his silently suffering wife (who would end up doing more traveling than anyone else), and in the other was a close friend, Frank Palmer. Part of the adventure arose from the fact that their instruments were crude and minimal. There were no charts and what maps could be found were delightfully unreliable. Neither were there any posted landing fields nor navigational aids nor weather stations nor repair facilities nor anything else that would invite anyone to make such a trip. Their speed was slow, their engines of dubious vintage and reliability, and their experience at this sort of thing somewhat limited.

The aerial armada of two airplanes chugged its way northward from Sea Breeze along the Florida east coast to Pablo Beach, 110 miles from their point of takeoff, and eighteen miles south of Jacksonville, Florida. It was a pleasant trip and the navigation proved to be superb; you could hardly get lost following the white Florida beachline. Equally superb were the emergency landing facilities: virtually the entire coast of the state. The two pilots and Marshall's wife basked in the safety of the beach, for they realized they would be likely to remember with great fondness what lay below them. They had taken off from the beach and at Pablo Beach they again landed on firm sand. That night the Marshalls retired to a hotel. Palmer, anticipating what might lie ahead of them and wishing to get in practice, curled up on his leather coat and slept beneath the wing of his airplane.

The pattern of what was to come became clear the next morning. The pilots planned to fly on to Savannah, Georgia, but immediately faced a major problem. No one knew where the field was at Savannah—nor even if there was a field. The two pilots sagged down in easy chairs while Mrs. Marshall hustled aboard a train to reconnoiter things on the ground. By the time she was at the station a visiting pilot informed Marshall that there was indeed a Savannah airport; the adventurers got word to their female bird dog to proceed to Augusta, Georgia, where she should await their arrival. For the rest of the day, while Mrs. Marshall studied the countryside from a train, Marshall and Palmer installed reserve tanks in the front cockpits of their airplanes. This would give them about six hours' endurance with a lot of throttle bending.

Their next flight was made with the beach below them obscured with thick clouds, and a clammy feeling of being forced to fly far out over the ocean. During this pleasant leg the engine of Palmer's airplane coughed and belched mysteriously—and alarmingly, since he lost altitude rapidly and began circling down into the clouds for the kind of a forced landing that ties butterflies in any stomach. Then, just as mysteriously, the engine blatted out whatever had caused its mechanical woes, and picked up power. A grateful Palmer clattered his way back up to cruising altitude and the two planes pressed on.

Right into gathering darkness . . . with no maps, no lights on the airplane, no instruments for night flying, and most of the earth as black as the inside of a dead cow's belly. To add to their discomfiture, Palmer's Canuck was painted a deep black color and kept fading from Palmer's sight. And then—in the words of Tex Marshall at the time:

Pretty soon we see the lights of Savannah and the next problem is where the hell is that landing field? I was flying lead, and thinking furiously to find out just where we were. I chewed over what meager details I had. The field was *supposed* to be about two miles southeast of town. I almost popped my eyes trying to make out details on the ground but all I could see was a park with a cement walk about fifty feet broad. I eased down closer to the ground and spotted a clearing and there, glory be!, a Jenny was parked alongside a bandstand. That was good enough for me.

Without a moment's hesitation I closed the throttle and nosed her down. Frank was somewhere around in the black sky awaiting developments. He was barely able to see me slip down onto the park and immediately afterward his Canuck eased its way to a bouncy landing in the gloom. I felt like a fellow who had just dreamed he has been run over by a steamroller and awakes to find it isn't true.

For the next two days the two-plane formation remained bogged down by low clouds and glowering storms that passed overhead, venting their energy with sudden, steaming showers. Not until the fourteenth did the biplanes creak their way into the air, and bound along the 140-mile air journey to Augusta, Georgia. It appeared to be a pleasant trip, for the airplanes could follow the course of the Savannah River directly to their destination.

Unfortunately, the weather became "one humdinger of a wild wind and rainstorm," as Marshall recalls. "It was a ripsnorter, all right. We were flying close together, and I started off a little to the right, following a railroad I was pretty sure was the right one. Frank kept signaling me to bear off on a railroad leading off to the left, but I felt sure I was on the right road and persisted on my original course. Frank followed me, but with some misgivings. . . ."

For three hours—filled with moments of near-hysteria—the two airplanes slammed and lurched their way through the air. The wings moaned and quivered visibly in the violent wind. Sometimes unexpected currents flung one airplane sideways through the pounding rain and only frantic movements with the stick and rudder and throttle prevented the two machines from crashing into each other. Keeping Marshall in sight was a bone-wearying job for Palmer; it's always much more difficult to follow a plane than to lead a formation. The lead airplane just plows right on along, while the pilot who is trailing must always be compensating for speed and altitude and course changes. In the tumultuous conditions of the storm, Marshall's plane bucked and slued about, yawing with the wind gusts, rising and falling like a demented trampoline athlete. Thus Palmer was constantly on the throttle, making minor power changes; no sooner would he catch up with Marshall's airplane when it seemed abruptly to slow in the air, and Palmer would frantically back off on the throttle and skid sideways to keep from mashing the wings together, and even as he did so he was working his way back in again so as not to fall too far behind.

Lightning flickered evilly at them from the shifting blackness of the storm, making the raindrops glisten like a million shining beads. And immediately afterward, especially when the bolts were nearby, came the ear-ringing smash of thunder that inundated even the roar of the engine, the pounding hiss of the rain and the scream of wind.

It was a miserable, stinking three hours. When finally they burst out of the storm—"we were vomited out," muses Marshall—it was with the unhappy realization that they were fifty miles into South Carolina, far off course, and starting to run low on fuel. When they were down to ten minutes' flying time, they pinpointed their position. It couldn't have been worse; they were almost midway between their takeoff point and their destination. Below them stretched an array of Georgia farms.

Seeing farmland below when the fuel tank is gurgling its last bubbles of petrol usually brings a sigh of relief from a pilot, but Marshall and Palmer reacted with groans. Marshall wearily recalls the sight:

> The queer part of the Georgia farms is that while there are lots of large fields, the damned things are all terraced. You can't land an airplane on that surface without tearing up everything in sight—including the airplane and the pilot. Hell, a balloon couldn't get down there in one piece. I circled a village from one side and Frank scanned the area from the other side, and the only thing we could recognize clearly was that the both of us were worried.

But time was fast running out, and there was one wheat

field that seemed better than the others—at least it appeared that I might be able to walk or crawl away from the wreck instead of being rolled up with the mess after it came to a stop. However, being able to survive that field meant, first of all, being able to slip in between some trees along the border of the field. I decided to try it, said decision being prompted by gasping sounds from the engine. Not even enough time left to circle the field for a proper drag. With the last fuel sputtering through the engine, I cut the switches and shot for the field.

The things you see clearly at the last moment . . . When it was too late to do anything about it I discovered that the wheat field was only a bald mound with patches of wheat about four feet high in spots; some areas were thick with the wheat, but the rest of the field made me turn cold. It was filled with gullies deep enough to break the Jenny's back and mine along with it. But I couldn't do a thing; the wind moaned through the wires and the braces as I sailed on down.

By some miracle I slipped through the first barrier. I whipped right through those trees and kept on going. My feet never moved so fast on the rudder as they did during those seconds—that seemed to last hours. The Jenny fishtailed and yawed like a thing berserk as I kicked and banged and by some freak of good fortune I missed about six or eight really bad ditches and gullies. It wasn't a landing. It was a splattering, bouncing, jerking, whipsawing motion which ended with me in complete disbelief that the airplane was still in one piece.

I leaped out of the cockpit, signaling Frank with wild motions to land *anywhere* but where I was . . . it was too late. He saw me on the ground and the airplane still with its wings on, and besides, his fuel was about gone. He made a sudden dive for the field from the opposite side where I'd landed. Oh, brother . . .

I saw him go out of sight over the top of the mound. For a second it was quiet, and then I heard a terrific rattle, a horrible scraping sound, a crash, and then an awful quiet.

I hustled up to the top of the knoll and sort of half-shut my eyes, afraid of what I might see; I was certain the Canuck would be a crumpled mess of kindling wood. I must have stared like an idiot, because there came Frank, grinning his way up the hill, and without a scratch on him.

Even more unbelievable was the sight of the Canuck, right side up and undamaged. Frank had dodged some ditches, weaved around a thicket of stumps and screeched to a stop in the middle of a nightmare of stumps, ditches, and rocks—in a perfect landing! The man was incredible. . . .

Now began the series of events that made Iron Men out of the old barnstormer pilots. The owner of the field, after screaming, cursing and threatening a nightmare of physical harm to the two pilots for chewing up his wheat field (to say nothing of the damage caused by a thousand people who tramped through the wheat to see the planes), finally calmed down and grudgingly consented to help the two pilots get back into the air. But he wasn't in any hurry.

Marshall and Palmer had made their emergency landings on Friday. The farmer agreed to cut the wheat on the following Monday, and nothing could convince him that the departure of the two planes was imperative. Marshall sighed resignedly—a characteristic of fliers of his day—and cabled his wife in Augusta to meet them in Sylvania, the nearest town to the field.

On the day following, the three partners in the aerial misadventure went for spine-jarring rides through the local countryside. Their tour had nothing to do with any sightseeing urge; they were trying to find any field in the area which might provide a better takeoff sight than the horror into which they made their emergency landings. No luck; they were stuck with the horror.

Monday morning the farmer chopped down enough wheat to form a crude runway path. The poor choice of that path meant the pilots must await a favorable wind for attempting their takeoff—which didn't happen until Wednesday, May 19. Unfortunately, with the wind came a thundering line squall with heavy rain. Marshall and Palmer groaned in unison, but agreed that it was "now or never."

Marshall was to be first off, and he studied his takeoff path with dismay written visibly across his face. "We had to roll uphill for about 250 feet," he explains, "then straight and level for another fifty feet, and then damn quick make a turn of about forty-five degrees into a big ravine. Just the other side of the ravine was a sharp upgrade with tall trees. They got taller every time I looked at them. The rub was that we had to get off the top of the knoll, and then climb like hell to clear the trees, because there wasn't any room in which to turn. If you didn't climb fast enough or the engine coughed . . . oh, well, we would damn well know what was happening to us at that point. We decided that if we weren't off the ground by a certain point—we jammed a stick in the ground to mark the distance—we would quit right there. The way to quit was pretty miserable, too. We would have to ground loop quickly so that the airplane wouldn't roll down the hill into the gully. I think we were mad even to try it."

Frank Palmer and Marshall's wife watched helplessly as the Jenny lurched its way down the deadly takeoff path. At the top of the knoll, with the help of a stiffening wind, Marshall dragged the Jenny into the air. The trees across the ravine rushed at him with alarming speed. Wisely, and with teeth-grinding discipline, Marshall held the Jenny straight and level to pick up airspeed. And then, at the last possible moment, he horsed back on the stick. The treetops brushed against the wheels as the Jenny clawed her way into free air.

Moments later Palmer was circling upward through the rain. The two pilots didn't mind the bouncing flight of seventy minutes up to Augusta, flown scant feet above the Savannah River. Behind them, suffering silently, Mrs. Marshall hurried to catch up with her "speed demons on wings."

The financial standing of the small group was rapidly becoming perilous, what with the drain of the constant delays. Why not remain in Augusta until the weekend, then, to ply their trade as barnstormers and carry local citizens about for their first flights? Why not, indeed? For the next three days Marshall and Palmer invested their money in advertisements splashed in the leading papers, and worked on the planes to return them to top shape for the passenger-carrying flights.

Nobody wanted to fly.

This astonishing fact became more and more conspicuous as the hours passed at the small airfield, with not a single visitor with whom to bargain for the price of a ride. The dismay of the trio abated somewhat when a friend flapped his way into the field in another Canuck. This pilot was being sponsored by the Coca-Cola Company, and was able to afford half-page advertisements for the barnstormers. By Sunday night, notwithstanding a small fortune spent on the newspapers, the three airplanes managed to accumulate only seventy dollars. Their friend in the Coca-Cola Canuck took obvious pity on their plight and gave them forty dollars of that amount.

Part of which Mrs. Marshall spent immediately on a train ticket to Findlay, Ohio. She had decided that the best way to accompany the two misadventurers was to wait for them at their destination, at which, they all hoped fervently, the pilots would arrive (eventually) safe and sound.

ONWARD!

The trouble with "pressing on" is that certain ingredients are needed to carry on with a flight. Pilots need food, airplanes need fuel and oil, and all these items need money to be purchased. The overriding problem of Marshall and Palmer was that of all the things in their possession, the one they needed the most, and of which they had the least, was cash.

Augusta was dead for any barnstorming with passengers. The two men spent the entire week following Mrs. Marshall's departure searching for a town or village within fifty miles where they might find people who were anxious to be carried aloft for "the thrill of a lifetime." Instead, they found only grubby fields, latticeworks of ditches and gullies, and an astounding number of stumps.

The following weekend their hopes soared. "About a thousand autos drove out to the field," Marshall explains. "We were delighted with the sight of all those people. Finally the word had spread about our airplanes. But then our delight turned sour on us. Those people were interested in airplanes, all right, but not one of them had any intention of flying with us. It seems there had been several fatal accidents there in Augusta, and the crowd had come to see somebody *else* go up and get their fool necks broken. Well, there just wasn't anybody around who would do it. When the weekend finally passed we were still on the ground. And now our problem wasn't even remotely funny any more. Either we got some cash in hand or we were liable to remain in Augusta as real down-and-outers. . . ."

A renewed search of likely prospects for barnstorming rides focused their attention on the town of Edgefield, South Carolina, identified on the map as having a population of 1,500 and stuck on the end of a spur railroad. Desperate now for *any* business, Marshall grabbed a ride on the backwoods train crawling along the spur. He was delighted not to find the sleepy town he expected, but a booming lumber town with 4,000 people and growing in leaps and bounds.

Marshall walked into the office of the Chamber of Commerce, shook hands with the secretary, and went right into a simple sales pitch. "Mr. Secretary, I have a couple of airplanes," he declared, "and I would like to bring them up here and give some flying exhibitions and carry passengers."

The secretary stared at Marshall as though he were an escaped lunatic. Then, abruptly: "How much room you need to land those things?"

"One thousand feet level ground with no obstacle higher than a five-foot fence to get over," Marshall snapped back.

"Hell, man, there ain't that much level land in this whole county!"

As Marshall's face fell, the secretary held up his hand. "Wait; I got me an idea. I'll introduce you to a big real estate man who's going to put in a big project, and maybe he can help you."

Marshall sold the real estate tycoon a bill of goods on the favorable publicity; but there still remained the problem of the field. The men trooped out to examine the location, and Marshall felt that he could have wept. Here he had finally sold the best prospect he had ever encountered—and Marshall stared at the "only level piece of ground" as though Fate were deliberately trying to give him heartburn (and succeeding). He recalls:

> I decided there was only one possible place on that field we might be able to use. It was in a corner of the field, and it was exactly a thousand feet long and nearly two hundred feet wide. But that was only a starter. The damned strip of ground had gullies in it four feet deep, there were ridges as high as six feet, and there were all sizes of rocks and I don't know how many tree stumps crawling all over the place. On three sides of the field there were high trees. It looked like a battlefield that had been left to rot after one hell of a fight. It was a bad dream from one end to the other, and it was the best piece of ground in the whole county!
>
> But I wasn't about to quit, because I was desperate. I had visions of myself and Frank cooking sleazy soup in tin cans over an open fire along a railroad track unless we got our hands on some money, and I was willing to try anything. With a grand flourish I proposed to the man from the Chamber of Commerce and the big wheel who was in

real estate that we declare a holiday. Why not, I suggested, get the whole blamed town to the field to assist in clearing off all the obstacles and then leveling the field? That way we could get the job done quickly and without great expense and we would be flying in two or three days.

I was amazed when everyone thought it was a smash idea. There wasn't a single human being in that town that could even lay claim to ever *seeing* an airplane, and they were crazy to watch one fly. *Two* planes struck them as a sensational event. The idea of actually being able to fly just about set them afire with the urge to get that field cleared off. It was—after long last—a decent dream instead of a nightmare coming true.

You never saw anything in your life like that clearing operation. It was like getting ready for a war. We had forty men in there working like mad, and they churned the field up with huge ten-ton tractors and a bunch of smaller tractors, with enough dynamite to blow up a mountain, and picks and shovels swinging left and right. Drag out stumps? Hell, no; they had plenty of dynamite, they said, and what good was dynamite except for setting it off? They sure had an enthusiasm for blowing things up. I think some of those stumps went flying clear into the next county, they used so much dynamite.

With all that, the field was so bad that it took four and a half days of the hardest work I ever saw just to get that field *fairly* smooth. And at that, there was only a bare possibility that we could use it. I was afraid that in places the field was too soft. The big road graders had neatly filled the ditches and the gullies, but the men didn't try to compact the soil and so it stayed soft. My concern was that our plane wheels might sink in. Then we might even turn over, let alone be able to take off. If the wind happened to blow from the wrong direction or if it rained, we were goners.

But I had seen those people breaking their backs for nearly five days of blistering labor, and I knew that if we didn't give it the old college try with our airplanes, they would probably string us up from the highest tree right on the edge of the field. And I couldn't have blamed them. . . .

*   *   *

Frank Palmer flew up from Augusta; Marshall warned his partner by telephone of the field conditions and also warned him that if Frank ever wanted to see his partner alive, no matter what that field looked like, by God, he was to *land*.

At 6:30 P.M. sharp, Palmer eased his way cautiously from the air. He circled the field and dragged it once to check the runway, and the sound of his engine brought people tearing out to the field. By the time Palmer bounced to his landing the mayor and a huge mob was there to cheer his arrival. Marshall climbed in the empty cockpit so that they could test the plane on takeoff with full weight aboard. The Canuck scrambled its way from the field with about an inch and a half clearance to spare. The two men crisscrossed the town to assure everybody they were in the area, and then Marshall gave the watching throng some excitement by blowing a tire on landing.

It was worth it. They could fly the Canuck with less fuel than usual and the lowered weight would help in getting into the air. Marshall's Jenny had a greater wingspread and more lift and could actually climb faster than the Canuck, so all the effort wasn't going to be wasted, and the vision of a rope around Marshall's neck faded swiftly. That night, while the lumberjacks gave Palmer a roaring dinner, Marshall was on his way by train to Augusta to pick up his plane.

They say good fortune sometimes comes in bunches, and neither Palmer nor Marshall would argue the point. The next day broke clear and with the wind no more than a gentle breeze; overnight the field seemed to have settled and hardened a bit, and flying was much easier than they anticipated. At 9:00 A.M. their passengers were lined up waiting for the first flights in their life.

All day long the flying continued, the two airplanes taking off and landing, taking off and landing, stopping only to exchange passengers and pour fuel into the tanks. "We carried nearly fifty passengers," Marshall said, "and without a wind down the runway, every time we started the takeoff run it was pretty hairy trying to get over the fence at the end of the field. If either one of our engines had coughed once during that period we surely would have slammed right into the fence. We had some close calls that I tried to forget as quickly as they happened. But the passengers didn't realize how close they had come to continuing from their takeoff run straight into heaven, and we kept at it. When darkness came, there were still people waiting to go up. The next day we started out with the same roaring business, but then the wind shifted, and we knew we could never get into the air safely. Besides, we were dog-tired and desperate for a rest."

On Tuesday, June 1, the two men declared their visit to Edgefield, South Carolina a "smashing success," and, with the happy cheers of the townspeople to bid them farewell, roared off for the return to Augusta, Georgia. In their pockets was a total of more than five hundred dollars.

The old barnstorming biplanes had saved the day for them . . .

Friday, June 4, the two planes were in the air, once again bound toward their original destination of Findlay, Ohio. Thick clouds separated the pilots, but possible danger evaporated with the rapid dissipation of the cloud layers, and they met once again at the airport outside the town of Athens, Georgia. With plenty of fuel in their tanks, they decided not to waste time, but to take advantage of the favorable weather and press on to Atlanta. Having the opportunity to refuel, and wasting it, was a mistake they would never make again, for they ended the day with disaster averted only by skill and another break from the Fates. As Marshall tells it:

At 3:45 P.M. we hurried into the air from Athens and set course for Atlanta. It was another one of those question-mark flights as to our destination, because no one in Athens really knew much about where to land once we got to Atlanta. We were told that the *only* place to get down safely was along the back stretch of an old abandoned racetrack—and that rested in a big cut sliced from a mountainside, about thirty feet deep. That should have warned us, but we were so eager to get on with the trip, we rushed ahead like the fools that we were. The rest of our directions were also pretty sad. An Athens pilot told us to fly due west until we came to Stone Mountain, a huge bloated stone monster that reared up 1,800 feet from the level plain. We were to fly directly over Stone Mountain, and continue due west along a railway. Atlanta would be just about fifteen minutes' flying time from the mountain.

Our engines had operated perfectly in the dangerous takeoffs from the Edgefield strip, but now mine began to act up. We were only a few minutes out of Athens when the oil pressure dropped like a rock going down a deep well. Then I began to heat up; low oil pressure and high temperature is a hell of a way to fly. I cut power until the Jenny just about stumbled through the air on the edge of a stall, wallowing about like an old drunk. Frank's Canuck had a higher stalling speed, and we must have looked pretty silly, me dragging along like a crippled bird while he flew lazy circles around me just to stay in sight.

But not everything is going wrong. Stone Mountain looms out of the horizon like the bloated carcass of a dead, gray whale; the damn thing is absolutely unmistakable. I picked up the railway and it veered off slightly to the southwest; this didn't seem right, but what the hell, these are general directions anyway. Only Frank once again appears upset at my sense of direction. The Canuck races ahead, and comes chasing across me and Frank is obviously trying to head me off. But I'm sticking to the instructions I received and I stumble along. Soon the fifteen minutes are gone, Atlanta is nowhere in sight, my gas gauge shows three gallons left, and once again I have demonstrated that I am a stinking navigator. The only bright spot in a rapidly worsening situation is that my engine is behaving somewhat better.

Frank drew alongside and I signaled him that I was lost. His answering shrug is pure eloquence; so is he. Great! Suddenly the Canuck sticks its tail almost straight up in the air and dives for the earth. . . .

Frank Palmer had spotted a small town and was wasting no time as his fuel supply steadily ran lower; three times he roared past the railway station directly below them as Marshall circled patiently, hoping that Frank might read the station signs and get them out of their mess. Far below Marshall the Canuck veered sharply and sped off to the east-northeast, skimming the treetops; Marshall shoved his stick forward and raced after the other airplane. Ten miles south of Atlanta industrial smoke rose against the horizon. Almost at the same moment that Marshall brought the old racetrack—his destination—into sight his fuel gauge needle sagged a bit and then pegged hopelessly on EMPTY.

On the way down, working with infinite care to keep his wingtips from scraping the sides of the cut along one edge of the track, Marshall discovered that a huge barn loomed dead center in the racetrack. Once again both men were forced to turn what should have been an ordinary landing into a slueing adventure that could prevent, at the last moment, a disaster.

Their gratitude at a safe stop was somewhat greater than they might have anticipated. As each plane whistled down from the air, fuel supply and ignition cut off, the pilots glanced down—at the mangled wreckage of a new Jenny that had failed to make with mangower what they were doing deadstick.

Saturday and Sunday gave the two men an intimate look at the interior of a haystack along the edge of the racetrack. No lodging was available near the airplanes except some ramshackle structures which Marshall immediately denounced as "filthy, miserable and absolutely ridden with cooties." Their choice was then narrowed down, during two days of winds and rain, to burrowing as deeply within the haystack as was possible to keep dry and somewhat warm.

Recalled Marshall with a grimace:

The colder it became, the further into the haystack we burrowed. On Monday morning it was particularly cold, and by the time daylight came around we were *lost* somewhere within that blamed haystack.

Finally I tunneled out, but there wasn't a sign of Frank anywhere. I let out a shout, but got only silence for my pains. So I shouted louder; in fact as loud as I could. From far away I heard a faint answer. It seemed to be way off in the distance. I walked around to the other side of the haystack and yelled again. The reply was even fainter than before.

This was ridiculous. I kept it up for some time and I was mystified by the whole thing. It seemed that Frank was either burrowing deeper into that stack or he was circling around inside it like some idiot lost in the night.

So I just sat down to await developments. It proved to be rather interesting; soon the haystack seemed to shudder through its length and then there was a terrific upheaval. And there he was, every inch of him a straw man. That straw was everywhere—in his clothes, shoes, beneath his clothes, in his ears and his nose and his mouth and his hair. I suggested we go eat breakfast before the gas truck showed up. Frank spat something angrily and said nothing doing. He had always suspected what they had used to make breakfast food with and now he was dead certain; they used hay, and he had already had more than his share for any one man. He sat down and brooded while I went off to eat.

ONWARD AND HIGHER

Chattanooga, Tennessee, their next destination, lay far ahead of the two aerial tramps. But from this point on in the flight the conditions changed. Flatlands characteristic of what lay behind them were to be a rarity. Atlanta itself nestled in the foothills of mountains, and along with the more rugged terrain over which they would now have to fly there would be several major problems: First, getting enough altitude to clear the terrain that would rear up at them. Second, a lesser number of emergency fields than even what they had left behind them. Third, clear-air turbulence from winds sweeping down the ridges. And fourth, the particular dangers of severe weather—before they could drop down to the trees. Now, the trees might suddenly loom up before them as the crest of a steep hill. Things were going to be different, mused the two friends.

Early Monday afternoon the two airplanes squeaked into the air with heavy fuel loads from the precarious Atlanta racetrack, setting their course for Chattanooga. Overburdened with their extra tanks, the pilots fought to get the airplanes to as great a height as was possible as they left Atlanta behind. For thirty minutes the biplanes tossed gently in the afternoon air, but the two fliers were unhappy with their altitude.

One hour after takeoff there loomed before them the range of mountains that barred their way to Chattanooga. Marshall, in the wide-winged JN4B, had lifted to a height of 3,500 feet, but Palmer was not quite so fortunate. Flying the Canuck with less lift than the Jenny, he was also cursed with a balky engine that failed to deliver full power. By the time the two planes were ready to hazard the mountain range Palmer was still at 2,500 feet, struggling vainly to claw his way to safer height.

A thousand feet above him, Marshall squinted at a mountain pass to the west, and headed for the opening through which he would try to squeeze. But he was deeply concerned about Palmer; squeezing over level ground is one thing, trying to beat your way through rugged terrain with unpredictable and balky winds and downdraft is something entirely different. The Canuck swung about easily to follow the Jenny, and Marshall smiled as he watched Palmer bring his seat-of-the-pants flying lore into practice.

Palmer sidled the Canuck close to the steep mountain slope while flying parallel to the range. Gingerly he tested his airplane for the wind effects he sought and then, finding his quarry, he grinned up at Marshall as the Canuck slipped into a gentle breeze rising up the slope. The airplane sailed steadily upward; by the time the formation was at the mountain pass the Canuck cruised at 3,500 feet and Marshall in the Jenny was 500 feet higher.

Recalls Marshall:

It's a beautiful, clear day, and we have a nice tailwind, and glory be, as soon as we cross this range of mountains the farmers seem to have lost the habit of terracing their fields. We are now in hilly country but it's just beautiful, a sweet sight for any pilot to behold. All around us and in front of us there are plenty of wide and long fields into which we could slip with ease if we suddenly lost the engine. There are just wisps of clouds along the horizon, and through the mountain pass the air is calm, and the sun a wonderful shining bright. We now swing up along a great, broad valley, and the flying is perfection itself, the two airplanes slipping through the sky without any effort at all. We have plenty of height with the fuel we have burned off, and we sail with ease over another mountain range. Lookout Mountain slides beneath our wings and there is the city and, finally, at last! we have a real airport at which to land. Down below us is the field used by the Chattanooga Airplane Company, and it's big and smooth and they have hangars and plenty of facilities waiting for us, and we're as happy as larks as we sigh our way back to earth and cut the switches as we land. The sun is about to nuzzle behind the distant mountains as we get back to the ground, and if ever there is a time to say it, this is that time—it's been a perfect flight.

At noon the following day, June 8, the formation lifted easily from Chattanooga, bound ninety miles up the Tennessee River for Kingston. The two fliers planned to spend the night at Kingston as their preparatory stop before attempting to cross the Cumberland Mountains into Kentucky, the most difficult leg of their flight. Their trip along the Tennessee River proved to be a repeat of the delight they had found the day before; the airplanes drifted along pleasantly, flying down a broad valley flanked on either side with towering mountains that provided scenery instead of obstacles.

Good fortune deserted them as they landed just outside Kingston. The field into which they descended proved fine for landing, but promised only ill for their planned takeoff the following day. A round hump loomed from dead center of the strip, and that obstruction could easily wreck an airplane on takeoff.

It didn't do their mood any good to discover, after they were on the ground, that they had landed at the wrong field. Their chagrin turned into a "who cares?" shrug when they discovered that their intended point of landing was just as bad as the mess into which they had flown. A foreboding of some disaster came to them early in the evening as they were being rowed across the river to reach Kingston, a mile away from the field. That all was not right came slowly to Marshall who discovered to his horror that his shoes were wet, and getting wetter, and that water was slowly creeping up his ankles. Marshall and Palmer stared at one another in disbelief as the skiff in which they sat gurgled its way lower and lower into the river. With a last, furious gasp of foamy rowing the farmer managed to get out of deep water into mudbank shallows, just as the skiff sighed and settled to the bottom. In a black mood, with the mud sucking and plopping beneath their shoes, they staggered to the shore.

Early the next morning, the planes filled to the brim with fuel and oil, they made another of their "just-squeaked-through" takeoffs. A stiff wind helped to get them into the air by bouncing from the hump in the center of the field to an altitude where their wheels skimmed the ground; by holding straight and level flight the airplanes quickly built up enough speed to start the long climb that would enable them to cross the Cumberlands.

Their first leg took them up a branch of the Tennessee, allowing them to climb slowly without worrying every moment about ground obstacles. By the time they reached the entrance to the pass, through which they hoped to cross the barrier before them, Marshall was at twenty-five hundred feet, with Palmer slightly below him.

Marshall explained:

We were in the air about an hour when we swung into the pass. If two poor devils ever faced a prospect more forbidding than trying to break through that pass in our overloaded and tired airplanes, I sure don't know of them. Where we began to enter the pass the ground rose steeply. The sides of the pass were about a quarter of a mile wide, and suddenly that precious altitude we had fought to reach began to vanish. The pass was about a thousand feet below us when very suddenly it angled sharply; it was almost as if the damned thing had turned a square corner. It wound along beneath us and then shot off at an angle.

A railroad wound along the bottom of the pass, and instinctively you try to follow the railroad because you know the thing can't go wandering off somewhere. That's what you think, anyway, until the first time that you have to fly through the Cumberlands in two old airplanes like the ones we were in. Every mile or so the railroad disappeared. It just passed completely out of sight. The tracks had disappeared into a tunnel, of course, but those tunnels came so thick and fast it was hard to believe.

What made everything so sticky was that we didn't have any room in which to turn around. Once you pushed your way into that pass that was it. There was only one way to go and that was where the pass happened to wander. If the air got rough, or clouds came down suddenly, you *might*, you just might, be able to make the tightest turn you ever did in your life and reverse your course. I think the only way that could have been done, would be to bring up the nose, and then slap her around in a wicked stall-turn, because a normal turn was simply out of the question. The mountains towered as high as two thousand feet above us on each side and we could never have climbed over them with our fuel load. So it was a case of pushing on with your heart in your mouth and your feet shaking just a bit on the rudder, and staying very alert every second of the time. If that pass had ever closed, with the railroad disappearing into a really long tunnel, the game would have been up for us. We would have been forced to dump the planes when the ground rose up to meet us, and frankly, we were never really sure if this wasn't going to happen. But it didn't, and we bumped and bounced and yawed our way along.

After forty minutes of this jarring nonsense, of winding

around corners so sharp we almost stood the planes on their wings, and would actually lose sight of one another, we started to get worried about the direction in which we should keep flying. It sounds ridiculous, but it was true enough. There were so many coal-mine branches running in spurs off the main rail line that we could hardly tell which was which. A wrong guess could have killed us very quickly. The only way we could tell where the main pass went was to watch the rails at a distance; the trick was to follow the brightest set down a straight stretch of the canyon. The brighter the rails, the more they were in use, and that *had* to be the main line we were supposed to follow.

And then we were in trouble, and it wasn't the laughing kind. We saw the rail lines disappear off to the left. I suppose the unhappy thought came to us at the same time: what the hell do we do if the tracks tunnel out and we are facing a mountain? We were still well below the tops of the mountains. I had the Jenny up to 4,000 feet, but Frank was fighting the Canuck like mad for altitude. She just didn't have it, and he was pooping along at 2,500 feet with the mountains far above him on either side. We were so deep into the pass that Frank could never have turned around unless he would have been able to loop the airplane and do a half-roll coming out of the loop. But he had as much chance of doing that kind of maneuver as he would have been able to fly by flapping his arms. We were stuck, but at least I had altitude on my side.

Well ahead of me—about ten miles up the pass—I could make out a gap in the mountains. No question but that with my height of 4,000 feet I could get through. But what about poor Frank? He was liable to run out of air without warning.

You never know when bad luck can hit—or good luck, for that matter. Without warning the canyon broke away sharply, and the tracks gleamed in the light and there, right in front of and below us, was the town of Jellico, Tennessee. One moment we were worrying about even surviving the flight, and then right below us there's a town and a decent field, and we sure did barrel our way right into that strip, two very relieved and happy pilots.

*   *   *

The town of Jellico lay in a deep pocket in the mountains; a rough bowl that seemed to have been cut by nature out of the surrounding hills. But no more than twenty-five miles ahead of Jellico, the mountains dropped off sharply and a wide prairie stretched along the flight path of the airplanes. The two men refueled, and at 3:25 P.M. were back in the air, climbing steadily above the depression within which lay the Jellico airfield. With enough altitude to slide through the final canyon of the mountains, the airplanes moved on—and left the worst stretch of the Cumberlands behind them. Happily, without further incident.

For nearly three quarters of an hour the flight continued smoothly. Then the level ground began to break up with hills rising sharply and "soon we were over the hilliest country I had ever seen in my life," explained Marshall—

There wasn't a place in which a man could even land a kite, and that damned railroad began twisting and turning like a snake gone berserk. We had to guess which way to follow the railroad, because it pulled its disappearing acts again, vanishing suddenly into long tunnels. For the first time on the trip I guessed right about which way to go; we hit a long stretch with the railroad out of sight, and I veered off to one side, and was grateful to see the tracks reappear suddenly.

There had simply been too much beating of our emotions, I guess, because both of us were feeling down in the dumps. We thought we had finally reached some decent country over which to fly and all we could see in every direction were hills, hills, and more hills. We both had visions of getting to Lexington, Kentucky, when it was dark and that didn't please us one little bit. We had only rumors to guide us as to the landing field, and rumors have a habit of being all wrong when you're trying to land in sky so black you can hardly see your hand in front of your face.

And then, suddenly, just like before, the country smoothed out. We were about twenty miles from Kentucky when this happened and we were caught by surprise. The ground looked as if a child had used it for a sandpile; as if he had built a range of hills, and then swept everything clean with a board. The change was that abrupt. One minute we had hills beneath us, and then suddenly

everything was flat prairie country. The change in color
was most striking. With that same startling suddenness the
earth became an extremely dark green, but with a definite
bluish tinge to the coloration. It stretched in every direction.

Aside from the beauty of the scene, which caught us
with impact, was the knowledge that we were out of those
infernal hills and that with all that flat land beneath us we
were safe. As things turned out it was vital. The racetrack
to which we had been referred as the landing field had
been turned into a trap with all sorts of structures all over
the place. But there was all that wonderful level ground
and that beautiful grass. We just picked out a nice field
that was close to town and settled to the earth as pretty
and gentle as you could please. That landing sort of made
up for the mess we had been in during the day.

Early the next morning, with the weather holding, the two
pilots pushed on from Lexington, Kentucky for a nonstop
flight to Dayton, Ohio. If they could just stay out of any
emergencies—and the mountains were now well behind
them—they could refuel at Dayton, and press on the same
afternoon to Findlay. But wise old pilots firmly believe that
when everything is going well and things look even better for
the future, well, that's when to look out for trouble.

Marshall was at a thousand feet and six miles north of
Lexington when trouble descended upon him like a thunderbolt. Only this was a thunderbolt that came with a crash—of
silence. Without any warning his engine quit. "The thing just
stopped dead," he said wryly. "Not so much as a poop out of
it. But wonder of wonders, I was right over a tremendous
meadow. In fact, it was the best field we'd been in since
starting on that miserable journey. Frank landed easily alongside me. . . ."

The magneto of Marshall's Jenny was completely shot, and
an all-day effort to fix the mag produced only skinned knuckles and grease all over their clothes. The next morning, June
11, the pilots dismantled the fuel tank from the front cockpit
of the Canuck and set off together for Cincinnati. They hadn't
planned to land there, but with only twenty gallons and extra
weight in the Canuck the refueling stop proved necessary. By
now what good luck they had been experiencing was vanishing like sand through open fingers. The Canuck's engine lost
oil pressure on the way in to "a terrible, rough, bumpy, short

field near Cincinnati." Marshall boosted the engine just enough to make the field.

But after takeoff the oil pressure dropped again, Marshall pumped like mad, and suddenly the engine had too much pressure. The specter of fire frightened the adventurers, who dove back for the field they had just left—and whistled in to a wild landing made wilder by a thirty-mile-per-hour wind on their tail. After emergency repairs (feeling much at home again), they staggered out of Cincinnati, neatly clipping tree-tops with the Canuck's wheels in a terrifying takeoff. At 3:00 P.M. that same day they landed in Dayton. That night, while Palmer slept in Dayton, Marshall glowered from the seat of a train that carried him, along with a new armature for his Jenny, back to Cincinnati. He rejoined Palmer in Dayton the afternoon of the twelfth.

By now, with Findlay so close, nothing could keep the two men from fighting their way on to a completion of the "flight." At sunset of June 12—*more than a month* since their Florida departure—the Jenny and the Canuck rolled wearily to a stop at Findlay, Ohio.

The final landing certainly proved to be in keeping with the nature of the expedition. Marshall broke a wing skid—the *only* mishap of the entire wild misadventure!

There is an interesting postscript to the saga of Tex Marshall and Frank Palmer. Marshall himself penned the words, one year later; the reader will find this diary postscript more revealing than any other document:

It is now May 10, 1921, exactly one year from the day that Frank Palmer, Mrs. Tex Marshall and myself lifted into the air from Sea Breeze, Florida, that I am writing this account. I am writing these words within one hour of the time that we began our flight one year past. It is with the dearest of memories of my life that I place those experiences, and the others that followed our arrival in Ohio. The two airplanes are stored away now; perhaps they will never again be flown by us.

Frank and I are both flying the United States Air Mail now; Frank is a regular pilot on the run between St. Louis and Chicago. Today he is a married man, making his home in St. Louis. As it happens, he is just starting a vacation of two weeks, and I am doing the same. We will meet later on this date and we will be able to talk about and to relive many of the experiences and the adventures we shared just a year ago. This anniversary of the start of our pilgrimage by air is somehow a fitting occasion for our meeting.

Today I fly 425 miles from Chicago to Omaha in a new de Havilland, a Mail Plane with 450 horsepower, and I make the flight in just three hours and thirty minutes. There is already a vast difference in the aircraft, the experiences of flight, and the country between one year ago and now. . . .

A NOTE TO MYSELF: The field at Findlay where we landed was one that my wife, Katherine, had picked out herself, and marked for us to see with a huge cross of wrapping paper she obtained from a grocery store. When we landed it was just that—an open field and no more. Now it is the Findlay Municipal Airport, and a very fine one. We have been back to look at it, and we can hardly believe what we saw. That rough field strewn with boulders, from which we operated through most of the summer of 1920, is now such an outstanding facility. We find it so difficult to believe because we used Findlay as our home base for barnstorming throughout that summer.

Those months of barnstorming were simply marvelous, and a fitting culmination to our rather hectic journey to reach Ohio. We hooked up with some of the carnivals that were playing the county fairs, and we traveled to the fairs with them, and operated as part of the whole show. In fact, we ourselves became real carnies before the fall of 1920! And we made money at it; we did a lot of fine business by hopping passengers at three dollars a head. Those flights were short. We took off, made a short climbing turn and hustled back in to land. The fields were short and some of those takeoffs and landings were pretty tight. But think of all the practice we had on the way from Florida to Ohio. . . .

9

The Sharpsters

During the years of the early 1920's, the town of Clarion, Pennsylvania, laid boisterous claim to being the most air-minded and air-active community in the entire United States. Clarion was a small collection of people, industries and homes that nestled in the northwestern part of the state, and every year hosted the surrounding communities by being the seat of the annual county fair. This countrified derring-do, with its razzmataz of carnies, sideshows, huge vegetables and glowering cattle, meant plenty of people with enough money in their jeans to attract barnstormers, just as winos are drawn eagerly to a half-empty bottle of muscatel. Not only did Clarion enjoy this happy state of affairs, but the townspeople prided themselves on their community's position as an historical center of things and events aeronautical.

Earlier—much earlier in the still fledgling history of aviation—the Clarion fairgrounds had been witness to virtually every hot-air balloonist on tour doing his best to impress the ladies and collect coins from their menfolk. A collection of bulging and pulsating bags had wheezed and snorted their precarious passage over the town rooftops and along the fields and hills, while the daring aeronauts waved and shouted at all below, bringing forth the customary response of barking dogs and shrieking children.

And then, men with wings clattered their way through the cool air over Clarion—among them such famed pioneers as the redoubtable Eugene Ely. The burgeoning position of Clarion in the dawning air age received further impetus when the granite-jawed biplane pioneers selected the town as one of the major way-stops for airmail pilots who were inaugurating the initial pathfinder flights. Such honor was not to be dismissed lightly, and the city fathers were swift to agree that the old fairgrounds would be a splendid site indeed for the Government's new project. Hastily they dubbed the fairgrounds their municipal airport, creating the airport by a hurried nodding of heads. And there half the town gathered one day, impatiently awaiting the fluttering arrival of airmail pilot Max Miller, the man delegated with the signal honor of being the first Post Office contract pilot to touch down at Clarion.

Max, flying a Hisso Jenny with a huge mailbag painted in atrocious colors on both sides of the creaking fuselage, managed to find his way to Clarion. Staring down at the ex-fairgrounds airport, he looked with misgivings at the great number of people unconcernedly thronging onto the field. Crowds, he had learned bitterly, were unpredictable creatures. All too often, and always at the worst possible moment, they had the nasty habit of staging wild cavalry charges onto the center of a field—exactly where he intended to land. Not only did this chew up the propeller, but the propeller chewing up parts of the crowd made the remainder very unhappy. They also became unfriendly to the pilot, and were liable to vent their wrath on the hapless airman.

Considering all the unhappy possibilities, Max was distracted. His preoccupation with such dire happenings lasted longer than he expected; Max discovered quite abruptly that not only was he going to miss the milling throng beneath his propeller, but he was also about to overshoot the entire field to go sailing into unpleasant terrain beyond. His descent was, however, not unusual for that era.

Max blithely sailed directly over and then beyond the upraised heads of the good people of Clarion. Despite the frantic waving, gesticulating and frenzied shouts of the townspeople, the Jenny rumbled out of the sky to settle to earth on the east side of town. Max barely skimmed his wheels over a nasty barbed wire fence and then slammed against the earth in a crunching three-point landing that jarred him from spine to teeth and stampeded an entire herd of cows that had been peacefully grazing directly in the path of the Jenny.

Well behind him, feet thudded against the earth as people scrambled for cars, trucks, carriages and horses, and went pell-mell in clouds of swirling dust after the errant Max

Miller. The mayor and the townspeople came upon their aviator sitting comfortably in the lush grass, casually puffing away on a cigarette.

Thus it was that Max Miller made permanent his mark on history. With deceptive ease he disposed of the herd of cows, caused the fairgrounds to be instantly dismissed as the new airport, and established for the Air Mail Service its new stopover point on the haul from Cleveland to Bellafone.

Max was unaware that he had also set the stage for the operation of two of aviation's wildest, sneakiest, shrewdest, stop-at-nothing operators in the vicinity of Clarion. These gentlemen were the irrepressible Parker Cramer and Jack Barstow. They seemed to be only one step removed from the back of a mule-hauled wagon, shouting at gathering crowds and selling Indian Cure-all Snake Oil. Cramer and Barstow showed up one day at the new Clarion airport with a bedraggled fleet of barnstorming planes, including in the motley assortment surplus Jennies, Standards, and Thomas-Morse Scouts.

The latter machine was a terrifying abortion of mechanical and aeronautical incompetence. It was a single-seater with a rotary engine (in which the entire engine rotated at great speed and with brutal torque) which once had been the great white hope of the U.S. Air Service. Gazing fondly upon the fabric apparition, Army pilots training in Texas—innocent as babes of the facts of life—had cried loudly that they would take their machines to France and wipe the skies clean of the filthy Boches and their dirty Fokkers. Fortunately for the nation, the "Tommy Morses" never reached France, thus robbing the Germans of easy victories and saving the Gold Star Mothers of America from an unnecessarily long list of members.

According to one veteran aviator who knew the two partners, Cramer and Barstow reached Clarion "during one of their frequent forced landings while flying cross country in marginal weather. To this pair, 'marginal weather' meant what the Weather Bureau now classifies as zero-zero or slightly worse. Because they were efficient at the stick, each managed to guide many a disabled plane to terra firma—visibility and ceiling be damned—without great loss of skin or bone. When such flights ended in the treetops or volunteer firemen were forced to respond to handle the situation, the event was shrugged off with the adage that any landing a man could walk away from was a good one."

The Cramer and Barstow method of operation was as shady, blunt, and seemingly haphazard as one might imagine during a nightmare. These two worthies resurrected from an evil-smelling junk heap a drugstore scale thrown away by its previous owner as worthless, beyond any hope of repair. Entirely unconcerned with accuracy or anything remotely associated with the concept, the partners shined up the scale and dragged it with them to whatever field might be selected as a destination. The scale was mounted prominently near their airplanes, and prospective passengers smilingly invited to step upon its platform. With solemn manner the partners then handed to each individual a slip of paper stating their weight and also listing the charges for a ten-minute flight around the pea patch. Their concept of operation was based on the system that the epic aerial journey would cost the passenger one penny per pound.

The fact that the scale was impossibly erratic was ignored. Sometimes the mechanical refuse employed for enticing customers would sag badly, and a slender, young high-school senior would be charged twenty-five dollars for her flight. The next customer might be a tight-fisted farmer's wife who ordered her dresses not from Sears, but from Omar the Tentmaker—and who would be charged only a two-dollar bill.

One should not draw the hasty conclusion that Cramer and Barstow were dishonest. They were not. One might classify them as "fiercely enterprising," for this certainly they were. For example:

The potential customers of the day often included those very tight souls who would rather cut off their arms than spend even a dime outright to purchase flight time. Yet they were eager to fly, if only they could figure out some method of wrangling "free" flying from the two partners. Thus it was that the smart ones often outsmarted themselves (with some help from Cramer and Barstow) by flinging money about with abandon in order to cadge a free ride. Whiskey and good steak were especially dear in those days, and it was evident that the pilots were not averse to partaking of sumptuous repasts.

The local con man would conduct himself in a grandiose manner and escort the two pilots to the Busy Bee Cafe, where he would then spend perhaps thirty to forty dollars in order to get the pilots into a congenial mood. At that point the con artist would introduce the friendly question of, "Say, we're good buddies now—right? How about a ride just for me, your buddy!" The pilots would ponder the question slowly—to the con man, anyway, since they had long made up their minds to follow exactly this procedure.

Sated with superb food, belching happily and aglow with good liquid cheer, the pilots finally nodded agreement. "Hell, it was a great system to be 'taken' by a local con artist," exclaimed an old-timer. "We loved to find one of those types. We could seldom afford a meal like that on our own money more than once a year!"

And then there was the delicate matter of building up a fuel reserve for future operations . . .

Cramer and Barstow let it be known that they were never above "making a deal" when it came to bartering for flights, instead of settling only for cash. Everyone loves to outsmart his neighbor, and the flying partners were experts in acting like wide-eyed sheep just drooling to be led to slaughter. Airplanes need gasoline, gasoline costs money, and the Indian traders fairly leaped at the chance to cut the pilots' profit by offering them fuel instead of hard cash.

"Why, hell yes!" Cramer would exclaim to such an offer, "just fill 'er up!" The smug customer forked over enough money to top the thirty-two-gallon tank. Confident that he had outwitted the sharpster fliers, he would then be treated to a flight of fifteen minutes that he might have bought in cash—for two dollars.

Other customers eyeing the proceedings were also quick to make the same deal. Neither of the two pilots could ever be accused of sleeping on the job of "how to be fleeced and make a profit." With potential customers in sight, a local kid was hired to stand by and immediately after each flight drain any fuel in the airplane into a steel drum. Thus the next local con artist in line always paid the full freight, but went aloft convinced he had outsmarted the barnstormers by only partially filling the tank. If there was no steel drum handy, the kid was always ready to help push another plane out from the hangar, after making certain that the tank was bone dry and ready to sop up the maximum in the best grade of gasoline offered at the field.

*   *   *

In 1925 the two men, by some devious process of thought never explained, decided that they were ready for a momentous step forward in aviation affairs. This lurch into the future was their first transport airplane. They looked upon its increased seating capacity as virtually a guarantee of additional dollars per flight and, while the machine might admittedly be somewhat modest in size, it could also be regarded as a stirring forerunner of things to come. Enthused with visions of great machines rumbling through the air and bank vaults steadily being filled on the ground, Cramer and Barstow began to bastardize a surplus Standard fuselage.

This took the form of additional structural strength with many stringers, cross-members and piano wire. With the hull ready to be abused in the form of extra weight, they installed a new Hisso engine, and looked with evident fondness on their creature.

Alas, but they yet lacked wings. Unable to find any lying about that would fit their needs, they declared themselves to be aeronautical engineers and set out to design and build their own set of airfoils. What the partners did not have they did not purchase if it could be borrowed, and they marched in triumph from the home of a civil engineer, carrying with them a drafting table, pencils, markers, T-square, triangle and other assorted oddments of the trade with which they were totally unfamiliar. After prodigious scratching and clawing at blueprint sheets they arose wearily, and turned over to their boys in the hangar drawings which were unintentionally but undeniably sidesplitting to any engineer worth his salt. The hangar crew, following orders, built the wings exactly to the specifications as laid down by Cramer and Barstow.

The results were then mated to the fuselage, control systems installed, and the whole of it ruggedly attached. After a brisk paint job the machine was trundled out of the hangar for its public debut.

While visitors stared in disbelief, Cramer and Barstow glowed with pride, pounded one another on the back, and mentally added up the incoming profits their machine was certain to bring them. They had added considerable isinglass in the back of the fuselage to form an enclosed space that would accommodate two passengers. The cabin was rough-hewn, and while it might have kept out falling snow in a dead calm, clearly it would not keep out the wind, and was guaranteed to be a center of howling drafts. Aware of this problem—

and entirely unconcerned about the warmth of their paying passengers—the pilots decided that the machine should be flown from the front seat. Here the pilot sat directly behind the bellowing Hisso, and gained all the advantage of the warmth exuding from the engine.

It must be duly noted that this creation of Cramer and Barstow, this insult to the science of aeronautical engineering, this pox upon all engineering graduate schools, *flew*. Not only that, but it flew *well*. It did everything that its designers had hoped it would do, and perhaps more, for it was likely they had patched together the sturdiest machine ever to take to the skies in its time.

And it made them money. Within the second day of rolling the new biplane from its hangar, the pilots were taking turns in the air, doubling the take of former passenger flights. Where other towns spurned flying—as Tex Marshall and Frank Palmer had learned to their sorrow—Clarion instead clutched the world of flight to its collective breast and gasped happily.

Overhead for operations at Clarion airport was a pleasant joke to be ignored. The expense of keeping mechanics and line boys was neatly obviated by taking full advantage of the airminded youth of the town who flocked to Cramer and Barstow as though they were Charlemagne and Roland reincarnate. The kids kicked and jostled one another to be first in line to push the heavy biplane in and out of hangars. The kids fought to help prime the engine by pouring raw fuel onto the priming cups atop each cylinder. And the kids were just wild to wipe oil from the fuselage, to clean the wheels, polish the windscreens—*anything* just for the privilege of being near an airplane, and receiving every now and then the breathless honor of a pat on the head from the pilots.

Barnstormers invariably regarded the coming of night as equal to an overflow of the River Styx. The nocturnal mists were no place for a smart man, for one was quite likely to stumble badly—with much crunching of airplanes and bones—while attempting to alight from the darkness. But not Cramer and Barstow, because they had Clarion at their beck and call. And Clarion had hundreds of parents who were as wild about flying as were their kids. The elders exhibited this zeal by willingly driving their cars en masse to the airport and sundering the night with banks of headlights so that Cramer and

Barstow could fly in illuminated splendor, and charge higher prices for the wonder of sailing the night skies.

Cramer and Barstow had the greatest thing going since mass adulation was invented. Just being on the periphery of their exciting aviation business brought about an unmistakable giddiness among the middle-aged and even the old duffers of Clarion. Shining eyes were the lot of the wee ones and their tottering grandparents when flying was involved. And the performance put on by the townspeople startled even the leathery piloting team.

The social betters and the ancients of Clarion—accustomed to nothing more dashing than wearing a heavy gold chain across their ample middles—became positively glamorous through their addiction for aviation. They appeared at the Clarion airport adorned in lace boots, oversize leather jackets, riding breeches, leather helmets and goggles, and gloves of the finest leather.

Did they fly?

But no.

Could they fly?

Heavens, *no!*

Did they wish to learn to fly?

NEVER!

No, these good folk wished nothing more than to array themselves in the fashion of members of the eighty-eighth Observation Squadron, their spirits raised by visions. They turned their failing eyes to the heavens where through the mists of age and soggy emotions they saw themselves engaged in swirling, dramatic dogfights with the treacherous Hun . . . struggling through terrible storms (the mail *must* go through!) . . . or delivering a rare medicine to a rich man's daughter gasping away her beautiful young life in a snowbound mountain lodge.

One should not underestimate the intensity of these feelings. The amazed team of Cramer and Barstow did not. Indeed, they were lightning-swift to seize upon the golden opportunity handed to them by the Walter Mitty characteristics displayed by their camp followers.

They rushed off one morning from Clarion, carrying with them their entire cash reserves. This alone was stark proof of their convictions. Later that day they spent every nickel they had between them at a U.S. Air Service surplus auction. And that night they slipped back into Clarion, driving a truck with its springs sagging under the weight of hundreds of brand-new aviator uniforms. The rest of the night was spent in neatly clipping off the quartermaster tags.

In the ensuing days and weeks Cramer and Barstow carried out one of the most sensational business deals in their entire career of happy chicanery. They sold the flying uniforms—with a profit markup of roughly *one thousand percent*—to drugstore clerks, harness salesmen, bakers' assistants, retired farmers and anyone else in sight.

On Saturday afternoons, the crowd that gathered at Clarion airport to watch their heroes, Cramer and Barstow, could easily have been taken by an outsider to be a reunion of half the surviving fliers who had gone Over There.

Yet it would be grossly unfair even to suggest that Cramer and Barstow grasped (or clutched, as some have said) at *every* opportunity to snare a buck. There was, for example, the case of Red Gahagan . . .

Red was a gas-pump jockey who roared loudly on a motor-cycle from work to the Clarion airport every Saturday after-noon in order that he might splurge his pay on flying lessons. There came one afternoon in particular when Red showed up earlier than his usual arrival time. He was observed to be strolling about the parked Jennies and Standards muttering to himself. At this point Cramer and Barstow appeared. They stared at Red as their student mouthed such foreign words as *empennage, l'aile supérieure, manche à balai* and other weird phrases that, due to a monstrously atrocious pronunciation on Red's part, could only be guessed at as to their origin.

After several moments of this performance both Cramer and Barstow advanced menacingly upon Red Gahagan and asked him just what in the name of hell he was doing with his tongue. With visible pride Red revealed that he had discov-ered a French Army pilot instruction manual that was being translated for him by a Butler University professor (who obviously had nothing better to do with his time). Aghast at this confession, the two partners grounded Red for a week, with the severe admonition that he stay the hell away from book learning and stick to what he could and should learn in the cockpit.

It was only a moment later that Cramer and Barstow were thunderstruck by their deed. They had turned down money from a paying student! Before running Gahagan off the field, they warned their zealous student to be sure that he saved his pay for a double lesson the week following.

Red was morose. With hunched shoulders and a black look upon his brow he climbed aboard his two-wheeler and crackled off in a roar and a cloud of smoke. Several minutes later he stopped at a diner to drown his sorrow in a cup of coffee. At that moment Fate intervened on behalf of Red Gahagan . . .

Noticing Red's new goggles jutting out from his jacket pocket, a customer inquired if he was an aviator. Pride rushed through the blood of young Gahagan. Didn't he have at least two hours of dual instruction? Hadn't he flown an airplane?

"Hell, yes!" he cried with bubbling friendliness, "Sure, I'm an aviator!"

"You're hired," snapped the stranger, immediately grasping Red by his jacket sleeve and dragging him bodily outside to his car.

A short time later the stranger braked to a stop at the edge of a cow pasture, where Red stared in wonder at a Hisso-Standard that was almost gleaming new. The stranger explained that he had just bought the airplane, but faced a serious problem. The previous owner had collected cash for the machine, and then departed the premises without so much as a brief explanation of how the thing should be flown.

"Now, friend," explained the man with the airplane who didn't know how to fly, "I want you to teach me how to fly that damned thing out there. I didn't buy that blasted machine so that it would stay with the cows in this here field." He paused briefly and smiled. "But first, young fellow," he added, "first you take her up for a little hop. Feel her out and see how you like her, and then we'll settle down to business." The invitation to Red for flight was tendered in a pride-of-ownership tone of voice usually reserved for those who have just purchased thoroughbred horses, sports cars, a yacht, or a nine-passenger limousine with built-in bar.

Red gulped a few times, swallowed a huge air bubble in his throat and looked at the airplane. "Sure," he said casually. "Sure. Why the hell not?"

So saying, he whipped on his goggles, clambered into the cockpit and began an uncertain groping for the proper switches. After several minutes he shouted his readiness. The owner swung the prop, the Hisso exploded into thundering life, and at the same moment Red was busy gritting his teeth and rushing down the field. The elation that came with his first

solo takeoff must have been something to behold. Red's spirits soared even faster than did the airplane. *Solo!* He was one
with the gods! He was . . .

With treacherous speed Red's feelings of Absolute Power
melted into a mixture of alarm, fear and chagrin. What sparse
knowledge that Red had of aircraft engines was limited to
small Curtiss power plants, and that proved worthless to him
now. The vagaries of the blatting Hisso with its ailing oil
system were strictly Greek to Red (who struggled with his
native tongue), and when the engine began to lose oil pressure Red could only watch dismally as the needle flopped to
the left. He grew even more dismal as the Hisso belched a
cloud of evil smoke and expired.

Red shoved forward on the stick and jiggled the rudder
slightly to continue straight ahead, where there lay a broad
field of new oats. Red thanked the gods for small favors—at
least it was an open field. Moments later he skimmed the
fence and flared out for his landing. The gear, propeller and
wings were instantly caught up by the tough, slender stalks,
and a horrified Red thought the airplane was being lashed by
a horde of maddened octopi. After a lurching, staccato-
hammering stop, Red crawled unhurt from the cockpit. It
would take no more than a big pot of glue to fix the airplane,
but as far as the owner was concerned all bets were off with a
snotty young pilot named Gahagan.

Basking in the glory of his first solo, Red waved off the
angry mutterings of the airplane owner. He was now ready to
become a barnstormer himself. He had proved he could fly.
Who the hell needed more lessons?

Thus did Cramer and Barstow commit the dastardly crime
of losing a student who, if not promising, at least was
paying.

Pay.
That was the unending nagging problem faced by Cramer
and Barstow. *Pay.* Following the defection of Red Gahagan,
business seemed to evaporate. The crowds that drifted to the
airport in their surplus-uniformed finery began to thin. Even
thinner were the ranks of those who wanted to pay for the
privilege of looking down upon the earth. The great fad of the
flying partners, once clutched to the bosom of Clarion, shriv-
eled rapidly, and the warmth of adulation began to be replaced with the cold grip of financial reality. Even the killing

made in the sale of the surplus uniforms vanished in the need to keep eating and living.

The harsh facts of life came on the afternoon that the local grocer met the pilot team with an upraised hand and the imperious announcement that their credit was now exhausted—finis, kaput, no more! Cramer and Barstow left the premises with their stomachs growling and their heads held high. Several minutes later, however, a stony greeting at their favorite hash house, where they stopped in to bum a meal, demolished even *their* lofty pride.

Broke! That dread word so well known to so many other barnstormers tasted like wormwood in their mouths. But they had to eat; what to do? To go into any other line of "work" was monstrous; unthinkable!

"Who," they asked one another in soul-searching honesty, "are even bigger bums than barnstormers?" The answer came with a glare of realization—newspaper men, that's who. Immediately Cramer and Barstow attired themselves in clean and pressed aviator togs and paid a friendly call on the editor of the local rag. His reply to their conversation was offered in a tone of acid honey.

"Money?" he shrieked. "You two nuts want *me* to loan *you* cash money?" His tone was incredulous and he sagged back into his chair, rolling his eyes in an impassioned plea to heaven that he might be spared such moments. Then, after shaking his head and leaning forward, he seemed to realize that he had two hungry types before him, and his tone became more friendly.

"Listen, birdmen," he said, "let me tell you guys something. The last subscription I sold for this crumby paper was traded for two bushels of potatoes and a dozen eggs . . ."

The editor went on to explain in gruesome detail that the entire town had suffered a disastrous financial blow due to the closing of the local highway for repairs. Farmers from outlying districts no longer were able to come into town; for three months they had bought no provisions in Clarion; and the local merchants, added the editor, "are beginning to button their shirts on the knobs of their backbones." (So that's why the flying business was about to roll over and die like a parched cockroach . . .)

The editor rubbed his chin; Cramer and Barstow sat up a bit straighter in their seats as they saw a gleam appear in the eyes of their host. Abruptly the editor leaped from his chair and shouted: "I've got it! I've got it!"

Cramer looked at Barstow. "Hooray! He's got it!"

Barstow stared at Cramer. *"What* has he got?"

Cramer barked, "How the hell should I know? He's got it—hooray!"

Barstow shrugged. "Hooray," he said.

The editor dashed around his desk and grabbed the two aviators by their shiny leather labels. Talking rapidly he ad-libbed a total promotion scheme that, even if it failed to make them rich, would crack the money drought. The editor in a spume of words outlined a mammoth shopping event. He described hundreds of free prizes from the cobwebbed shelves of the local merchants. And the lure, he explained, the sure-fire, catchall, snag-'em lure would be a wild and thrilling air show staged by none other than the one-and-only redoubtable flying team of Cramer and Barstow.

"By God!" shouted the editor as he slammed a skinny fist again and again into his palm, "we will get every last dime those blasted farmers have been saving since the highway closed!"

Before the day was out the great scheme was under way. The merchants shook the dust from their clothes, cleaned their stores, dressed up their windows, and dug into dwindling cash reserves to lavish their last money on huge newspaper ads (which did not make the editor unhappy). Colorful posters went up on trees, poles, buildings, buggies, automobiles—anywhere and everywhere. Cramer and Barstow cleaned their goggles and polished their airplanes and prepared for their huge aerial circus.

On the appointed day Clarion swarmed with visitors from miles around. Heading the vanguard into town were the greedy farmers and their wives who had rushed to enjoy the dare-deviltry and take advantage of the discount prices on everything from liquorice to corset stays. Even Cramer's young brother, Bill, was called into the act. He promised to make a parachute jump and, as an added fillip to wow the crowd, he would play the sad refrain of "My Old Kentucky Home" on a harmonica while drifting earthward. Wisely, unfortunately, depending upon the point of view, young Bill suddenly remembered a pressing engagement in Pittsburgh, and he left it up to Cramer and Barstow to carry on the show by themselves.

The morning was witness to an orgy of spending by the farmers and little cries of delight from the merchants, who were doing more business in three hours than they had in the previous three months. Following the great splurge, the sky circus went into action.

Barstow appeared first in his Hisso Standard, and dazzled the crowd with a half hour of low-level aerobatics the likes of which hadn't been seen since Roy Brown and Wop May played tag with von Richthofen over the Somme. He went into loops by starting his pullup at treetop level. He spun to dangerously low heights and came out of his whirling plunge with a sudden zooming roar. The Standard slow-rolled and then barrel-rolled. He did falling leaves and Immelmanns, chandelles and figure-eights, stall turns and split-S maneuvers. He hung the Standard on its back and stood it on its nose and wing tips. Twice he narrowly missed clipping off the weathervane that jutted above the courthouse roof. When his fuel began to run out and his nerves were ragged, Barstow returned to the field to pick up Bill Cramer for the promised parachute jump.

His face fell when informed of the defection of young Bill. What to do? There was a mob waiting; they simply had to deliver. The ingenuity that had kept them so long in the barnstorming business came to their rescue; inspiration lit up their faces. Working quickly, Cramer and Barstow tied knots in the sleeves and legs of a pair of mechanic's coveralls; then they stuffed the garment with straw. The dummy was dumped in the rear cockpit of the Standard and Barstow took off in a rush to "thrill the hell out of those yokels." That he did . . .

High over the river Barstow slow-rolled the Standard. He kicked in just enough rudder to give the dummy a sideward motion, and the straw man was flung out into space. Far below, craning their heads back to watch the wonderful scene of the parachutist, women fainted, strong men cursed, small children cried in fear and the inevitable dogs barked and snarled.

Poor Bill's chute, it was obvious, had failed him. And he was so young to die! A crowd of stunned, heartsore and wailing spectators stampeded toward the river to gather in the crushed remains of the hapless, courageous youth.

The wailing choked off to a snarling gurgle when the mob discovered the bloodless dummy reposing peacefully along the riverbank. Sorrow changed swiftly to wrath. Hoaxed! The crowd turned itself about, the angry murmuring growing into shouts and threats as it stalked purposefully back to town.

Uncaring and unknowing of the train of events, Cramer and Barstow sipped coffee in the Busy Bee Cafe. A pleased look was visible on their faces. And then they heard a distant roar, like a tidal wave grinding its way along the street. No tidal wave this, but the enraged mob tramping with menacing intent up the main street.

"Now what's wrong with *them?*" queried Barstow, in all innocence. He and his partner found out quickly enough as the mob surged into the doors of the cafe, intent on an old-fashioned tarring and feathering.

From within their jail cell—where the sheriff had locked them for their own protection—the birdmen spent the rest of the afternoon trying to explain their innocence and their good intentions. The shouting mob quieted only when the barnstormers promised them a free jump the day following. "Even," Barstow affirmed, "if one of us has to make the jump himself."

Free from confinement, the intrepid aviators discovered that they lacked even the vaguest idea of where they might locate a parachute in that part of the country—but they knew they had better find one someplace, and soon. The vision of bubbling tar and clouds of feathers spurred them on. All through the night they drove, eventually digging up a chute that resembled a museum piece and which, they prayed, had not yet provided unknown moths a satisfying meal.

As Saturday dawned, an angry Barstow struggled into his flight gear. "Damn it," he muttered to his partner, "somebody is sure gonna get some surprises today!" Cramer agreed sleepily; he was too shot from the all-night driving search for the parachute to once again review the plans for the climax of their two-day airshow.

Not only were they going to keep their promise of the parachute jump, but Barstow, his anger growing at the previous day's threats of the mob, was going to give them a demonstration of low-level flying guaranteed to whiten every freckle in the county. He had made his decision to fly beneath the bridge that spanned the new dam above the town. And for this little caper he would use the single-seat Thomas-Morse. The Tommy, as he affectionately referred to the machine, in comparison to the Standard or the Jenny was firefly-quick on the controls. It could respond to a nudge of the stick with all the alacrity displayed by an aging virgin being pursued by a horny gorilla.

Barstow fired up the rotary engine and took to the air in a light blue cloud of carbonized castor oil. He was at maximum power when he slid down from the air to start his run toward the bridge. The airplane trembled slightly in the air currents sweeping over the ground, and Barstow felt the keen thrill of a mastery of the medium. The earth rushed closer and closer, the airplane flung itself toward its goal, and Barstow exulted in the moment.

Then the thrill vanished and the exultation threatened to gag in his throat, all of it replaced with the feeling of arrogant stupidity and utter helplessness. At the last possible moment Barstow realized that he had neglected several matters which were of the utmost importance to his continued survival.

For one thing, he had forgotten that the new dam had raised the level of the river. With care and a hell of a lot of luck he just might be able to keep his wheels from hitting fish and his skull from going *splat!* into the lower span of the bridge—all at one hundred miles per hour.

With no more than scant millimeters to spare, the Thomas-Morse streaked in a blur beneath the bridge. Barstow's explosive sigh of relief was sucked back into his lungs with sight of the new horror now looming in front of the whirling propeller blades. He broke out into a cold sweat as he stared upon rows of high-tension wires that crisscrossed his path, spanning the river in a lethal cobweb that could snatch him from the air and kill him instantly.

Barstow raged at his own insanity in not studying what lay on the other side of the bridge before starting his suicidal run. The wheezing Le Rhone lacked the power to zoom him up and over the wires. Moreover, he was now snared within the downdraft corridor of air usually experienced in river valleys that are flanked with high ridges.

Flying with consummate skill Barstow whipped beneath the wires, avoiding obstructions by inches. His feet danced gingerly on the rudder, and he used as much body English as he did control pressures to snake his way along the river. If he so much as slipped once, or yawed unexpectedly, or allowed a downdraft to steal away altitude from him . . . With a rush he escaped the trap in the valley; free of the obstacles, he horsed the stick back in his stomach to grab for altitude. Relief flooded through him as he flew home to land. Cramer noted with alarm that his partner was dead-white in appearance and that the wheels were dripping . . .

The pair then drew lots out of a helmet to see who would have the good fortune to fling himself bodily into space with the ancient and seedy parachute. Cramer lost; that is, he received the dubious honor of making the jump. A huge crowd had gathered at the field to witness the takeoff and, as well, to take appropriate action if there was no jump or if the aviators took it upon themselves to try another hoax. The pilots were dead-certain that somewhere on the field, within easy reach, the suspicious rednecks had secreted a barrel of tar and bags of feathers.

High over the crowd, Cramer released his seat belt in the front cockpit of the Standard. As he stood up the crowd murmured. Cramer shut his eyes and flung himself away from the airplane. The sight of his body tumbling wildly through the air brought a tremendous roar from the hundreds of watching spectators. As Cramer fell, he pulled mightily on the D-ring. Silk fluttered into view. Then there came a faint *crack!* as the canopy blossomed out fully, and Cramer was drifting earthward. In the pleasant silence of the parachute descent he heard a swelling roar and was amazed to hear the mob cheering him with enthusiasm.

The pleasant ride ended with a bone-jarring smash into a cornfield. Cramer climbed awkwardly to his feet, pain etched on his face from a severely sprained ankle. He watched Barstow bang to a landing; Cramer limped to the Standard while Barstow gathered up the chute.

Back at the airfield the crowd surged about the airplane. Flushed with pleasure at their reaction, Cramer tried to stand in the cockpit to receive their cheers. His face whitened as pain surged through him from his ankle—and he tumbled unconscious from the airplane onto the ground.

It would seem that this was climax enough for any local airshow, but Cramer and Barstow as a team weren't through. Their big act of the circus was a promised takeoff of the Thomas-Morse from the main street of Clarion. Every farmer, farmer's wife, their kids and the assorted mutts of the town, to say nothing of the town populace, was on hand to watch the grand finale. With great ceremony a Model T towed the little biplane along the street while people waved and shouted. At the intersection of Main Street and Sixth Avenue Barstow made a great fuss over aligning the airplane down its improvised runway.

Russ Brinkley, himself a barnstorming pilot and a witness to the great airshow, recalls:

> Those of us in the know were aware that the Morse couldn't take off from Main Street. To make the deal look a little more impossible, Barstow had the nose of the ship pointed down Sixth Avenue. Now, Sixth Avenue was just about twice as wide as the wingspan of the plane. Add to that the fact that blossoming maple trees and some huge oaks lined the narrow cartway all the way to Wood Street. At the end of Wood Street there was a stone church with a high bell tower. And there were plenty of wires overhead leading to the local telegraph office. The whole situation took on the aspects of a birdcage, but this didn't seem to daunt Barstow who went right ahead with his preparations.

The local gendarmes managed finally to clear the street of automobiles, but nobody could have budged the excited spectators, most of whom had never seen a fatal accident, and were fairly slavering at the rare opportunity. People were piled six deep along the curb. They roosted in the trees along the takeoff route, shinnied up poles, and clambered onto the tops of roofs, porches, cars and buggies. At the end of the street willing hands held the wings of the Thomas-Morse while the rotary engine was pulled through prior to starting. Curious kids milled about directly behind the airplane, in the path of the slipstream from the prop—they would smell for weeks afterward of castor oil. Other kids jostled each other just so they could touch the doped fabric of the fuselage. *That* was a thrill . . .

In the cockpit Barstow listened carefully until the engine sounded as if it had reached peak rpm. He jerked down his goggles with one hand, shoved the stick forward with the other, and nodded to his helpers to release the wings. The howling little machine bounded forward along the paved thoroughfare.

Quickly Barstow brought up the tail. For a moment it seemed that he would really make it into the air despite the birdcage obstacles. But a capricious gust of wind blasted out from an alley to send the Thomas-Morse careening wildly to the left in a semiflying ground loop. Onlookers dived out of the way as the flashing propeller whirled directly toward them, and by the miracle that protects fools and innocents there was no bloodshed as the airplane smashed itself into wreckage. There was a jarring, crunching scream of tearing wings and fuselage as the Thomas-Morse slashed through a fence and piled up at the wall of a hotel. Outside of a few spectators who were jarred from their perches in nearby trees by the impact, there were no casualties.

The pilots paid gladly for a new fence. Everybody agreed that the airshow had been a tremendous success . . .

That episode marked the beginning of the end of the partnership of Parker D. Cramer and Red Jack Barstow. Private enterprise took over the airmail routes. The inflammable De Havilland DH-4B's were replaced with longer-ranged, new Douglas biplanes, and Clarion suddenly was no longer needed as an intermediate stop by the pilots flying the mail. Fuel sales plunged. It was not long before both the pioneer barnstormers and the local airfield operator were forced to sell out, dead broke.

Barstow slipped quietly from public view, but not his part-

Stinson

ner. Twice Cramer tried to fly the Atlantic Ocean. The first time his airplane failed him and he crashed into the sea; rescuers pulled him to safety before a swarm of hungry sharks got to him. He tried once again, with Fish Hassell, in a Stinson. But the airplane crashed on a glacier in Greenland, and Cramer was killed.

His only monument to fame is the wing of the Stinson, which may still be seen by passing fliers winging their way to Europe.

10

King of the Stunt Pilots*

It looked for all the world as if time had gone mad in the sky high above the Normandy Coast, as though the clock had spun backward into World War I. Far above the earth fighters of the Royal Flying Corps jockeyed into position for a massive clash with the German Air Force, preparing the stage for the greatest aerial dogfight in history. Maltese crosses and brightly colored roundels flashed in the sun . . .

But the war was nine years done, nine years in the past, and in the thin air thousands of feet above San Francisco Bay, two score of the most skilled and daring pilots in the world were about to clash in a deliberate melee that would surpass most of the great air battles of World War I.

Gleaming white cumulus clouds towered miles into the blue heavens, forming a backdrop of gargantuan proportions for the winged contestants. Breaking suddenly through the mists, there streaked a tight formation of weird biplanes, an aerial armada the likes of which had never before been seen. The airplanes snarled in an angry cacophony of engines; the dawn patrol of oddball crates made up of SE-5's, Sopwiths, Avros, Snipes and Canucks. They looked for all the world like a swarm of maddened hornets stirring for trouble.

At almost the same instant, from the opposite direction, rushed a second formation of warcraft. These were German Fokker D-VII's, their coffin-shaped black fuselages silhouet-

*The writer is especially indebted to Don Dwiggins for this chapter, and expresses his gratitude to Mr. Dwiggins, superb pilot and one of aviation's most thorough and competent historians.

ted against a massive cloud as they raced into combat. In the lead fighter huddled a German pilot garbed in black, a white scarf streaming back from his tight leather helmet. Quickly the pilot glanced over his left shoulder, his eyes flashing behind oval goggles. Below the rim of the cockpit, in stark white letters, was emblazoned the dreaded name: von Richthofen!

The German killer raised an arm in signal to the other pilots. Then the Fokker banked over, half-rolling into a screaming dive that led directly toward the formation of white enemy planes . . .

Frank Clarke, greatest of all stunt pilots, felt a strange exhilaration as he led his group into a bruising melee that would make aviation—and cinematic—history. Following his lead, more than forty World War I fighters swiftly mixed it up in a whirling, diving, spinning, screaming dogfight more exciting than any ever watched from the trenches of the Meuse-Argonne.

Hell's Angels, the most extravagant aerial epic ever to emerge from Hollywood, was swirling into its triumphant sequence. The battle was unreal, but death still lurked in the sky, and Frank Clarke was acutely aware of its presence. Not death from stuttering Spandaus, of course, but from the danger of collision never more than an instant away in the incredible flying of the craziest squadron of stunt pilots ever to shove a control stick or slam a rudder in their violent maneuvers. One mistake, one error, one belated second in midair maneuvering, and two men's lives could be flicked out.

For several months of grueling work, Clarke had led his motley collection of stunt birdmen through one scene after the other of the flight extravaganza. He had suffered rising anger and mounting frustration from the myriad problems of the great air battle. Every time the planes assembled for the swirling dogfight something had gone wrong: the cloud background was poor for flying or for the cameras, the fighters drifted out of camera range, cameras jammed, or half a dozen pilots would spiral earthward from the mock battle with all-too-realistic engine trouble.

Now, late in December of 1927, Clarke meant to conclude the epic air struggle with a flourish that would never be forgotten. As his Fokker plunged in its inverted dive into the "enemy" formation, he singled out the lead ship, an SE-5 flown by Roy Wilson, another man famed for his daring and reckless maneuvers in the air.

The cameramen were especially on their toes for this take, because Clarke had a grudge to settle with Wilson—and a grudge pushed to its limit by two madmen could produce anything for the rolling film. The day before Wilson had sliced away part of the Fokker's tail in the air; he had spun against Clarke, broken away from their midair collision into nearby clouds to return to their airport without being recognized. Late that night Clarke found the damaged SE-5 in the hangar, and exploded in fury against Wilson.

"Sure, you've got to get in close to make it look realistic," he shouted, "but damn it, Roy, you could have killed me!"

Wilson turned to Clarke with a sardonic grin on his face. "What's the matter, Frank?" he sneered, "you getting old?"

Clarke had reacted almost with violence to the dig. "Listen," he snapped, "any time you want to play chicken, waggle your wings and let me know. And then get the hell out of my way!"

Clarke remembered his own words—and he saw Wilson's wings suddenly waggle at him as the formations closed. "Okay, Buster!" Clarke shouted into the screaming wind. Signaling his wingman to break away, Clarke rolled swiftly right-side up and aligned his gunsight dead on Wilson's SE-5, approaching from dead-ahead on the horizon.

Above and behind him Harry Perry, Hollywood's top aerial cameraman, had his camera glued to "von Richthofen" as the two-seated photography plane rushed after the diving Fokker. Clarke grinned as he thought of what Perry might get on film as he shot from the Thomas-Morse Scout, piloted by Frank Tomick. Clarke hoped it would be good, for Hughes already had more than three hundred thousand dollars wrapped up in getting this single sequence. This one was for the jackpot.

As Clarke bored straight ahead the SE-5 loomed larger and larger in his sights. A nerveless man, lean and muscular, Clarke hunched low his six-foot frame and tensed. Hughes had insisted that the pilots wear parachutes, and while Clarke felt that was for sissies, the chute on his frame also made him, for the first time in his unusual flying career, careless.

"Okay, move over!" he yelled explosively into the wind. "I'm comin' through!"

Crouched in the cockpit of the SE-5, Wilson felt his mouth go dry as Clarke's Fokker bore down on him. "Son of a bitch!" he muttered. "The bastard meant what he said!"

For Clarke to pull up now would mean a personal defeat. He knew that Wilson was one of the finest pilots in the world. But he preferred to have the two fighters slam together in a head-on flaming crash than to swerve away.

Closing on each other at more than two hundred miles per hour, the black and white airplanes seemed bent on suicidal destruction.

In the camera plane Perry stood up in the teeth of the howling wind. He knew no one could hear him, but the words burst from his lips. "Pull up! Pull up, damn it, *pull up!*"

One fighter swerved—at the last split second. It was the white airplane.

Clarke felt the sudden sharp jolt as Wilson's landing gear slashed across his top wing, ripping open the fabric. A second later and he had the Fokker screaming up through a steep Immelmann turn, climbing hard. Under his cowling, Clarke had mounted a Hall Scott L6 engine that gave him a power edge over the Hisso-powered SE-5. The Fokker arched over through the sky in a dramatic, silhouetted turn against the white cloud; then the airplane dropped swiftly after Wilson, closing in on his tail.

All about him, Clarke saw the sky filled with airplanes swirling about in the mad dogfight, but he was intent on only one ship. Gradually he closed the distance on Wilson. But that man wasn't going to just wait for Clarke. The SE-5 suddenly whipped its nose upward and shot into a vertical climb. Clarke clung grimly to its tail.

A split second before his fighter stalled, Wilson jammed in full right rudder, kicking the SE-5 over through a violent stall-turn. Again he tried for the advantage, diving straight down at the climbing Fokker. Clarke hesitated barely a second, then jerked the stick over and slammed rudder to put the Fokker into a whirling spin as the white biplane streaked inches past him in a dive. He saw Wilson thumb his nose as he flashed past.

Clarke hauled the Fokker out of the spin and slowly closed on Wilson. This time he slid in tight by cross-controlling. A moment later he had locked his wingtips with those of the SE-5.

"Okay! Okay!" Wilson shouted across to Clarke as the two fighters dove earthward in a tightening spiral. "You win!"

Laughing, Clarke pulled away and headed once more into the thick of the dogfight. He saw with a shock that two fighters above him had collided and were spinning out of control. He recognized the ships as being flown by Ira Reed and Stuart Murphy. The latter abruptly hurled himself from the cockpit of his demolished SE-5; the body continued to fall as Murphy made a delayed drop to clear the tumbling wreckage. Reed's Fokker limped off in crazy maneuvers and disappeared.

Later, on the ground, Clarke met Reed walking home. He had flown his battered fighter forty miles before all the fabric ripped away from one wing and exposed two broken spars.

"Hey, Spooks!" he yelled at Clarke. "I won't get fired, will I? I got her down okay."

"Hell, no," Clarke grinned at him. "You looked good on film."

Clarke had won the nickname "Spooks" from Hughes because of a gag the millionaire producer had pulled on him during a table-tilting seance. With one side of the table in the air, Hughes slid a Coke bottle under a table leg and nearly choked laughing at Clarke's consternation when the table wouldn't level itself.

Clarke was a strange contrast. He was a fun-loving and easy-going individual who seemed to be almost completely relaxed. Nevertheless, he was one of the coolest pilots ever to ply the barnstormer's trade or to risk his neck before a camera. He loved his job and he was fiercely proud of the men who worked and flew for him, and he took it as a personal blow when three fellow pilots died in the filming of *Hell's Angels*.

First to die was Clem (Little Phil) Phillips, who shared ownership of a Waco with western actor Ken Maynard. Phil was told by Clarke to fly an SE-5 from Glendale Airport north to Oakland, where the big dogfight scene of *Hell's Angels* was to be shot—there weren't enough clouds over the San Fernando Valley to please perfectionist Howard Hughes. At one hundred feet on a steep takeoff climb Phil's engine quit, and he spun in, breaking his neck in the crash.

Al Johnson was the second to die. In a low-level maneuver

he tore out some power lines, crashed, and was burned alive in the wreckage.

What horrified the pilots most of all was the death of a young mechanic, Phil Jones, who was operating the smokepots in a German Gotha bomber, apparently spinning earthward on fire. Jones had volunteered to go up with Al Wilson, one of the greatest of all aerobatic fliers, and pull off the stunt in the Gotha for a fee of ten thousand dollars. Two expert pilots, Clarke and Jimmy Angel, Hollywood stunt fliers of unquestioned nerve, had already refused the offer. The Gotha was a flying wreck and might come apart at any moment, and they wanted nothing to do with the machine.

Wilson kicked the Gotha into a spin at 7,500 feet. As the big airplane lurched around Wilson heard a wing spar snap. Instantly he shouted to Jones to jump, and then bailed out himself. But Jones, huddled in the nose over the big smoke pot, failed to hear the warning. As Clarke in a camera plane followed the crippled bomber spinning down through the sky, he saw the smoke stop, and then start again. At once he realized that Jones was unaware of disaster and was hard at work, lighting the second pot.

Clarke shoved forward on the stick and pushed into a vertical dive. He was trying to slam his wheels hard enough against the Gotha to alert Jones to his plight and give him the chance to bail out. But before Clarke could get into position, the bomber smashed into an orange grove and exploded in a mushrooming ball of flame.

Throughout his years of stunt flying, death was a constant companion to Frank Clarke. Somehow, through skill, meticulous planning and a good share of luck, he managed to stay one jump ahead of the grim reaper. That task kept him hopping.

Caddo Field, named for Hughes's production company, was run under the rigid supervision of Clarke. The job demanded almost constant supervision, for the field was a complete military airport in San Fernando Valley, with hundreds of mechanics and ground crewmen who kept the old combat crates and camera planes in flying condition. There were enough incidents and near-accidents to drive to distraction all but the most hardened veteran, but even Clarke paled one day when Howard Hughes insisted upon personally flying a Thomas-Morse with its infamous Le Rhone rotary engine.

At twenty years of age, Hughes was a "boy genius" who

had already brought home a celluloid money-maker known as *Two Arabian Knights,* starring William Boyd and Louis Wolheim. Hughes defied tradition and the box office by not including any women in his picture, and stunned everyone by bringing home a box-office smash.

In addition to his management and planning, Hughes learned to fly and spent many months in assembling the aerial fleet for *Hell's Angels.* The first ship he brought into the fold was a vintage Sikorsky bomber which his mechanics converted into a German Gotha for film work. Roscoe Turner flew it cross-country to the West Coast.

The Thomas-Morse incident began with Hughes berating Ben Lyon, his male lead, for excessive flying. Lyon, a private pilot as well as an actor, laughed in Hughes's face. "I'll knock off the flying if *you* do the same," he said.

Hughes accepted this retort as a personal challenge, and stalked angrily into the hangar. Moments later he rolled out the Thomas-Morse, fired up the engine, climbed in and took off. But you didn't "just fly" the vicious little airplane. Unaware of the overpowering gyroscopic torque of the spinning rotary engine, Hughes completely lost control in his first turn and spun wildly into the ground. Horrified, Clarke dashed out to the wreckage.

"You okay, Howard?" he shouted as Hughes crawled out.

"I guess so," Hughes replied weakly.

"Thank God," sighed Clarke, "I thought for a moment that we'd lost our meal ticket!"

Hughes grinned at him.

Frank Clarke received his apprenticeship as a fledgling pilot at the old Venice Field, on the edge of Santa Monica Bay. It was a perfect setting for the neophyte, for barnstormers and carnival fliers spent much of their time at the field inventing new ways to cheat death for money in the good old wood-and-wire days of open cockpit flying. It has been said that more stunt flying and barnstorming acts were invented at Venice Field than in all the rest of the world put together—although the claims always brings cries of outrage from veteran barnstormers who plied other parts of the country.

In 1918 Clarke made his first solo flight. It was a bright Sunday morning and no one could ever accuse Clarke of moving slowly into the barnstorming business. That same afternoon he took up twelve passengers at ten dollars a head, and was fast on his way to making aviation pay off handsomely. Two of the best-known early birds, Al Wilson and Swede Meyerhofer, were his instructors, and what they failed to teach Clarke he invented for himself.

For the first two years that Clarke flew at Venice Field, operations in the air were unblemished—there wasn't a single fatality. And then, as so often happens, within one month Clarke watched six of his closest friends killed before his eyes.

First to go was Joe Hoff, a Venice tailor who had built Clarke's first airplane, but who personally lacked skill as a pilot. He dove straight through the Venice Pier one afternoon while stunting on the deck with a passenger, killing the second man as well. Herb Wilson and his mechanic drowned when their flying boat plunged out of control into the ocean. Then B. H. Delay, flying with a close friend of Clarke, Ruel Short, tore the wings from his plane while trying to pull out of a vertical dive. Finally, rounding out the ghastly month, Swede Meyerhofer ended his life in grisly fashion. He died despite the sign on his own hangar that read: "Pilots may come and pilots may go, but the Swede goes on forever!" The Swede simply forgot to let go of the propeller on his Standard one morning when the engine backfired. That lapse was his last—the blade sliced his body in half.

Frank Clarke maintained that a stunt pilot had to be born; you couldn't make one if the raw material wasn't there. He once explained to friends: "I never heard of a man coming to the flying field and saying, 'I want to learn to be a wing-walker.' Flying stunt men just *appear*."

The first plane change on record was carried out in 1919 by Lt. Omar Locklear, who startled an audience of Texans by pulling off the trick with a rope ladder. When word of Locklear's feat reached the men at Venice Field, the barnstormers and stunt pilots flatly refused to believe what they heard. They ridiculed the whole thing as so much bushwa. But a producer at Famous Players-Lasky Studios wanted to use the routine in a Houdini movie and Lt. Al Kennedy, spanking-fresh out of the air war in Europe, said he'd give it a whirl.

C. V. Pickup and Tommy Thompson talked it over with Clarke, and they decided to risk the stunt. They were grimly sorry they ever started the "fool thing." When they actually began the maneuver, the two airplanes locked wings. The pilots fought wildly at the controls but without avail. Helpless, they watched their two airplanes swing around to grind head-on at each other, so that each propeller chewed into the opposite plane like a mad dog. Thompson spun crazily into a field a mile away and by a miracle survived the crash. Pickup and Kennedy—the latter clinging grimly to his rope ladder—glided into a bean field. They had their second miracle of the day when both men walked away from the wreckage without serious injury.

Clarke hated to send up men on something he hadn't done himself, and he announced he would make the next attempt. The only ladder he could find, however, was rotten, and Clarke volunteered to do the trick bare-handed. No one had ever done that before.

At three thousand feet Clarke crawled out onto the wing tip of Howard Patterson's Waco. Al Wilson flew a Standard above and behind Patterson. But this wasn't going to be any easy job . . .

Unexpected turbulence threw Wilson's judgment off badly, and his wing tip smashed Clarke in the jaw, sending him sprawling ten feet back along the wing, his feet tearing through the fabric of the center section. That little accident saved his life. Clarke was out cold.

When he revived, his head a pinwheel of bright stars, Clarke started crawling back again to the top wing tip. Any other man would have called it quits and still have been acclaimed a hero. But Clarke was now blindly determined to go through with what he had started. Atop the wing, he signaled Wilson to return to position for the change. Wilson slid his wing in close, Clarke lunged out to grab the wing—and scrambled aboard!

In one way that first plane change might have been a bad mistake for Clarke; he had the fever now and he was eager to try just about every stunt in the books, or those that he and his fellow pilots could dream up. He went in for exhibition wing walking, a peculiar sort of suicide put together the year before by Mark Campbell who worked the East Coast. Clarke went on a barnstorming tour with his mechanic, Wally Timm, who was just learning to fly. (Later, Timm taught Art Goebel, winner of the Dole Race to Honolulu, but at this time he still didn't know how to take off or land.)

Once they were in the air, Clarke turned the controls over to Timm, who put the ship into a shallow dive while Clarke crawled back to the tail. Then, bracing himself, he leaped forward to land in the cockpit. It scared the watchers on the ground, and it scared the other pilots as well.

It also scared Timm—but for a different reason! "Don't ever miss that cockpit, Frank," Timm pleaded with Clarke. "Because if you do and fall off, how am I ever going to land this thing?"

Clarke once *did* miss the cockpit. Good fortune had it that Ray Goldsworthy, a veteran flier, was at the controls instead of Timm. Clarke bounded forward from the tail, missed the cockpit, and smashed with the seat of his pants into the turtleback. His butt end crashed through the fuselage structure and he was stuck as though he were on flypaper. Still in this ignominious position he was brought safely back to earth by Goldsworthy!

On another occasion Clarke decided to outdo himself with a spectacular never-before-done stunt: he would leap from the ground onto a speeding plane that descended from overhead. He planned to pull this trick by running along the ground and snatching at a rope dragged by the airplane. His friends told him he was mad; Clarke agreed and grinned at them.

Airmail Pilot E. L. Remlin came across the field, flying low and slow with the rope trailing. Clarke took off in a cloud of dust to build up speed before the rope reached him. And then he snatched at the rope, clamped his hands on hard and was promptly towed down the runway in enormous one hundred-foot strides that made him appear to be hurtling through the air in balloon-like impossible leaps. But he couldn't get his body into position to climb the rope and finally, gasping for air, relinquished his grip and forgot the whole thing.

Whatever else he might do, Clarke was always busy plotting new stunts . . .

One day he terrified an audience of thousands of people—to say nothing of his friends and fellow pilots—by taking off solo and then climbing back to the tail of the airplane! His idea was to fly the ship with a rope that ran through a pulley system to the control stick in the cockpit. It was a fine idea, but Clarke never seemed to follow up his ideas with quality equipment. On his first attempt, with his legs straddling the rear fuselage and flying the airplane as if it were a high-speed horse, the rope broke. Immediately, with Clarke's weight at the tail, the airplane clawed upward into a violent whipstall. It hung on its prop while Clarke clung for dear life, knowing what would come next. And it did, with violent fury, the nose snapping down like a whip and trying to fling Clarke wildly through the air. Finally the airplane plunged earthward in a screaming power dive. Sans parachute, the frightened Clarke crawled his way forward in the teeth of the howling wind and managed to drop into the cockpit without a moment to spare.

The next time he used a new rope . . .

With extensive barnstorming experience behind him, Clarke felt he was a natural for the hair-raising stunts demanded by the movie industry of the time. His first movie job lived up in every way to its billing as a "hair-raiser." Clarke dressed as a cop and then chased Mark Campbell (dressed as a convict) all over an airplane in flight. To accomplish this neat trick, Clarke had to tie down the controls with a rope. Then, with a constant shifting of weight and air drag because of the two lunatics cavorting about on the airplane, and with no one in the cockpit, Clarke crawled out over the wings, down through the undercarriage and back up the other side!

After this episode he hit the barnstorming trail again. He was particularly vexed at the public when folks who had never before seen an airplane fairly stomped their way about, over, and through his ship. They clambered into the cockpit, tore holes in the wings and ripped instruments by brute force from the instrument panel, then they secreted them within their clothes to drag home as souvenirs. At the Venice Pier Midway, Clarke borrowed a rattlesnake from a sideshow friend, and carried the reptile with him. Whenever he had to leave his machine unattended, he removed the snake from the box and left it free in the cockpit. The approach of an instrument-happy souvenir hunter was met with an angry rattle from the snake, guaranteed to send any visitor scurrying off to a safe distance.

Even the best of pilots, if they pursue the mad world of barnstormers and stunt men, inevitably run up against the odds—and Clarke's first crackup came one day as a result of his discretion being overcome by an urge to valor. He was flying an old Canuck and appeared determined to outdo some of the old masters by looping near the ground, but pulling out beneath some trolley wires. Coming down from the backside of the loop and rushing earthward he suddenly spotted a huge electric sign he hadn't noticed before. It was a case of looping before looking, and frantically Clarke maneuvered to avoid the sign. He missed it, all right—and flew smack into the wires. The first person he saw when he crawled from the wreckage was Charley Crawford, who ran a Venice junkyard—for stunt planes cracked up by fool pilots!

Clarke alternated at times between barnstorming and the insanity of movie flying. In 1920 he was hired to fly in a "super air melodrama" with the unlikely title of *Stranger Than Fiction*, starring Katherine MacDonald. After perusing the script, Clarke decided it was a lot stranger than fact. The scenarist had dreamed up stunts that had never been invented by a pilot.

Perhaps the wildest of them all was a scene where a gang of villains was to chase the hero to the top of a skyscraper. And there, for some reason inexplicable to Clarke, would be waiting the hero's airplane. The script called for Clarke, doubling as the hero, to leap into the airplane and barely in the nick of time to rush from the skyscraper roof into space. Nobody had ever before flown an airplane from the top of a skyscraper, although plenty of pilots, starting with Lincoln Beachey, had buzzed around the buildings. Clarke shrugged; if anyone could do it, *he* could.

He visited downtown Los Angeles and selected for special study the new Los Angeles Railway Building, a thirteen-story structure with a rooftop ninety-five feet wide. It wasn't much, but added to the safety factor of height when taking off from the building, it would have to do. With a select crew Clarke dismantled his old Jenny and hoisted it to the building roof. Then the men built a plank runway just wide enough for the wheels, with an incline at one end to help lift the plane into the air at the end of the very brief takeoff run.

When the owner of the building, on the East Coast, heard of the mad stunt, he sent a frantic wire forbidding anything to do with Clarke or with airplanes. Clarke read the telegram, shoved it into a pocket and dismissed it from his mind. But *other* people could interfere . . . Hurriedly he started the engine of the Jenny, climbed into the cockpit, and waved the "start grinding" signal to the cameramen. Then—full throttle, while two assistants struggled with a rope tied to his tailskid to keep him from moving as the engine spun to maximum power. Clarke signaled, the rope was released and the Jenny shot down the wooden runway. It hit the incline and did a tremendous bounce of thirty feet into the air above the rooftop. Thousands of amazed pedestrians on the streets below cheered as Clarke dropped the Jenny's nose to pick up airspeed; then he dipped down to slide along Broadway, past the Examiner Building. He waggled his wings happily at the crowds before setting off for the airfield in Hollywood.

Two glaring motorcycle cops were waiting for him when he landed.

Two thick fingers pointed at Clarke "You're under arrest!" snapped the owners of the fingers.

"For *what*?" demanded an amazed Clarke.

There was a long silence as the two cops looked at one another. "Well, uh . . . well," said the first cop. He looked at Clarke. "Damned if I know," he admitted candidly to the pilot. Then, as an afterthought: "But why the hell did you do it?"

Clarke grinned. "I got rolling and couldn't stop," he said. "It was either take off or fall into the street and kill a lot of people. You didn't want *that*, did you?"

Clarke grinned some more. The officers left in disgust. Clarke roared.

Another stunt only one step short of insanity dreamed up by the script writer for *Stranger Than Fiction* was to begin with an actor diving from an airplane while wearing a parachute (thank heaven for small favors, thought the stunt men). But then . . . ah, then a second plane was to appear. The latter machine was to trail a three-foot barbed grappling iron. It was to buzz the falling actor, hook his parachute with the anchor, and then the actor was supposed to climb up the rigging like a monkey into the second plane.

The old-timers called the whole thing mad, but Clarke and his associates went ahead with the stunt. Clarke in the camera airplane circled the jumper, Sgt. Ray Sauren, as he leaped away from his airplane. But there are just some days . . . when Sauren's chute cracked open, his body whirled, and he fouled a line. As he plummeted earthward, Sauren with detached coolness snapped open a knife, cut away his main chute, and deployed his reserve canopy.

Lt. Ray Robinson in the second airplane failed to see this little train of events and he bore down against Sauren. Clarke knew Sauren's danger—a mistake that fouled his reserve canopy would seal his doom—and he dove at full speed directly across the nose of Robinson's airplane.

Robinson pulled up, circled, and again sliced in to snag

Sauren's parachute. Once again Clarke intercepted him, forcing away Robinson's airplane. He broke free only when he saw Sauren on the ground, safe and sound.

They tried once again. This time the anchor jerked through Sauren's canopy with brutal force. It snapped the riser cords and nearly broke Sauren's back. Grimacing with pain, Sauren again managed to jerk the ripcord of his reserve chute. He hit the ground with a crash. They never tried the stunt again.

Whenever movie work fell off, Clarke and his gang swung to the open road. On one barnstorming tour the men organized a Wild West Flying Circus. Their first stop was El Centro, California, and preshow notices brought ranchers in from many miles around. The pilots were astonished to see the ranchers park their vehicles a good distance from the airfield, then climb atop their cars to watch the show—without paying admission. Clarke's anger boiled up; the deal for him and his men was based on a percentage of the take at the airport entrance, and road parking added up to strictly a no-profit deal.

But Clarke never failed for solutions. He took off from the circus grounds, swung around sharply and then roared down the road with his wheels only inches from the ground. At the last instant he pulled up to skim the tops of the parked cars—his flashing propeller and wheels sending the ranchers diving for safety. They got the message, and headed quickly for the safety of the grandstands.

At Yuma, Arizona, promoters booked the Flying Circus for a death-defying race from Los Angeles to the Arizona border. The hoopla about the intense competition built up tremendous interest in the event and also raised the prize ante. The night before the race Clarke, Ray Goldsworthy, Howard Patterson and Swede Meyerhofer slipped out of town, caroused uproariously until the wee hours, and exactly at race time straggled into the air. They flew lazily along until they had Yuma in sight, then with throttles wide open and flying precariously close to one another, they sprinted across the field in full view of the waiting crowd, giving them their money's worth. They also cleaned up enough "prize money" to move on to Tucson in financial comfort.

It was in that city that Clarke's cronies saw another—and to them, delightful—sign of the ace pilot. Clarke was described as "a handsome dog with a pencil moustache, a fondness for Irish whiskey, and a penchant for pretty girls." In Tucson he fell madly in love with a dark-haired cabaret singer who lived in a big hotel smack in the center of town.

Following a wild party one night, Clarke wrote her a passionate love letter, crammed it in his leather jacket, and at dawn stumbled into his plane. As he neared Tucson he dropped to just above the ground and then roared down the main street of the town straight at the hotel. At the last possible moment before impact he hauled back on the stick. His airplane shot vertically into the air—Clarke rolled his wheels up the side of the building and flipped the note into the windows of his beloved! He burst away from the building, rolled into level flight and disappeared. Behind him the uproar was frantic.

Clarke's buddies decided that the opportunity was too much to miss. They planned a frameup and went in a group to have a private talk with the sheriff, who went along with them, and issued an arrest warrant for Clarke. It was, to be sure, a false warrant, for in those days there weren't any laws forbidding pilots from flying vertically up the sides of hotels. When the sheriff served the warrant and then unexpectedly demanded a fine of ten dollars, Clarke's buddies hastily, and testily, interceded.

"Hell, Sheriff," they cried, "he's just an inexperienced pilot who doesn't know any better!"

The Sheriff tightened his lips and shook his head slowly. "Ten dollars," he repeated.

Clarke looked him straight in the eye. "Tell you what, Sheriff," he said. "I'll pay you off with a plane ride."

"No, thanks!" shouted the lawman. "Fine suspended!"

On another occasion the irrepressible Clarke clattered noisily down a Tucson side street and buzzed a milk wagon. The sudden roar and sight of the airplane frightened the horse so badly it dashed a hundred yards and collapsed in a heap— stone dead. The irate, shouting milkman demanded $150 for the dead beast. It took all the eloquence he could muster for Clarke to convince the man that his horse had simply died of a heart attack.

Barnstorming meant much more than buzzing horses or flying up the sides of hotels or performing aerobatics; the barnstormer learned to make his dollars in any way possible. It was shortly after Swede Meyerhofer was fatally bitten by his propeller that Clarke went after side money as an instructor. His first pilot was a young Japanese who was sadly lacking in proficiency. This he made up for in the possession of a war-surplus Fokker. Came the day when the neophyte decided he would fly two hundred miles north to Fresno.

"Be sure to send me a telegram that you landed okay at Fresno," Clarke told him.

The student nodded, gave him a toothy grin and clambered into the cockpit. He staggered north into headwinds and approaching dusk, blissful in his confidence. Dark fell, and Clarke had no wire. The stars came out, and still no message. Clarke began to chew his fingernails until, at 11:00 P.M., a Western Union messenger arrived. Hastily Clarke tore open the envelope and read:

"Landed Fresno. Okay. Upside down."

It has been a trademark of aviation that flying fields attract a swarm of strange characters, and that the only difference among them is that some are stranger than the rest. One such character was Chief Whitefeather, a powerful, dark and stocky fellow with thick black hair that hung down his back. He explained to Clarke that he was a full-blooded Cherokee Indian and also an experienced parachute jumper. But he lacked thrills. He wanted, said Chief Whitefeather, to hang from the landing gear *by his hair* and fly all the way across town in this fashion.

Why not? Sensing the chance for a profit, Clarke immediately called the newsreel cameraman. The two men then tied Whitefeather's hair with catgut and propped him up on the undercarriage. After a wild takeoff, Whitefeather was swinging gaily by his hair as the airplane trundled across the town, and waving happily all the way to the cameraman.

Clarke sighed contentedly. He had visions of a veritable fortune, touring the nation with Whitefeather sponsored all the way by a hair-restorer company.

Alas, it was not to be. Fate intervened, in the form of a bright idea of Whitefeather's. He decided to introduce a spectacular parachute fall—a series of cutaways—in which he would leap from an airplane wearing *ten* parachutes. First, he said, he would open one chute, then cut it free and open the next chute, and so on down to the tenth chute.

Clarke watched him jump from Howard Batt's ship at a height of five thousand feet. The first chute opened perfectly, it was cut away, the second chute blossomed, and so on right down to the fifth chute. And then, for some unknown reason, Whitefeather rode that canopy to within a hundred feet of the ground when he cut loose again. Before the sixth chute could deploy, Whitefeather made a sickening *splat!* against the ground, and the dreamers of hair-restorer financing vanished with the end of the strong-haired Indian.

It was said that the Fates must have tired their facial muscles in smiling down upon Frank Clarke. Once he pulled off a stunt that by all that was holy should have snuffed out his life. He decided to thrill a barnstorming audience by climbing all over a speeding airplane—*while his wrists were handcuffed.*

He was at 2,500 feet in his madman's act, working his way out along the lower wing, when his foot slipped. Instinctively he grasped for a flying wire with his right hand, forgetting all about the handcuffs. It was almost a lethal lapse of memory. The sudden lunging motion jerked his left hand free from a strut and Clarke toppled backward in the howling wind. His body fell against a drift wire, preventing him at the last second from tumbling to his death.

Each miraculous escape seemed only to urge Clarke on to other stunts that taxed the imagination. One of his most dramatic acts took place on the occasion that he blindfolded Al Johnson, put him in the cockpit, and then had Johnson, *still blindfolded,* crawl out to the top wing and stick his feet up in the air. As Johnson hung in his precarious position Art Goebel flew in from the rear, and maneuvered a hook on his wingtip to adroitly snag Johnson between the legs. He then pulled Johnson into the air where he could remove the blindfold (at last! at last!) and climb to a safer perch. Even Clarke admitted the danger of this stunt, and flew directly beneath Johnson just in case he dropped off! Somehow Johnson climbed, still alive and whole, into Goebel's cockpit.

Clarke never missed an opportunity to play a hilarious and heart-sinking joke on his friends. During filming of the picture, *Eagle of the Night,* Clarke flew Jerry Fairbanks (producer-cameraman) and a friend on a sightseeing trip along the Mexican border. Before taking off he warned Fairbanks that he was subject to strange spells and every now and then was possessed with the uncontrollable urge to leap from the cockpit. Jerry laughed weakly and climbed aboard.

While his passengers were enjoying the sights Clarke slipped down into the rear cockpit and started flying by pulling with his hands on the control cables. He put the airplane into a dive, then suddenly pulled up. He repeated the maneuver a second time until Fairbanks looked around to see what was going on. With a shock he stared at the empty cockpit. Neither Fairbanks nor his friend could fly (and Clarke had removed the controls from the front cockpit).

While the two passengers hung on and clutched each other in terror, Clarke kicked the airplane into a screaming spin. Fairbanks and his friends knew this was the end, and they braced themselves for the impact that would snuff out their lives. But the ship lurched; miraculously the nose dropped steeper and then began to lift above the horizon. It was an unbelievable reprieve. But to what avail? Death was certain . . .

Then Fairbanks looked behind him. There was Clarke sitting with a poker face, totally unconcerned, flying the airplane as though nothing had happened.

Fairbanks didn't speak to him for a month.

Clarke couldn't escape forever the accidents that plagued the barnstormers and stunt men. He splashed into a frightening experience one bitter winter day while flying his Standard with his mechanic, Jimmy Hester. A mile offshore, the engine quit. Clarke spotted a Japanese fishing boat and glided toward the vessel, pancaking neatly onto the water without damaging the airplane.

Half awash and half frozen in the cold water, Clarke saw that Hester, pockets filled with wrenches, was starting to sink. He threw him a line just as the fishing boat with jabbering Japanese sailors pulled alongside. Both men then crawled onto the tail to keep the engine dry as the fishing boat towed them to the shore.

After pushing and dragging the airplane onto the beach, they drained the carburetor, poured five gallons of borrowed gas into the tank and took off again! The only aftereffect of the incident was a bad cold that plagued Clarke for a week.

In the old stunt-flying days necessity mothered a multitude of inventions. Once a wheel tumbled off a plane that Howard Batt was flying. Clarke and Al Johnson, witness to the incident, took off hurriedly in another plane, carrying along a spare wheel. Clarke strapped the wheel to his back and stood up on the top wing while Batt flew overhead. Clarke grasped the undercarriage, pulled himself up and in midair bolted the new wheel into place. The idea worked so well that Clarke and Johnson later capitalized on it by using it as a movie stunt.

During his career Clarke broke up, pranged, crunched and

smashed up a considerable number of airplanes—but only twice as a result of accidents he didn't want. One crash took place during filming of *The Woman with Four Faces*. Clarke took off from the Santa Monica cliffs and turned to wave good-by to actress Betty Compson. He looked long and hard at Betty, and so failed to see the tree that loomed up before him—into which he smashed at full speed. The crash demolished the airplane and tore it into a ball of splintering wreckage. A disgusted Clarke crawled out from under, sat down under another tree, and lit a cigarette while he contemplated his own stupidity.

Betty Compson and the director, Herbert Brenon, ran over and began searching the wreckage for Clarke's body. Finally Clarke rose to his feet, walked over and tapped Brenon's shoulder from behind.

"Looking for something?" he grinned.

Brenon turned chalk-white and almost fainted.

Clarke's second crash—accidental, that is—virtually duplicated the first. Only this time the event occurred in a Beverly Hills pine grove, then a far-out community next to nowhere. He got off easier—he broke the prop and bent one wing, leaving the wreck to be salvaged and to fly again.

When a relative of Wally Timm died, he and Clarke decided to pay a final tribute to the deceased with an impromptu airshow, tossing flowers over the grave from a plane. Together the two men searched for the cemetery, found the mourners, and then streaked low over the grave, inverted, tossing out violets.

When they landed they learned they had buzzed the wrong funeral.

A Fourth of July celebration prompted Clarke to stage a brilliant fireworks show at Venice Field. It proved to be a wild and gala occasion. The people came in thick droves and the liquor flowed freely, and finally Clarke decided that it would be much nicer and certainly more interesting if he watched the show from the air. Ed Remlin fired up a Canuck and Clarke crawled out on top of the wing, clutching a bottle to him, while the Canuck flew lazy circles through the searing starbursts.

It wasn't until the pyrotechnic show ended that Clarke discovered he was blinded from the lights. He groped his way back toward where he knew the cockpit to be—and stepped off into space.

Frantically Clarke flung out his arms (dropping the whiskey bottle, he explained later) as he fell away from the airplane. His fingers gripped a wire. Superb coordination, great strength and an unbelievable grip on his own fear enabled Clarke to hang on, and then to pull himself bodily against the wind back onto the wing. He realized then he had committed the almost-fatal error of walking out on the right wing instead of the left.

The impact of brilliant lights at night came home to Clarke in yet another way, when he watched two pilots die because the man at the controls was blinded by pyrotechnics during a movie night sequence. Omar Locklear, the first man to make a plane change, and Skeeter Elliot put their ship into a whirling spin high above Wilshire and Fairfax, while Clarke dove alongside in the photo plane. Clarke looked on in horror as the other airplane spun all the way into the ground to explode in flames.

Al Wilson owed his life to Frank Clarke's quick thinking, when Wilson once attempted a plane change without a parachute. He was hanging by his knees from the wing skid of Wally Timm's ship while Clarke flew up from behind to pick him off. As he approached, Clarke spotted Wilson in trouble.

Just as Wilson lost his grip and plummeted away, Clarke rammed the throttle to the firewall and dropped into a desperate dive directly beneath Wilson's falling body. Fifty feet below Timm's airplane he made one of the most spectacular midair catches in all of aviation history. Wilson plunged head-first through Clarke's upper wing and remained there—five thousand feet above the ground. Clarke brought him down to earth in a feather-light landing.

To provide realism to the old airplane action serials, Clarke dreamed up an endless variation of old tricks. On one occasion he rode a galloping horse alongside a plane speeding down a runway during takeoff. Clarke didn't just climb aboard—he leaped from the horse onto the tail of the airplane. Or he would hang from the axle of an airplane and drop onto a racing passenger train, in which badmen were carrying off the heroine, who shrieked and kicked appropriately.

Clarke was, in fact, the first pilot ever to land an airplane on a moving train. It was a feat infinitely more difficult than it seemed, because of the turbulence whipping up from the cars.

In 1937 Clarke made headlines in a unique accident. He broke an ankle while stepping off a six-inch curbing.

In 1938 he narrowly escaped death at the National Air Races, looping in a formation billed as the Hollywood Aces. Following close on the wing of the leader, the famed Paul Mantz, Clarke felt a tip vortex suddenly slam one wing so that it intruded between Mantz's left wing surfaces. By a miracle they pulled apart.

For more than thirty years the incredible Frank Clarke laughed death in the face, performed the impossible, defied all the odds—but in the end he finally pushed even his luck too far.

On Friday the thirteenth in June of 1948—a date that should have been a warning to Clarke—he flew a surplus BT-13 Valiant trainer to a mountain mine owned by his old flying buddy, Frank Tomick. He hadn't seen Tomick for a long time, and decided it would be great fun to surprise him by buzzing the mine. That way Frank could drive out to the airport at Kernville and pick him up.

BT-13 Vultee "Valiant"

Clarke invited Mark Owen, another friend, to go along for the ride. For a final touch of genius he loaded a sack of manure into the back seat of the BT-13. It was his plan to slow roll over the mine and christen it with a spray of cow dung.

Standing outside his mine, Tomick heard the characteristic high whine of the BT-13 as Clarke shoved the propeller into fine pitch. He saw the ship dive straight at him.

"That can only be Frank Clarke," Tomick grinned.

Then his face froze. He watched in stark disbelief as the airplane started into a slow roll, hesitated upside down, and plunged straight into the ground.

Almost at Tomick's feet it ripped the air with a terrifying explosion of flame. It was all over instantly for Frank Clarke.

Tomick discovered later that Clarke's own sense of humor had killed him. The manure sack had jammed the control stick so that Clarke was unable to move it.

All the old timers and a great many other people went to the funeral of Frank Clarke. But there weren't many tears. Clarke had died the way he would have wanted to go, pulling off a gag for a friend.

The only real tragedy was that another man had died with him. Clarke would have been deeply sorry about that.

11

Ragged but Rugged

On March 20, 1919, a young man named Frank M. Hawks happily held out his hand to a uniformed adjutant. The man's expression was unreadable, but Hawks couldn't have cared less—for in his open hand he received his honorable discharge from the United States Air Service. At twenty-two years of age, Hawks was filled with that brash optimism common to youthful fighter pilots. He had not a shred of doubt in his mind that shortly he would become a millionaire.

He glanced down at his uniform and smiled. Not, however, as an aviator. To hell with that. He would make his killing as a *farmer*. Wartime prosperity had made rich men out of those who were even illiterates, and Hawks was determined to cash in on the golden opportunities offered to men of the soil.

He therefore traded his leather helmet for a straw hat and his shiny uniform for some sturdy coveralls. He bought some acreage near Lewistown, Montana, rolled up his sleeves and went to work. Good Lord, how that man worked. He labored mightily from sunup to sundown for two long years. He worked seven days a week and every week of the year. At the end of the two years he straightened up his aching back, looked upon his murderous labor, and realized that he was dead broke. Poor seasons and a sagging economy had wiped out his savings and made a lewd mockery of his dreams.

Recalled Hawks: "The flying bug, of course, was still in my veins. Once a man is bitten by it, I doubt that he ever really recovers. He may think he is cured, go along for months or even years without a twinge of homesickness for the widened horizons that are the heritage of the airman—and then the sight of an airplane against the sky, or even the roar of an unseen engine, will . . . bring the malady back upon him more virulent than ever."

It was a good philosophy, considering the sad state of affairs into which the pauper farmer had fallen. Things could hardly have looked blacker to the ex-fighter pilot when, out of the blue, Hawks's wife received a thousand dollars from an insurance loss payment. His spirits revived, Hawks returned to the world of aviation by using seven hundred out of the thousand dollars for his half share of an "ancient, weather-beaten crate with a Thompson radial engine . . . it was not an encouraging sight." But neither were the bare fields of agriculture that had failed Hawks in such devastating fashion, and ragged wings appealed to him much more than stooping over an unyielding furrow in the soil. Besides, Hawks's partner was allegedly a man of many talents and much experience, and in his wisdom he foresaw the two men on a barnstorming venture that would cover the nation and line their pockets with gold.

That airplane cost Hawks and his partner one hundred dollars a mile. Hawks managed to fly cross-country in the $1,400 machine for exactly fourteen miles. At that point the engine seized with a grinding moan and a disgusted pilot set down the weary biplane in an open pasture. It was a good landing and the plane was undamaged; the engine could be repaired without too much difficulty. There was but one small problem to overcome: money. Hawks didn't have any more, and his partner, while perhaps blessed with wisdom, was woefully short of ready cash. Thus handicapped, they were forced to store the wings in a barn, and in a disconsolate journey they hauled the fuselage home behind a truck, towing the remains to their home airport where it was interred within a hangar. Alas, the plane never again took to the air. The only thing that flew away was their investment.

Hawks turned to new fields, not to conquer, but to eat. He took a job with a man named Charles Heddon, a fishing tackle manufacturer of Dowagiac, Michigan, who exhibited a rare form of enterprise. It was Heddon's ingenious scheme to fly his tackle to dealers throughout his area, and to defray the flight expenses by barnstorming along the way. Heddon purchased a Jenny and a Canuck, painted them in outlandish, eye-stabbing colors, and in grim seriousness christened them the "Flying Fishes."

"We always put on a few stunts above the town," Hawks said of his delivery stops, "in order to lure some prospective passengers to the pasture I had selected for a landing field. Of course, the first thing to be done on landing in some farmer's hayfield or pasture was to negotiate for the use of it while we were in that neighborhood. Sometimes I got the use of the field for taking the owner up for a free ride; other farmers drove shrewd bargains and insisted I take aloft the entire family. Then there were genial, cautious old codgers who would neither charge anything for the use of the field or trust themselves in 'one of them fool flying machines.' These were the salt of the earth as far as the barnstorming era was concerned and we gave thanks when Providence brought us into their fields."

Wanderlust was the malady common to barnstormers, and before long Hawks rid himself of the flying fish-tackle delivery game and moved his family to California. He wangled a job with Emory Rogers, who had just opened a new airport on Wilshire Boulevard in the Los Angeles area. As chief pilot Hawks received the magnificent salary of fifty dollars a week— and was glad enough to get it.

One of his first passengers struck a forceful impression upon him. She was a lanky, red-headed female with a face full of freckles. Following the thirty-minute tour over Los Angeles, Hawks returned the excited girl to earth. On the ground she was still burning with her new-found enthusiasm for the world of flight. "Now," she affirmed, "I *must* learn to fly myself."

Hawks believed she had the makings of a good pilot. The lanky redhead didn't disappoint him. Not at all. Her name: Amelia Earhart.

Shortly after Hawks joined Rogers he was approached by "a sleek stranger with breezy ways and an air of prosperity." The dark and mysterious stranger called Hawks aside and tempted him with dazzling promises of big money for a man who could fly well and fly hard. With gold glittering just around the next thundercloud, Hawks resigned his newly found job and, impressed with the stranger, flew the man's gleaming new OX-5 Standard to San Diego. Here he was to wait until his mysterious benefactor contacted him with instructions. Hawks was willing to wait, for the future could not have looked brighter.

He waited—and waited, and waited. Now, no one buys an airplane for what is obviously a high price, hires a pilot by dragging him away from his job, and lets everything stew around in a big pot of nothingness. Not if things are normal, they don't. Hawks's nose began to wrinkle and there came to him the odor of a very large rat. Sure enough there was one—without whiskers—in the shape of the stranger of the gaudy dress and the smooth tongue. The stranger was a crook, an out-and-out thief who was simply setting up a neat killing. Confronted with Hawks, he admitted that some "special flying" would be needed. The "big money" would come, he explained, when Hawks began flying narcotics into the States from Mexico.

Hawks couldn't believe it. He raged at his unknown employer. The stranger responded with his own particular brand of verbal vehemence, and from this bitter and heated argument Hawks stumbled away the loser.

Or so the stranger thought.

Later that afternoon, with the gaudy dress of the stranger removed from sight, Hawks topped off the tanks, climbed into the Standard and buzzed off across the mountains to Arizona. Whipped into anger at his own innocence in being dragged into a deal that could have tossed him into a cell for many years, he became a frantic, one-man air circus. He clattered and thundered his way from one town to the next, landing at field after field. He put on wild demonstrations of aerobatics that strained the Standard to its limit and awed his gaping onlookers. Each time he landed after a demonstration he filled the rear cockpit with eager passengers; he flew so many people the rear seat cushions never had a chance to cool off from the proximity of passenger rear ends—which also added to his fast-growing kitty. After a hurried dinner meal, he worked on the airplane and, as quickly as night fell, roared again into the air, drawing even bigger crowds than under the sun. His night specialty was a nocturnal exhibition of aerobatics carried out with fireworks.

Hawks admits:

> My activity was a little feverish, because I didn't know what minute the consequences of my wholly justifiable but illegal act might catch up with me. Almost before I knew it

my bankroll had attained the size I had set for it and I flew back to Los Angeles with a certain grim satisfaction.

The stranger had been looking for me and the ship and he finally found us where we had all started out with such great prospects, at Rogers Field. He was sore, all right, but everybody knew what a four-flusher he was, and I had plenty of backing. We parted company, he in an ugly mood from having been beaten at his own game. . . .

I later teamed up with Earl Dougherty and a wild man named Wesley Walker. Mere acrobatic flying had become a drug on the market, so to revive the flagging interest of the public we began wing-walking and transferring from ship to ship and parachute jumping. These stunts palled in an amazingly short time, so I dreamed up something really sensational, and, as events were to prove, highly useful in a strategic sense years later.

What we did was to strap a five-gallon tin of gasoline on Wesley's back. Wesley crawled up on the top wing of the Standard, and off we went to perform history's first midair refueling act!

While the barker on the ground was building it up to the huge crowd, Dougherty was jockeying his Jenny around until his lower wing overlapped our upper one. Then the daring wing-walker, doubly handicapped with his awkward burden of fuel, reached up and grabbed the wing-skid of Dougherty's ship, lifting himself calmly onto the other plane as I dropped to give them leeway. Then, in full sight of the crowd and to the accompaniment of mad cheering which none of us could hear, he walked down the length of the wing to the fuselage and poured his can of gas into the Jenny's regular gas tank.

Poor old Wesley! Hardly a year after our refueling stunt, he met his death in a manner as ironic as it is given to a daredevil to die. He had just completed a parachute jump from a speeding plane, landing unhurt in a tree. Finding himself quite safe, he unbuckled his parachute harness and started for the ground, only to slip and fall. His neck was broken and he died instantly.

It was in the fall of 1921 that the lives of Frank Hawks and his wife—and barnstorming for him generally—went blithely to hell. Hawks chanced into a representative of the Mexico City Centennial Committee who was looking for a plane and a pilot to perform stunts for the mammoth celebration that was being planned. Immediately Hawks hit the man with a demand for high fees. He wanted, he said, a guarantee of $350 a week no matter if he flew or slept under the wing of his airplane. He also demanded a flat price of one thousand dollars for every stunt flight performed in the daytime, and double that amount for flying at night with appropriate fireworks. To his delight the Mexican official agreed, and told Hawks to get under way.

The happy barnstormer took with him his Hisso Standard, a mechanic named Tom Sketchley, and a wing-walker named Auggie Pedler. Because the mechanic tipped the scales at two hundred pounds, he was banished to a train to make the trip to Mexico City.

Over the desert on the first leg of the southward journey, Hawks almost immediately ran into the bane of the itinerant barnstormer: a balky and coughing engine in the middle of nowhere. Hawks's trained ear diagnosed the trouble as fouled plugs. With all that money awaiting him south of the border, Hawks wanted nothing to stand in his way, and the prospect of crisp, green cash set him to thinking furiously.

A short shouted discussion with Pedler led the passenger to rummage around in his flight kit. It was with a slightly unhappy look on his face that he came up with new plugs and a wrench, for he knew what was to ensue. He nodded to Hawks as he received his instructions . . .

At nine thousand feet, Pedler crawled out from the front cockpit and prepared to perform a feat of derring-do in midair that had never before been attempted, and that also earned Pedler a very special niche in aviation history. He was going to change the plugs on a running engine (the only engine of the airplane) while they were en route to their destination.

With Pedler in position, Hawks cut the ignition. As the big wooden propeller slapped to a halt, he put the Standard into the flattest glide possible while Pedler braced himself and went speedily to work.

Three thousand feet above the ground the amazing Mr. Pedler had completed the change of the plugs! Windblown and aching where he had braced himself, Pedler crawled back into his seat while Hawks restarted the engine and climbed again into the sky. Later that day they landed safely in Yuma.

But their engine was not one to accept defeat so easily, and three more times en route to Mexico City it coughed black smoke, vibrated and shook badly, belched raucously and threatened to commit internal mayhem upon itself. So three more times the redoubtable Pedler wearily left his seat and crawled forward where, with the switches off and the airplane gliding earthward over the mountains, he performed his mechanical legerdemain upon the engine with a change of plugs.

At Mexico City, Pedler was more enraged than he was tired, and the first thing he did in that mountain capital was to tear apart the entire engine and put it back together, so that it ran with a smooth song of power. Then both men varnished the Standard and polished it a dozen times until it gleamed in the sun like burnished gold.

In retrospect, Hawks said about his frame of mind as he set out to give the Mexican population a flying demonstration long to be remembered:

> In those days I was accounted by many—and with cause—a wild and reckless flier. Part of my daredeviltry was talent and part, no doubt, was due to the mood in which I constantly lived as a result of the recent upheaval in my personal affairs—a sort of devil-may-care, let-come-what-will attitude. Consequently I took long chances, ran spectacular risks and generally tempted fate more than a sane man should . . .
>
> Certainly no balanced aviator would loop, roll, spin and do wingovers with an old Hisso Standard less than fifty feet off the ground, even at sea level, much less in the rarefied and treacherous air of Mexico City where takeoffs begin at 7,400 feet—yet that is exactly what I proceeded to do when I went up to perform the first act of the *Circo Aero*. What a hand the Mexicans gave me, and how intoxicating was their wild applause after the bored crowds to whom I had been playing in the States! It is no wonder that I was inspired to outdo myself even at the imminent risk of breaking my neck. I gave them the best I had and that mob literally ate it up.

While Hawks handled the Standard through its paces with his consummate flying skill, Auggie Pedler further raised the blood pressure of the crowd by standing on his head on the wings, hanging by his hands—and then hanging by his toes—

from one of the wing skids. The crowd was already hoarse with cheering and handsore from applauding when Hawks went into his climax of the show. He slow-rolled the Standard while Pedler was seated on the upper wing.

That wasn't the specialty. He did this at what amounted to a suicidal altitude—with his wing tips nearly scraping a dozen sombreros from their owners' heads!

Later that night Hawks was in the air alone, splaying and streaking the skies with garish, brilliantly colored fireworks. Their first day went in a fashion that could only be described as fabulous.

In the ensuing days things could not have been better for Hawks. He flew his heart out, Pedler performed like a madman, and the crowd showered them with adulation. Then once again bad luck clung to Hawks's back. Sketchley, their mechanic, was overcome with a mooning case of homesickness for California and lit out for the north. A swift and unexpected bout of malaria knocked Pedler into bed with a raging fever, and doctors ordered his return to a northern climate.

Hawks and his Standard suddenly seemed very lonely in Mexico City . . .

He turned to other sources of income and his first solo mission was to fly a pair of very fat Mexican ranchers from Puebla to Mexico City. A ferrying job seems easy enough, but in this case Hawks demanded a fee that was as hefty as his passengers, for it was a flight that could be made only against forbidding circumstances. He would cross his first hurdle on just getting off the ground, no mean feat when one considers that his takeoff run was to be made from a plateau 8,600 feet above sea level. Many Standards could barely struggle up to that altitude.

Yet conditions were *worse* than they seemed. The takeoff was planned for midafternoon. At that time of day the air would be severely heated and would lose some of its density. The combination of altitude and heat meant that Hawks would have to take off at an altitude equivalent to about eleven or twelve thousand feet—and more than one pilot of his day had said that just such a stunt was flatly impossible.

And so it turned out to be! Hawks remembered that the takeoff run was the longest of his career. For an uncertain time he believed that the Standard might even make it to the Mexican capital without ever leaving the earth it apparently had come so much to like. Finally, after bouncing and vibrating madly during its long roll, the biplane staggered like a sick and dying bird into the air. Elated, Hawks eased back on the stick and brought the machine to the great height of one hundred feet above the ground. At this moment he realized that perhaps a bounce had sent him aloft in the first place. The Standard reached one hundred feet, sort of sighed in a dying expulsion of life, and began to settle back for the ground. Nothing Hawks could do with throttle or stick could prevent the earth from greedily claiming what had only seconds before escaped its grasp. Feeling extremely foolish, Hawks shrugged and plopped back to the ground.

Since he could not even babble like a child in Spanish, Hawks grinned like a demented idiot at his curious passengers. He pretended to tinker with the innards of the Hisso so that his passengers might believe that engine trouble, rather than a total lack of capability to fly, had kept them on the surface. Hawks stalled for time until the sun slipped for the horizon and the evening air cooled swiftly. He knew then that he could make it into the air.

Then started a night flight that lasted two hours, but which seemed to Hawks to last not one minute less than two years. There wasn't so much as a single light on the ground to guide him across the trackless and dangerous, sawtoothed wastes. He guided himself by the stars and, eventually, landed at what is now Valbuena Field.

There were times when Fate uses its fickle finger with great gusto and on Hawks's next night flight he was the unwilling target of that finger. Cruising through absolute blackness his engine gurgled to a stop. Hearing the sighing of wind through the wire and braces, Hawks eased the nose forward. He was not upset, for by great fortune the engine had expired over what Hawks knew to be a million acres of level ground.

That it was—except for a hayrick that stood directly before him in the murky night. Hawks plunged into the hayrick doing about fifty miles per hour. He came away from the hayrick without any wings or landing gear, and without any injuries either.

His miraculous escape seemed only to make the Fates angry and they did their best to bludgeon Hawks out of this life into another.

After wrecking his Hisso Standard, he bought a surplus Nieuport 28. Shortly after taking off on his first flight with the old French fighter the engine quit, and Hawks made history of a very special sort by dead-sticking the airplane into the middle of a bullring—without injury to man or beast!

He repaired the engine and took off again to the thundering cheers of the crowd, the salutes of the matadors and the bellowing of bulls. While the crowd watched, he hauled the Nieuport off the ground in a screaming zoom. Ah, when those Fates get busy . . .

At three hundred feet above the city the control cables tore loose and Hawks was in a runaway, uncontrollable airplane. Desperately he cut the switches. The Nieuport smashed into an apple orchard and a swift series of events ensued:

The seat belt snapped like rotten rope—catapulting Hawks like a bullet out of the airplane and onto the ground—a split second before the heavy rotary engine slammed backward into the suddenly vacated cockpit!

Shortly thereafter Hawks chanced upon a Belgian pilot who stared moodily at the world from behind a monstrous cast around a broken leg. Immediately, from the man's glowering, bloodshot eyes, Hawks deduced that he had run into another barnstormer. And so he had. The Belgian had shipped three war-surplus German L.V.G. two-seat biplanes to Mexico. The first plane he flew promptly snapped his leg when it ground-looped viciously during a takeoff roll.

The Belgian brightened. "Look," he said, "I'll furnish the airplanes, you furnish the flying." Hawks agreed and once again he was in business. They drove out to the field so that Hawks could check himself out in one of the L.V.G.'s.

He climbed into the cockpit, flicked switches, shouted he was ready to start, and then fretted impatiently while the mechanics tried to swing the propeller through to start the big in-line engine. "Aw, hell," he snorted, "here—let me show you birds how to do it."

He jumped down from the cockpit, grasped a prop blade, and gave it a mighty swing. A second later he lay groaning and cursing in pain on the ground, his left hand grasping his right. Four bones in that hand were instantly broken when the propeller kicked back with vicious force. Now there were two airplanes and two crippled pilots. It was a fine way to kick off a new business . . .

The hospital bill cleaned out the last of Hawks's money. He became so desperate for eating money he accepted a job flying a passenger from Mexico City to Tuxpan. His left arm was heavily encased within a plaster cast, but Hawks decided that he could manipulate both stick and throttle perfectly well with only one hand, and off they went.

"The proverbial one-armed paperhanger would have looked like a slow-motion movie by comparison," commented Hawks, "but I managed to stay with it—and that is about all that can be said concerning most of the flying that went on in those days." He earned four hundred pesos, and this kept him and his crippled Belgian friend in business.

Hawks learned quickly that in Mexico the zany and the unexpected were routine, that planning was held in utter contempt, and that *mañana* is the key word to all operations. No self-respecting Mexican would possibly do today what could conceivably be ignored until tomorrow—and there was *always* tomorrow.

His next passengers were an army general and a congressman, who wanted Hawks to barnstorm them around the country so that they might induce popularity because of their flying and thus invoke the peasants to vote for them. Few of the peasants, they were convinced, ever had seen an airplane, and certainly none had ever seen an airplane loaded to the cockpit coaming with ranking dignitaries. Of course, none of the dignitaries had been so foolish as to risk his life in the fabric-and-matchwood heaps that passed in those days for airplanes!

Before taking off for Huetamo, the general's home town, where he expected to be received as a conquering hero, Hawks inquired as to what type of landing field he might find in those distant parts. The general assumed a pontifical air and thrust out what remained of his chest (which strangely pushed against his belt). "Do not worry, my son," he informed the *yanqui* pilot with disarming charm, "just write down what is required and I shall see that it is prepared for our arrival."

Hawks looked at the general for a long moment, wrote down what he wanted, and the general fired off a wire. An answer was very quick in coming. There was, to be sure, a suitable field, but did the gentlemen understand the nature of a minor problem? There were a number of trees that dotted the landscape but, one should understand that they were lovely trees. Hawks ignored the beauty of the terrain and insisted that the trees must be felled before he would attempt a landing. The general shrugged, dispatched another wire with instructions, and only when Hawks received an answer that the trees were being removed would he consent to take off on their political barnstorming expedition.

Hawks managed somehow to stuff his two overstuffed officials in the rear cockpit of the L.V.G. and off they went to make political hay and history. Hardly were they airborne when there came an interruption to the flight. A hand tapped the pilot—politely, to be sure—on the shoulder. It was the general; would the gentleman flying the machine enjoy some of the cognac which the general was waving about in full view?

Hawks certainly would have enjoyed some of the cognac, because the air was bitterly cold at fifteen thousand feet where he was flying. And for the same reason—the rarefied air and lack of oxygen and the cold—he refused even this one drink. The general and the congressman were not so inclined. As the trip continued the blasting wind became colder and colder, the need for the cognac was appreciated by the passengers as never before, and by the time the old German airplane neared its destination, the two dignitaries were hilariously, blindly drunk.

Then: "Down, down, down we came in slow, graceful spirals. Every now and then I would clear the engine with a short burst from the throttle to make sure it wouldn't clog up and quit running before I was ready. At five thousand feet there was a sudden change in the atmosphere. We had dropped below the level of the mountains and the air became hot and stuffy.

"I looked around to comment on the quick change of climate and, to my utter astonishment and horror, found the general leaning far out of the observer's cockpit with the congressman holding on to his legs. . . ."

The general was waving enthusiastically to a waiting crowd below, bellowing hoarsely in drunken Spanish and lurching about against the side of the airplane, while the congressman fought a losing battle with the wind to keep him from tumbling away from the machine. The congressman thought the whole thing was a magnificent flourish on the part of his compatriot, and Hawks was deathly afraid that the congressman would soon start to wave also, with his frantic waving becoming, in effect, a good-bye to the general who would be falling to the hard ground far below.

Hawks screamed at them to get back in their seats, punctuating his remarks with a profanity that one may recognize in any tongue or dialect. Despite their obviously injured feelings the two officials subsided groggily, slumped back in the depths of the cockpit, and muttered slurrily while they drained what was left of the cognac. The L.V.G. fairly lurched with the powerful hiccoughing from the floorboards of the rear seat.

Hawks was unable to repress an involuntary shudder when he studied the landing field. The "prepared" airstrip was exactly as advertised in the telegrams: large, and treeless. The Mexicans were absolutely true to their word. But as Hawks committed himself to his final approach he saw to his horror that while the trees had been cut down, the Mexicans, never ones to overexert themselves, had left the stumps remaining. No one had said to remove the stumps? Then why bother? They didn't.

The field expanding before Hawks's agonized gaze was a maze of wicked stumps at least two feet high. Hawks began to sweat; if he cracked up and killed officials of the stature he was carrying, he would be drawn and quartered on the spot, *if* he survived, that is.

"Now commenced a reverse-English game of tenpins," recalled Hawks, "with the L.V.G. and me trying desperately to wiggle through the tree butts without scoring a hit. We were snaking along in great style until the ship began to lose speed and the undersized rudder of the L.V.G. would no longer swing right or left. I pushed up my goggles, cut the switches and began praying.

"One wheel smashed into a stump, and the gear collapsed. One propeller blade dug into the ground and was snapped off halfway to the hub. We ground to a halt in a cloud of red dust, and my relief at finding neither passenger hurt is beyond description. The ship settled back on her tail, and the general and the congressman were home in Huetamo."

Plastered as tightly as they were it did not occur to the officials in the back seat that there had been anything amiss with the landing. They were deliriously happy with their grand arrival. As for the villagers—well, they were ignorant in any case of the mysteries of airplanes, and they believed that *all* landings were executed in the manner so ably demonstrated by the *yanqui* pilot—by plowing with a horrendous crash into tree stumps. Had he not been selected by the general and the congressman as their skilled and brave pilot? Was this choice not obviously made of the best? There could not be any other method of landing, obviously! Thus there rang out cries of *Bravo! Ole! Viva!*

The officials, with much indecent posturing, extricated themselves from the machine. Reeling their way into the arms of their compatriots they were immediately smothered with hugs and garlic-flavored kisses, while an astounded Hawks almost had the clothes shredded from his back by the ardent enthusiasm of the swarming crowd. He nearly smothered in the close proximity of peasant breath.

One week later, a new propeller and wheel arrived by surface transportation. The stumps were removed by mule power and, to some extent, by a lesser sacrifice of human energy. Once again Hawks embarked with his passengers. On the previous flight they had become bombed while airborne. This time they arrived at the airstrip nearly embalmed from staggering amounts of tequila and other local firewater absorbed during the enforced but uproariously happy stay on the ground.

During the next aerial trek trouble visited Hawks while still airborne. He was over the mountains when a small leak appeared in the radiator. The leak was bad enough. The fact that the radiator was located on the top wing was much worse. Due to the partial vacuum always present atop an airplane wing in flight, the water in the radiator was literally siphoned out.

Without the water the engine began to heat up. As it heated up it started a tremendous thumping. The monstrous complaints from within the engine grew noisier and added great whacking blows to the process from premature explosions within the cylinders. Hawks switched off all power before the engine seized and climaxed its performance with the inevitable explosion.

He stretched his glide—a cardinal sin—almost to the suicide point, nearly sweating blood, seeking to reach a tiny pasture at the far end of a valley. In the back seat the general and the congressman were making evident their debonair dismissal of all danger. They ignored the perils of the emergency landing. Indeed, they were oblivious to it all, since they were draining the dregs of the last cognac bottle. In the gentle wind sighing past the powerless airplane, they bellowed the strains of "El Rancho Grande." Their volume was magnificent as the drunken cries echoed down the valleys and rebounded in shuddering tones from the mountain flanks.

Hawks with his customary expertise set the L.V.G. down without breaking or snapping anything. As the plane ground to a halt, amidst the carousing roars from the rear seat, it was surrounded at once by curious peasants. They stared agog at the distinguished government officials who had dropped in on them in such a splendid fashion—for dinner, of course. That night the overwhelmingly happy farmer slit the throat of his one and only chicken, bade his wife prepare extra tortillas, and held a primitive banquet by candlelight. There was, of course, much firewater present for one and all.

Senor Hawks collapsed into slumber on the floor. That he was not entirely welcome was a fact he learned during the darkened night. A disgruntled hog rooted and snuffled angrily at him; it appeared that the Yankee pilot had usurped the sleeping quarters of the hog, who cared nothing at all for dignitaries or officials. Hawks moved over, never one to argue in the middle of the night with an unhappy hog.

Early in the morning Hawks repaired the leak in the radiator. He amassed a quantity of chewing gum, grass, and mud to seal the opening. He also made a successful takeoff from the valley, which proves that engineering rules never really apply to barnstormers. And finally he returned his animated (and still drunk) cargo to Mexico City, where those worthy gentlemen remained entirely unaware how many times they had nearly reached the moment of their Last Drunk.

Hawks remained in Mexico only a short time longer. He never became rich, in cash, that is. But his experiences there he could never have bought for any amount of money, in dollars or in pesos, this side of the Rio Grande, or south of the border.

12

Historical Note

It was one of those beautiful mornings that every pilot feels is just made for flying. A gentle breeze sailed out of the southeast, bringing a sea crispness to the air as it carried across the Florida coast. No more than ten miles from where we sat there loomed the naked skeletal spires of Cape Kennedy, but here, on the grass strip airport of Merritt Island, was a world apart. The writer and several friends were sitting over heavy mugs of hot coffee, our conversation interrupted every now and then by the clattering roar of airplanes surging past the windows for takeoff. The morning had been, and was, wonderful. The writer and a close friend, John R. Hawke, had just completed an hour's aerobatics in the only Messerschmitt Bf-108B *Taifun* in the country, and that had included a rat race with a bright yellow Stearman. Rushing past the windows and swirling overhead were a dazzling variety of planes—everything from Super Cubs to Bonanzas and Skynights. This was a flying day, to be sure. And now we were relaxing, going through a hot-and-heavy session of hangar flying, and, of course, the old and woolly days of barnstorming.

One member of our group appeared vexed. "Look," he said, a hand waving in the air, "you've been banging my ear for an hour, nonstop, describing all these guys and their Jennies and other birds. Colorful—I admit it. Exciting—sure. But mostly, I gather, they seemed to be just a pack of irresponsible jerks. There's a sort of veneration about a guy who could fly like a dream, but ended up busting his butt in a stupid crash. The lot of them sound like hot-rodders with oily clothes and goggles, and a jolting whiskey breath. I mean *bums.* So their flying was great. Okay. But did any of them ever amount to a damn?"

Well, now, that *was* a different point of view. In his own way, and not being all-inclusive, my young friend wasn't far from pegging an accurate description of quite a few of the barnstormers. But I thought it painful to observe that he believed there is anything really *wrong* with being a bum, anyway. To be a bum with skill and talent takes a hell of a lot more work, guts, daring, and imagination than being a clerk shoving shoes on and off the perspiring feet of fat women in a shoe store! And there's something great about the professionally successful bum. But these young kids today . . . Well, on to his question about any of "those bums" ever amounting to a damn. Yes. Many of the fly-by-nighters sure did. And some of them even became famous . . .

They were over Minnesota swampland in the spring of 1923; the engine had been raising all kinds of sick hell for a while and now it threatened again to quit. The pilot, a slender youth with unruly hair, cursed softly and concluded that this was one of those days when you were better off in bed. Only a painfully short time before he had risked his neck and his Jenny by trying to bull his way beneath a local storm; the black belly of the cloud had poured forth an unbelievable concentration of water that changed his mind quickly enough. Now, his flight suit uncomfortably sodden and plastered to his skin, he was fighting the winds near the ground, hoping the storm would break enough to allow him passage through the violence.

His engine had other ideas; it didn't care about life any more. One cylinder abruptly cut out. Instinctively the youngster at the controls heeled over sharply and shoved down the nose, heading for a clover field. Then two more cylinders died, and with the ghost of an engine he was committed to an emergency landing.

His choice of where to alight was meager. He could select either the woods or a swamp, for the clover field turned out to be not much larger than a postage stamp. He chose the swamp, and from two hundred feet skillfully belly whopped the airplane down. The Jenny slithered along like a winged eel for perhaps ten yards; then the pilot felt the earth slam hard against him. The sky cartwheeled and the lights went out. When they came back on again the pilot was upside down, his face shoved in the tall wet grass.

The immediate urge at such a moment is to *get out from under*. And those pilots who gave in to that urge, not without understanding, often made the Fates double over in laughter. For when they released their seat belt gravity exerted itself and they dropped headfirst out of their crumpled cockpit. Such motion as produces a tremendous *thwack!* against the skull or the back of the neck can snuff out a life that has just survived a miraculous crash landing—and it has happened too many times.

So this particular young pilot stopped to think of where he was and what would happen when he cut loose. He grasped the cockpit ridge, braced himself and with his free hand released the belt—and eased himself gingerly from his machine. It was the kind of thinking that in the coming years would enable him to leap to the forefront of world flight . . .

The landing had been far better than he had hoped. After emergency repairs to the cracked spreader bar with a length of twine and some dope, the weary Jenny was once again ready to try her wings.

This young pilot found the financial take from barnstorming not enough to keep both his fuel tank filled and his stomach free from complaining, and in order to remain airborne he took to instructing hopeful airmen, no matter what their age or their occupation. One such student was a Roman Catholic priest. No man ever evinced more zeal and enthusiasm for the upper regions than he, and no man could have been a worse pilot. It was with regret that the instructor terminated the lessons; he felt fortunate indeed that the termination was voluntary rather than being enforced by a final and fatal crash. The padre, however, was quite happy about it all. He explained that his attempts at airmanship allowed him to be "brought a little nearer to God"—and he did *not* mean by a mere two thousand feet or so.

No matter how intensive his efforts to keep in the barnstorming game, the business simply wasn't there, and the young pilot threw in the towel. He enlisted in the U.S. Air Service. It was a move he made with some sorrow, for the step appeared irrevocable in clamping the lid on the independence so unique to the barnstormer. The world lay at any end of the compass. You knew a kinship with the feathered creatures of flight. Your home was a pasture beneath the stars, a roof, the wing of your airplane. A magic carpet presented you with drifting cloud mountains, with the vast sweep of the plains, the rolling wonder of the hill country . . .

Oh, well. The pilot decided to cancel out his barnstorming independence with a final fling. He would challenge the length of the continent in a Canuck that was owned by an old barnstorming buddy. It was a project that began badly.

The pilot went aloft on a solo test flight, the engine of the Canuck suffered its crash of silence directly over Pensacola Bay, and the pilot deadsticked the biplane down to a sand hillock. The abrupt meeting with the earth slammed the left wheel up through the lower wing and chewed the propeller into jagged and useless splinters.

The determined duo repaired the Canuck, loaded their sparse gear aboard, and trundled off for the West Coast. To lengthen their endurance between fuelings, they installed cylindrical, five-gallon fuel cans on either side of the fuselage by the lower wing. The tanks were lashed to the airplane, and performance became a matter of trading drag for range.

Once in the air and clattering over the landscape, it was the pilot's onerous task to lean far out of the cockpit, unlash a can, jam a hose inside its neck and then—in the teeth of the raging wind from the propeller—empty the fuel into the main tank of the Jenny. Surprisingly, the system worked well, and the two adventurers decided to install even more tanks. They purchased three surplus tanks, each with a capacity of nine gallons, and installed them beneath the wings. Now, with the original tanks, they had a theoretical range of four hundred miles. Tremendous!

Enthusiasm outran aerodynamics. Their new troubles began when they attempted their first takeoff from a Texas field, burdened with all their excess weight and air drag. It would not be wrong to say that the Canuck did not wish to fly. The old machine nearly burst its heart as it pounded and banged and shook for a half mile just to get the wheels off the ground. And that seemed to be just about all it could do. Despite the best efforts of the pilot he failed to nurse the wheezing and gasping airplane more than fifty feet above the ground. They were flying, but just barely.

Disgusted, the two men eased into a very gentle turn and wallowed back to the field. Here they removed one can from the airplane. Another was unfastened but, to save drag, if not weight, it was deposited in the lap of the passenger. Once again they struggled aloft and were able to plead and coax the Canuck to a height of several hundred feet.

Against a quartering westerly wind, with the engine whining at maximum rpm, their indicated airspeed actually reached fifty miles per hour. But then the sun rose higher in the sky, the temperature went up, the density of the air went down, and the earth began to reach up for their airplane once more. With low hills directly before the plane, the passenger heaved the remaining five-gallon can over the side into a stony ravine directly beneath them. The difference of about thirty-five pounds in weight meant everything—they scraped their way over the hills.

Near the hamlet of Camp Wood, Texas, the engine began to noisily suck up the last dregs of fuel. In all that vast area there was no place to land but the town square. Undaunted, the pilot slipped down from the sky and slapped the Canuck neatly onto the ground.

People fairly exploded from stores and buildings, and the Canuck soon was surrounded with townspeople pelting the two aviators with questions. To the adult voices there soon was added the shrill cries of children; the excited schoolmarm had dismissed all classes and locked the school door behind her. The townspeople fueled the airplane, and after tying down the Canuck, offered the pilots the hospitality of their town.

Early the next morning the fliers were dismayed to note that during the night the winds had shifted southeastward. Their planned takeoff across the square against the wind was now out of the question. Directly ahead of their path loomed a cluster of buildings.

The pilot surveyed the town and decided to use a side street as a runway. He realized that the choice was far from ideal, for several hundred feet from where he would begin his takeoff run there was a deep depression. The street was so narrow that the wings would be brushing tree branches all along the run. To add spice to the event there were two telegraph poles almost in the street, with no more than a foot of clearance between them for the wings. The passenger, to save weight, drove to another field outside of town while the pilot prepared for the do-or-die takeoff.

He aligned the Canuck's nose squarely in the middle of the street, gunned the engine to maximum power, and shot down the narrow passageway. Alongside him came the roaring cheers of the good citizens of Camp Wood, who had assembled en masse to witness the daredeviltry of the intrepid barnstormer.

The pilot failed to clear the right telephone pole by only three inches. That was three inches too much.

The momentum of the takeoff swung the plane around sharply and the nose of the Canuck slammed into, and then crashed through, the side wall of a hardware store. The din was earsplitting. The propeller flew to pieces, and the engine ground hoarsely to a stop. There was a moment of silence, and then a clattering bedlam as pots and pans tumbled and rained down from the shelves within the store.

The pilot was relieved when the store owner did *not* threaten mayhem. Indeed, he refused to accept a cent for damages from the chagrined flier. "Hell's fire!" exclaimed the merchant, "think of all the publicity!"

The men fixed the smashed propeller and repaired the wing tip and decided, wisely, to wait for a wind shift. This came three days later, and the barnstormers departed the town with their wheels several feet over the highest building.

Dusk caught the Canuck in a remote and deserted part of Texas close to the Mexican border. The airplane sighed its way uneventfully to earth between the sage and the cactus plants, and the pilots slept the night through beneath the stars. But that quiet repose was to be rudely shattered after daybreak; disaster caught up with them once again.

With the help of some Mexicans the pilots cleared a takeoff path through the wasteland. But by the time they were ready to fly it was Texas hot—a shimmering blur of heat with the air deathly still. The pilot managed to break free of the earth, but only barely, and the Canuck sagged wearily in the savage heat, rising no more than four or five feet above the ground. On and on the plane rumbled, gasping, its wheels sometimes bashing through sagebrush.

It was too late when the pilot saw the thigh-thick spire of a towering Spanish bayonet cactus poking up from the landscape directly ahead of him. It was too late to land and they were too low to bank, and the only thing to do was to cut the switches and wait for the crash. It came swiftly. The lower wing crunched into the thick trunk of the green cactus; fabric ripped and wood cracked. The bracing wires sheared off the bayonet and the plane slammed with a jolt against the hard ground and rumbled to a stop.

They were stuck. Smack in the middle of nowhere.

And then, unbelievably, came a shout. The pilots turned to stare at a freight train standing still on tracks they had never even spotted. The passenger of the Canuck held a hasty meeting with the brakeman, and clambered aboard for the ride to El Paso. As the train disappeared the pilot made himself comfortable beneath the shade cast by the Canuck's wing, and waited.

Many hours later his vanished companion returned in triumph, laden with dope, nails, screws, boards and cotton cloth. They worked through the blazing heat of the afternoon, a mishmash of patching, doping, glueing, hoping, sweating and cursing. Then, with fatigue etched on their faces, they climbed aboard and staggered successfully from the parched earth.

That was the end of their cross-country. They flew the Canuck to Brooks Field, near San Antonio, where they called it quits. The Canuck looked like a dead prehistoric bird by then.

And so the nation lost a barnstormer, the United States Army gained an SE-5 pilot, and all the world was gifted with a hero.

That "young pilot" about whom we have been reading?

Oh, yes. His name: Charles A. Lindbergh.

13

Cloudbuster

From two thousand feet the grass airfield resembled nothing so much as a small postage stamp. Standing on the wing, leaning into the wind and hanging grimly to a wooden strut, Tommy Walker made the big mistake of staring straight down. He squeezed his eyes tightly and gritted his teeth to overcome the sudden vertigo, a crazy, overwhelming crush of no-balance that threatened to spin the earth below like a pinwheel. He groaned quietly to himself.

The ancient biplane shook badly as it rumbled over the Orlando airfield at seventy miles per hour. The air between the flying machine and the hard earth far below seemed thinner and thinner and . . .

"How the hell did I get into *this?*" Walker asked himself in futile desperation. He pushed back the sensations that flip-flopped about within his stomach and threatened to climb with greasy tentacles up along the lining of his throat. "*Gaarghh,*" he said weakly.

Only fifteen minutes before he had been safe on the ground, a seventeen-year-old kid with more guts, it now seemed evident, than brains. Otherwise, what the hell *was* he doing up here?

He needed a job. He was down on his luck, he was broke, and he was hungry—all powerful arguments for trying anything that will fill the stomach and perhaps put a little weight into a trouser pocket. He walked to the small airport and asked for work. The airport manager waggled a greasy thumb in the air, pointed it toward the road, and muttered: "Beat it, kid." The manager looked as friendly as an orangutan with a fierce toothache, and Tommy walked away from him.

But he didn't leave the field. Not yet, anyway. He ran into three barnstorming pilots who needed a parachute jumper quick for their gypsy air show. Tommy approached one pilot lounging in a chair alongside a biplane. "I understand you're looking for a parachute jumper," he said.

"Yeah," the pilot replied. "You know somebody in the business?"

Tommy nodded. "Me."

The pilot sat up a bit straighter and stared hard at Tommy Walker. Sopping wet, Tommy could just top the 145-pound mark on a scale. The flier shook his head slowly. "*You're* a jumper?" He might have reacted the same way if Tommy had said he could fly by a vigorous flapping of the arms.

Tommy played it with care. "Hell, yes," he answered blandly. "I've had lots of experience."

The pilot's eyes narrowed. "Yeah, yeah. What kind of chutes you jump with?" he queried.

It was a long shot; Tommy took it. "Any kind."

Again came the slow shaking of the pilot's head; then, a "who cares?" shrug. He rose to his feet and his voice became friendlier. "Okay, kid," he said, "you're on. Let's see how you can do."

Two pilots helped him struggle into the harness of a seat-pack chute. Tommy acted as if the harness were a bit tangled. He wasn't only grateful for the assist from the men, he *needed* the help.

He didn't have the faintest idea of how to wear a parachute. He had never worn a parachute before. He had never *seen* a parachute.

In fact, he had never even flown in any kind of airplane!

One of the pilots took him aloft in an old Fleet open cockpit biplane, hanging her nose high until the ship settled down at two thousand feet. Through the takeoff and all the way to altitude Tommy stared in fascination as the earth fell away from him. For those minutes of delightful first flight he seemed to throw a wall against a subconscious memory of intense fear of height. He just didn't think about it; he drank in the wonder of soaring away from the world and thought of nothing else. At two thousand feet the ragged snarl of the engine settled down to a more comfortable roar as the pilot eased into level flight. With a jolt reality returned to the kid strapped into the chute harness.

The pilot turned to him. He waved his arm vigorously and

shouted for the "jumper" to climb out onto the wing. Tomm
stared at him as if he were mad. Climb out on the wing? Thi
guy was nuts! And then Tommy remembered . . .

His face half-frozen, his emotions numb, he followed the
order. He fought back the giddy sensation that swept over
him as he stood up, got one foot over the cockpit coaming,
grabbed for a strut, and staggered onto the wing. Beneath his
feet he could feel the trembling of the wing as the airplane
rode the currents. The tremendous blast of air coming back
from the propeller helped somewhat; along with the thunder
of the engine and the cry of the wind it helped to dull his
senses.

Two things aided him. First, his mind seemed to be numb.
Second, he was grossly ignorant of the parachuting facts of
life. He had no emergency pack; he didn't even know that
almost all jumpers wore two chutes for safety.

And then sanity came to him with a rush that nearly
staggered his body out on the wing. He realized what was
going on, as he clung grimly, sans helmet and goggles, eyes
watering in the wind, to the strut of the vibrating airplane.
The pilot glanced at the earth to check the relationship of the
plane to the airport and lifted his arm. Tommy opened his
eyes wide as the arm came flashing down.

He hesitated only a moment longer. Resignation shoved
aside his quaking fears and his startled thoughts.

"What the hell!" he muttered as he released his grip and
the wind snatched eagerly at him, "you gotta start sometime."

It was an auspicious start. The wing whirled crazily before
his eyes as the wind flipped him neatly into space. For a long
moment there was a gut-wrenching spasm of falling, falling,
falling . . . The sensation vanished as he stared in amazement
at a horizon that whirled before his tumbling body. It was all
impossible, all crazy . . ."*Count*, you sonofagun!" he cried
out to himself. The numbers spilled from his lips, five, four,
three, two, one, and he tightened his grip on the cold metal
of the D-ring, and pulled savagely, sheer instinct throwing
his arm far out from his body as he tumbled.

The world went mad. All at once a hundred fists smashed
into his body, a knee went *WHOMP!* into his groin, and his
plummet earthward stopped with a head-spinning jar. He
blinked his eyes and tried to make all those colorful comets
go away and . . .

And suddenly he was in that marvelous world of the airman, drifting earthward beneath a huge silk canopy, suspended in space, drifting with no more effort than a moonbeam. With ridiculous ease he sailed out of the sky, a gentle breeze wafting past him, the earth below coming up slowly toward his floating form. In a moment he ignored the pressure of the straps against his body. He marveled at the fact that there was no sense of height despite there being nothing beneath him. It was the most wonderful sensation he had ever known. From that moment on, Herbert M. C. Walker, known to one and all of his friends simply as Tommy Walker, was committed to a life in the air. It was to be, and it still is, a fantastic lifetime of flying skill and courage, a story of a man who, like Frank Clarke and other pilots, had been described as being absolutely free of fear.

The latter statement is, of course, not true. This is the most amazing aspect of these people. Without fear they would have killed themselves long ago. It is the acceptance of and the control over that fear that makes them stand out so clearly against the men around them.

Tommy Walker is one of those men who has never allowed his fear to openly bother him, or to control him, in anything he has ever done, on the ground or in the air. He went on from that sudden revelation discovered during his parachute descent to become one of the world's great pilots, a devil-may-care soldier of fortune who never once turned down what promised to be a good fight or a rousing challenge. Since that very first flight, his flying has subjected him to burns, gunshot wounds, gashes, cuts, bruises, broken bones, scalding and a wild variety of physical mayhem. From that first jump he went on to leap out of airplanes more then 360 times in as crazy a variety of aerobatic nonsense as has ever been seen. His career against even the background of barnstormers and stunt men has been one to evoke a slow shaking of the head, and the wonder of it is that he is still going strong, and looks forward to many years of even greater accomplishment lying ahead.

All this, of course, would be his life for the next thirty-two years, as the youth drifted beneath his silken canopy to the grassy airfield. He landed hard, but jumped to his feet with an air of aplomb that smacked of long experience at leaping into space. As he shucked his harness the other two pilots of the barnstorming trio ran to his side, grinning.

"Okay, kid!" one shouted. "You're hired!" The words came nice and clear. They also meant *food*.

That same afternoon the "experienced parachute jumper" sneaked over to the airport office to beg information on some fine points of jumping. In the next several hours a grizzled old hand taught Tommy how to control the billowing canopy in a descent, how to go into and get out of chute spins, how to work the shroud lines to select his landing site, and what to do in event of landing in electric wires, trees, water or other obstacles. He especially warned him of the obstacles that could snare the unwary jumper, of flat spins and tumbling motions, of twisted shroud lines and other malfunctions and how to get out of them *fast*. His advise was worth everything to the young neophyte.

Unquestionably the most outstanding aspect of Tommy Walker's explosive entry into his new career was his background. Tommy had, since he was twelve years old, suffered an overwhelming terror of height! If he looked down from a high window or over a balcony he was afflicted immediately with the shakes; his face turned a pasty white color and his knees threatened to buckle beneath him. Even today, after several decades of the wildest flying and jumping imaginable, he is still the victim of this terrible fright. The writer knows this only too well: I have more than once actually assisted him to return into a room as he stood rooted in one spot on my apartment terrace.

This paradox in life—and a measure of what Tommy had to overcome—stemmed from an incident that took place when he was twelve years old. It was in New York, and resulted from a dare by friends that Tommy didn't have the guts to climb the sheer face of an apartment building—six stories up to the roof.

Tommy started climbing. He used handholds in the bricks and chinked spaces to scale that building like a human fly. Up and up he went, while a great crowd watched from below, wrapped in silence. Tommy was at the level of the fourth floor when the brick beneath his fingers ripped loose. His body plunged away from the building toward solid concrete four stories below.

By a combination of a miracle and a natural acrobatic tendency he performed a complete somersault and *crashed to the ground on his feet*. For a few moments he sat on the sidewalk, dazed, but incredibly without a single injury. That night he didn't say a word to his family about what had happened.

The next morning he awoke wrapped in a spasm of fear. His body was completely paralyzed from the waist down. His legs were useless.

Doctors said he would never again walk. His parents were thunderstruck. And then his father, a man of old-country wisdom, gambled with the future of his son. He started an argument with the boy. Whereas everyone until that moment had poured sympathy onto Tommy, his father berated him for idiocy. He railed against the fates that gave him a son of such stupidity. He brought the flush of anger to the boy's face, until the shouting came from both of them. And then the father delivered a smashing palm across the boy's face. Tommy cried out in pain and rage.

His father stood in the middle of the floor, cursing his son to be a man, to fight back. In a blind range Tommy staggered from the bed, lurched three steps, and fell helplessly into his father's arms. The old man wept like a child—his son had walked. One week later Tommy walked and ran as if he had never suffered an injury. His doctors saw it happen, and still they couldn't believe it.

The fever of wanderlust carried Tommy Walker away from home when he was seventeen. In 1932, with his closest friend, Dutch Wendt, he took off from New York for Florida. Dutch, also seventeen, was already an experienced hand at hopping freights, and late at night the boys clambered aboard a freight moving slowly out of the Jersey City rail yards.

Four days later, after eating and sleeping in Salvation Army and Volunteers of America centers, the youths hopped off a freight just north of Jacksonville, Florida. It had taken only this long for the glamour of riding dirty, jolting freight trains to pall. And they didn't like taking handouts for the food they had to eat. The depression was at full swing and, fortunately for the boys, the nation was dotted with Government camps for transients and migrating workers. For youngsters of their age the work was exceptionally hard, but the food was also plentiful. Tommy and Dutch Wendt signed up, received their bunks and without further ceremony were put to work.

For the next month Tommy worked like a mule; the worst of the jobs was to help pull stumps from fields. He swung an axe, slammed sledges against stone. He had always been unusually strong; in school he had been captain of the soccer team, run for his track team, and was the bruising, leading contender in wrestling and boxing. The Government camp whetted his skill in wild and punishing ring brawls. Pitted against experienced boxers, he had his head rattled more than once, but ended every fight standing on his feet and as the winner of the bout.

But a month of back-breaking labor and slugging it out in the ring at night was enough. Tommy and Dutch took off to work their way south to Orlando. It was here that Tommy made his first flight, his first jump, and began his career as a wild and woolly barnstormer.

From that first heart-squeezing moment of dropping into thin air, the die was cast for Tommy Walker to become one of the most skilled and famous fliers and stunt men among the freelancers at this exclusive art. On the morning after his first jump the trio of barnstormers, their number now grown to four with Tommy, took off on a long gypsy tour through the southeast. It was a wild and a free life and it exhilarated Tommy. The four men bounced from town to town, landing on roads, in hayfields, within towns, and pulling wild stunts to drum up business for their winged caravan. The pilots took care of all Tommy's expenses, and, quite generously, gave him ten percent of the take from each show. A really good weekend meant crisp folding money in his pocket.

Sometimes Tommy would fling himself away from an airplane three or four times a day. A small crowd meant that for all this expended energy he would finish the day with only a twenty-dollar bill. But with a packed house on the field or in the grandstands the barnstormers could reap in two thousand—and two hundred dollars of this take went to Tommy. In 1932, this was money with dazzle to it.

True to the form he was to later display, drunk with the heady taste of success and local fame, confident in his own ability, and face grinning from the roaring applause of the crowd, Tommy lived high on the hog.

His first gypsy tour with the barnstorming team meant three months of flying from field to field. Day after day Tommy tumbled away from airplanes, piling up jump after jump, and every time gaining invaluable experience in the fine points of risking his life. Every new plummet through the blue gave him the opportunity to test stability in the falls. He had long ended the uncontrolled tumble or end-over-end drop of the inexperienced jumper. Strictly on his own, and cribbing points from other parachutists, he learned to stabilize his drops by going into a spread-eagle arch (the standard form for sky diving today), or entering spirals, or dropping through the sky along a slant he desired.

Of far more importance to him was the fact that the gypsy tour provided him with an unexcelled chance to learn how to fly—and to fly in the full sense of the word: fighting weather, navigating, making emergency repairs, getting in and out of small fields, meeting the unexpected. He learned his flying in the best possible way, through the practical experience of cross-country flights over all kinds of terrain and in all kinds of weather. His airmanship was instinctive and it was superb. His pilot soloed him after three hours of dual instruction.

By the time the three months were over Tommy had, in addition to his fifty-six jumps, qualified as a hot-rock pilot. Introduced to flying in the best barnstorming tradition, he considered loops and various aerobatic stunts as natural as flying straight and level.

But Tommy even today finds excitement difficult to fulfill, and at his tender and brassy age of seventeen he fairly slavered for new thrills. After his eighth jump the pilots introduced him to the gentle sport that has never really found many takers—wing-walking. The three pilots and the boy in their midst concluded that if they could spice up their air show of aerobatic stunts and parachute jumps they could also fatten the daily kitty. In addition to the regular gate admission charged for the audience, the pilots learned early in the game to pass among the crowd with a winning smile and an outstretched hand that held an oversized hat, into which the impressed local audience invariably tossed change and dollar bills. The more impressed was that audience, the fuller would become the hat.

So they mounted a special brace on the fabric wing of a Fleet, and convinced the boy to stand on that wing during flight. Tommy loved it from the first moment. What the crowd couldn't see, of course, were hidden wire braces that supported the wing-walker in the air and during the steep air maneuvers. To the onlooker from the ground, Tommy stood erect and waved his arms in brazen defiance of death, balanced by some sorcery against the howling wind. It was a tremendous act, and one developed to its utmost by stunt men and barnstormers throughout the country. Tommy excelled in it; he was wild about the performance and looked forward keenly to each new air show. His antics atop the wing caused many a feminine onlooker to faint as Tommy sometimes "lost" his balance and wobbled dangerously on the wing. But according to Tommy, up there he was just as safe as at home in bed, and, considering some of his bed company, a hell of a lot safer. Two slender wires reeled out from pulleys within the wing, which Tommy hooked to a heavy belt against his waist.

After a week of waving gaily to the crowd while his pilot flew him at low altitude past the grandstands, or swept into tight turns, the act began to pall for Tommy. It was too tame. He wanted to do more and, unknowingly, was developing on his own the same daredevil stunts that other men had planned in other parts of the country. With his pilot Tommy worked out plans to stand on the wing, half-turning his body and blowing kisses to the local beauties, while the old Fleet biplane whirled through successive loops close to the ground.

Tommy felt they weren't coming close enough. His pilot told him he was mad when Tommy insisted that at the bottom of the loop, cracking out and starting up again in a rolling turn, he wanted to be able to look *up* at the broads along the upper grandstand rows. So the pilot cinched his straps a little tighter and cut it finer and Tommy up on that wing had a ball, waving and flinging kisses to the females, who shrieked and screamed and kept coming back for more.

The act was sensational. The pilots were delighted and they let the kid in their midst have his own way, because he was now pulling off stunts they wouldn't dare to try, he loved every moment of it, and he was the best crowd attraction they had ever seen outside of a naked trapeze artist hanging by her toes. News of Tommy Walker's fabulous derring-do in the sky below the level of the grandstand preceded their barnstorming stops and the crowds slowly continued to grow larger. For a youngster named Tommy Walker, this was sheer heaven, a fascinating life of wing-walking, flying his first aerobatics before the crowd, and leaping into space.

Tommy, it seemed, never got enough of anything that he really liked, and soon he was shouting at the pilots to extend the wing-walking acts. Only this time the pilot assigned to carry him aloft balked at his enthusiasm and flatly turned down his ideas. Tommy argued all the louder. He wanted his pilot to whirl the Fleet through slow rolls and barrel rolls while he stood spread-eagled, feet wide apart, and waved at the crowd as he whirled around and around. The pilots sighed helplessly and agreed to the madman stunts—Tommy threatened to quit the show unless they went along with him. And how could they fight the kid who was filling their pockets, who wanted only to put on a wilder and a better slow?

On his own, Tommy dressed up the routine, but without telling his pilot. His pilot heard a strange sound and for a moment thought the engine was about to blow up. But this sound was different . . . he looked up and gaped at the youngster, standing erect and blowing a cavalry charge on a bugle as the Fleet whirled through a series of barrel rolls!

And still Tommy wouldn't quit; he just *had* to try new stunts. He thought it would be a great routine if he could transfer in flight from one plane to another. He had heard about such stunts performed by other barnstormers and, without his being aware of it, the plane change had already become one of the standby acts of the great wingwalkers in the business, as we have seen. But since he had never witnessed this stunt and knew nothing of its problems, Tommy decided it might be prudent to wear a parachute.

His pilot grinned at him. "Tommy," he chortled, "you're getting old."

Tommy donned a seat-pack and cinched the harness just tight enough to give him body movement. At two thousand feet he climbed atop the biplane and braced himself. The second plane came in low, rising and falling gently with the air currents as the wheels lowered steadily toward Tommy. As the undercarriage dropped within his reach he reached up suddenly to grasp a gear leg. He pulled himself up higher, swung around to the lower wing, grabbed a strut and scrambled into the cockpit of the second plane.

The barnstormers were delighted, but faced a thoroughly disgusted Tommy Walker. "I could hardly move with this damned chute on," he stormed. "It gets in my way. Stow it!" He never wore the parachute again during transfer from one plane to another.

It had become abundantly evident to his pilot friends that Tommy Walker would try *anything* in the air. He was fast becoming, and strictly on his own motivation and through his own ideas, a startling mixture of the great barnstormer pilots and stunt men.

He swung gaily beneath a plane, hanging on to the axle bar of the landing gear with one hand—sans parachute.

He stood on his head as the ship soared around the field in steep turns and other "hairy maneuvers."

He hung by his feet beneath the airplane. That not being enough for him, he hung by one foot. Even this became tame, and he braced his shoes, and hung by one ankle instep, waving gaily to the stunned onlookers.

He developed a disdain for his safety that became frightening. One of the team's most effective tricks began on the ground as Tommy climbed into his plane without a parachute, a point stressed most carefully by their announcer. As they climbed to 2,500 feet Tommy slipped into his seat-pack chute, unseen by the audience. Over and over the announcer chanted of the death-defying stunt to come.

"Mr. Walker will chance death itself!" he cried emotionally to the edge-of-the-seat audience. "Watch closely as he climbs from the cockpit onto the wing. You saw for yourself—he has no parachute! He is going to stand on the wing while the airplane loops . . . while the airplane rolls around and around! Watch closely, folks, don't miss a thing! *This is the most dangerous act ever performed!*"

As the crowd watched tensely, Tommy climbed onto the wing. First there were a few rolls to whet the crowd's excitement. Then came the shouted, frenzied announcement that the plane would not loop directly over the grandstand. It was a "doozy of an act." With the announcer whipping the audience into a state of taut nerves and emotions, the Fleet dove, gathering speed swiftly. The sound of the wind shrieking through the wires and struts came clearly over the howl of the engine, and in a sudden screech of power the biplane tore up from its dive and soared up and up, higher and higher, arcing over into the loop.

At the top of the loop, Tommy cut himself free. His body plummeted unexpectedly away from the airplane and tumbled into space. The announcer, by now a skilled veteran at his spiel, gibbered appropriately in horror as Tommy's body plummeted earthward, arms and legs flailing. At the exact moment, the pilot in the Fleet cut his engine, the announcer's voice ended in a rasping gurgle, and Tommy took his cue like a vaudeville master. A thin, wailing shriek sounded from the hapless man as he fell to certain death.

Pandemonium reigned. Women fainted, children wailed

and strong men turned white ("the chorus of the barnstorming audience," Tommy grinned in descriptive explanation) as his body prepared for its final bloody *splat!* against the ground.

At the last possible second, barely seven hundred feet above the ground, Tommy jerked the ripcord. The chute popped, and finally, at one to two hundred feet above the ground, he snapped into landing position, grinning broadly.

Sometimes the barnstorming group modified the routine with their star performer by staging a fight on the ground before the flight. As the announcer confided his fears with the audience, Tommy and the pilot tore at one another—ostensibly behind their airplane—in a fierce slugging match. The announcer poured coal on the fire by telling the story of a love triangle; he whispered hoarsely (into the microphone, of course) that the pilot had been overheard swearing to kill Walker. He kept up his running invective as other men separated the two "enemies," and declared that he had tried to call off the act. And sure enough, as his prediction of doom reached its peak, his voice cracking at just the right moment, and the biplane soared around over the top of its loop, Tommy was tossed helplessly into thin air, screaming horribly. No one ever seemed to match the sudden chopping of power in the Fleet to kill its noise as Tommy's last burble of shrieking life reached the ground. Never relaxing his hold on the audience for a second, the announcer gripped the microphone tighter and shrieked: "I knew it! Oh, God, I knew he would kill him!"

Arms and legs flailing, the twitching thing that was Tommy Walker's body hurtled to certain death. As Tommy said: "It always fractured hell out of the crowd."

The barnstorming act ran out of cash customers in Texas. For three months they lived and they flew gloriously, but the depression was just too rough to sustain all the gypsy flying acts beating their way around the country. Finally, after two solid weeks of collecting nickels and dimes and exhausting their cash reserves, the group called it quits. Tommy had made several thousands dollars and had spent every dime on wild parties, excellent whiskey and the best of companionship.

One of the pilots, who worked a smuggling deal on the side, invited Tommy in. He jumped at the chance—it was flying and it was money and it was a lot easier than some of their barnstorming routines. So, like many other barnstormers who were down on their luck, Tommy and his benefactor plunged into the shady part of flying. The pilot didn't know what his contraband cargo consisted of and, wisely, didn't want to know. That way he could never let anything slip, or drop a remark that could prove incriminating either to him or to his customers. He asked no questions, but ran his delivery service as agreed, and collected cash on the barrelhead. From Houston, the two men flew to a farmer's pasture outside of El Paso, where their contact delivered the cargo.

It was, strangely, a good life. Their contact paid them five hundred dollars before each flight, and a second payment of the same amount on their return. That meant a cool thousand dollars for less than two hours work. The trouble was that at the end of a month Tommy was still broke, since he lived like a drunken sailor, flinging money about freely just so long as it brought him what he wanted in the form of entertainment.

Things were just *too* good to continue. After weeks of being ridiculed by the will-of-the-wisp smugglers on wings, the Mexican *Rurales* went hot and heavy after the old Fleet. Neither Tommy nor his friend paid much attention to their brandished fists and their shining rifles. Hell, they were on *horses*, not wings . . .

But there was a problem. Tommy lived it up royally on the ground, but from the first of his flying he never went into the air with any liquor under his belt. Not so the Fleet's owner; he was happy when he was drunk, and he drank on the ground and he drank in the air. It was his playful disposition while three sheets to the wind that finally proved their undoing.

One night they hedgehopped over the border with their wheels skimming the brush. Under the full moon the pilot spotted a mounted Mexican border patrol, out in search of *him*. With a shrieking whoop of joy the pilot slammed the throttle forward, went up and around in a single banked roller-coaster turn and came out of the turn in a howling power dive to scatter the horsemen. The Mexicans, however, showed superb discipline, dropped from their horses, and set up a steady rifle fire. Finally a bullet smashed into a control cable as the plane swooped upward. The Fleet lurched badly and almost at once spun out of control.

Both men scrambled swiftly from their cockpits into the air, hauling on their parachute ripcords even as their feet cleared fabric. In the darkness, they signaled to one another, and sneaked back across the border.

For the next two years barnstorming remained the financial

playground of only a few well-heeled outfits, and there were more than enough pilots and stunt men to keep the planes and the parachutes filled with the best. Pilots who wanted to fly found all too often that they could stay in the air only so long as they were willing to give up eating. The barnstorming business was lousy; it was as simple as that. So for two years Tommy Walker killed time at home. From a high-flying daredevil who had earned a thousand dollars a week at his peak he dropped to performing odd jobs in his Bronx neighborhood for pin money. He and Dutch Wendt stuck together most of the time. Dutch had a powerful Indian motorcycle, and Tommy took out many of his flying frustrations on the beast. Wendt taught him the basics of trick riding, and within a week Tommy became the terror of the local roads as he practiced madman stunts.

In the summer of 1934 New York was closing in on them, hot, stifling, frustrating. They blew a kiss behind them to the city and took off on the motorcycle for Chicago, driving nonstop to reach the Century of Progress Exposition. Tommy Walker was a superb pilot, wing-walker, stunt man, and parachutist—but in Chicago his ability on the motorcycle paid off in spades. Tommy convinced authorities at the Exposition's Motordrome that he was an experienced trick rider on the hefty bike. He convinced them so well that immediately they gave him a job, on the Wall of Death!

For a month he rode a thundering, blatting motorcycle at breakneck speed *within a giant barrel*, sheer centrifugal force keeping the wheels glued to the side of the vertical walls when he roared up and around within the barrel. With other riders he crisscrossed in stunts that kept the onlookers gaping, and the lines moving through the viewers' stands. He also pulled more high g-loads inside that barrel during the month than he had in all his flying to date.

The Exposition over, Tommy bid good-bye to Dutch Wendt and worked his way south by hopping freights, just as he had done some years earlier. He kept a running check on air shows by stopping in at newspaper offices in different towns, and wherever the barnstormers showed up, the kid named Walker was on hand to offer his services for anything the gypsy show might need.

But the depression still hung on like a smothering blanket over the itinerant winged entertainers. A lucky break meant a week or ten days of money rolling in. Just as often, however, weeks went by without cash in the till. Tommy worked his way from Louisville to Memphis, using his growing talents to keep his stomach full. He had earned money at the controls of an airplane, as a wing-walker, a jumper and then a motor-cycle trick rider, and finally he turned to his fists. He stopped in at local promoter's offices, at athletic halls, anywhere they booked fights. It would be too much to call them boxing matches, for Tommy found himself slugging it out for his life with mean and experienced local boxers. By now he was a skilled and deadly ring veteran, and he needed everything he had in the way of startling speed, ring savvy, and his tremen-dous physical strength and endurance. The local promoters liked nothing so much as to pit a hometown favorite against some bum coming in off the road. They knew that the foot-loose fighter often was clumsy with his hands, hungry, and out of condition.

That didn't include Tommy Walker. He slammed his way through fifteen fights and won every scrap. He kept notices of his past fights with him, for the better the news stories on his prowess in the ring, the higher on the boxing cards he went, and the more money there was to earn. On the road he was booked for thirty-five matches, and won every fight. A natu-ral southpaw, his powerhouse left downed twenty-six of his thirty-five opponents for the long count.

As the months fled, Tommy found his life to be a combina-tion of an itinerant flying stunt man, daredevil parachutist and a mean and brawling club fighter. Finally he settled down for more than a month with an air show in San Diego, where he jumped every weekend when the weather permit-ted, and flew whenever he could beg or borrow an airplane.

It was "a hell of a way to live," he recalls wistfully. Three times a week, at the San Diego Exposition, he climbed into the ring to batter other fighters silly. He loved it; he was back to that carefree and wonderful life to which he had been introduced when barnstorming years before. He was flying again, and getting paid for it. He had all the parachute jumping he could handle, for he had developed specialties. And the best of these was to "see how close I could get to the ground before pulling the ripcord. We had 'em crowding in and screaming and falling all over one another when they started to faint. I pulled all sorts of stuff, from long delays to low jumps. But the long delays, say from fifteen thousand all the way down to two thousand, weren't nearly as hair-raising as the jumps from two thousand down to four or five hundred feet.

"When we used to have races to the ground—a couple of us throwing ourselves off the aircraft at the same time—well, it was *almost* like playing 'chicken.' Almost, but not quite. We had seen more then one guy play it too close and splatter himself into the next world."

In between his flying and jumping, he climbed between the ropes to grin at opponents who didn't know whether he was slaphappy or else supremely confident. It turned out to be the latter, as they discovered only too quickly. Tommy fast learned the financial advantage of taking every bet he could garner on himself—and he never lost. For now, at least, money sat fat and crisp in his pockets, and he was in the ring as much for the sheer joy of battering his opponents as the money in it.

In 1937 war flared in China. Tommy called Dutch Wendt and told his friend to meet him in Seattle, Washington. By the time Dutch arrived Tommy had visited the Chinese consul to offer his services as a fighter pilot. The Chinese signed him up. In a month or so they would call him, but in the meantime . . .

"This building," the consul informed Tommy Walker, "is under the constant surveillance of Japanese intelligence agents. I assure you that you have been watched and that before the day is out they will know your name and a great deal about you. Be careful. If you stay in Seattle until we call you, it would be prudent to avoid too many, ah . . . dark corners."

Tommy grinned. He didn't take the advice too seriously. It sounded like a Hollywood thriller about the mysterious Orient. He and Dutch—who nixed the idea of fighting for China, but agreed to stay with Tommy in Seattle until he was called—thought the whole thing was a great joke.

Three weeks later they discovered the Chinese consul really knew what he was talking about. Tommy and Dutch were in a Japanese restaurant, and they learned that the Japanese really had the Indian sign on him. (The restaurant, he learned later, doubled in brass as a center for Japanese intelligence.) Seated at the counter, the two men tried in vain to get service, and it was quickly obvious that the snub was very deliberate. Finally Dutch shouted angrily at a passing waiter. The waiter snarled in Japanese, leaned close to Dutch and spat deliberately into his face. Dutch blew up.

His hand flashed over the counter and a massive fist closed around the shirt of the Japanese. The enraged Dutch belted him with a thundering right straight to the face. There was a crack of snapping bone and the Jap folded like a rag doll.

For the next ten minutes that restaurant was sheer pandemonium. Tommy and Dutch mopped up the place with waiters and customers who were still willing to slug it out. The Japs were confounded by the piston speed and hardness of Tommy's blows, whose fists kept snapping Japanese heads back with lightning rapidity. The two friends waded through their opposition and then dove through the back windows just as the cops came pouring through the front door.

Two weeks later Tommy said good-bye to Dutch and returned to the Chinese consul to begin his new career as a soldier of fortune. The Chinese Government contracted to pay him—under an alias—five hundred dollars a month in gold, a bonus of one thousand dollars for every enemy plane destroyed (and confirmed) in combat, and bonuses for missions successfully completed against ground targets.

They gave him a .38 revolver and a shoulder holster and warned him to stay armed. He had been marked by the Japanese who had "lost face" in the slugfest and they would welcome the opportunity to toss his mangled carcass into the nearest sewer. The Chinese took care of the paper work, and Tommy's passport carried the notation that he was going to Australia "for his health." The next morning he was on his way to join Chiang Kai-shek's International Squadron, with the rank of captain in the Chinese Air Force.

The liner docked at Hong Kong, where agents of the Chinese Air Force took him to meet three other pilots newly arrived from Europe. Late that day they took a train to Canton, where they checked in at the New Asia Hotel. The sight of Hankow airfield the next morning sent the pilots into bitter laughter. The place was a sickly assortment of fighters, bombers, and trainers parked at random about the sprawling field. There were Russian planes, American fighters and bombers, Italian and British biplane fighters, a decrepit Savoia-Marchetti tri-motor bomber and—raising the envy of Tommy —six spanking new Gloster Gladiator biplane fighters from England. Envy was the closest he got to those ships . . .

For three weeks he languished on the ground, cheering himself up with personal research on the characteristics of young and beautiful Chinese women . . .

He then traveled from Hankow to Nanking, where the Chinese assigned him to the Fifth Pursuit Group. Here he made a close friendship with Claire L. Chennault, who led the Chinese Air Force (the American Volunteer Group, or Flying Tigers, were still some four years in the future). The two fliers hit it off perfectly.

The Chinese gave him a weatherbeaten Hawk III fighter, a weary biplane with single .30- and .50-caliber machine guns, each firing through the propeller. The Hawk III was an export version of a U.S. Navy fighter. With a 750-horsepower Cyclone, Tommy could barely hit 215 miles per hour in the old machine. But how she could maneuver! To Tommy she was an angel, weary wings and all.

Tommy flew patrol missions with three other Hawks, striking at targets of opportunity or trying to live through skirmishes with Japanese fighters. Every other day he flew one or two missions, except when special strikes or intercepts were ordered. So far it had been anything but a war for him, but the face of China beyond the front lines changed all that. Tens of thousands of troops locked in fierce combat. Towns burned on every point of the horizon, and masses of trucks and men choked the narrow roads. These were his main targets.

He strafed trucks and troop columns, swooping low over the roads and pouring slugs into the screaming men. Japanese gunboats infested the rivers and canals, and dozens of these were shot apart and sunk by the Hawk patrols. They attacked gun positions, observation balloons, bivouac areas, anything that was Japanese.

Tommy had been at Nanking for two weeks when he returned to his barracks white-faced and sick. He had just returned from a small village where the townspeople faced the grim task of disposing of the bodies of more than a hundred women and young girls, all of whom had been raped, tortured, and then killed.

From then on he took every opportunity to fly solo missions. On his off days, he was up before dawn and in the Hawk cockpit. With the first crack of light on the horizon, he roared down the Nanking runway on lone-wolf raids over Japanese territory. He was obsessed with the urge to kill. His favorite targets were troops caught on the narrow roads, naked to his wild strafing runs. He searched for barges bulging with troops; in a single run he could kill as many as forty or fifty men. He took every chance to fly his solo raids, shooting and burning wherever he could find Japanese. The other pilots thought he was mad to take such wild chances "in a war that really didn't matter anyway."

His flights also meant a great deal of money. Near the close of his tour Tommy was making an average of $2,400 a month. But this mattered little to the pilot carrying out his personal vendetta. He never had the desire to accumulate a fat bank account at the expense of his own principles. He always liked money, but cash and Tommy Walker never remained long together. As a border runner at El Paso he made a thousand bucks a week for four weeks, and when it was all over he had barely enough money to buy a bus ticket back to New York.

The Fifth Pursuit Group had six to ten Hawks ready to fly at any one time, a puny force to hold back Japanese raids of thirty or forty bombers with as many or more escorting Mitsubishi Type 96 fighters. Most of the time the International Squadron pilots didn't even try to fight against such odds. Chennault didn't want any dead heroes or smashed planes, and his orders were for the fighters to run for safety when an alert sounded.

Japanese Type 96 Fighter

Neither Tommy nor the other pilots enjoyed having to run whenever the Japanese came over in strength. When the spotter network gave them enough time they climbed high over Hankow, and then dove under full throttle into the bombers. The idea was to do maximum damage on a single pass and then to run like hell. And so down they came in their ancient fighters, the Hawks screeching and buffeting madly as they plunged at three hundred miles per hour. They had but this one opportunity to pour their slugs into the big twin-engined Mitsubishis before the enemy fighters slapped them out of the sky.

Most of the time, however, they never did make it to the bombers. The Jap fighters were faster than the Hawks, and the Chennault fliers were outnumbered usually as much as six to one. In man-to-man fights some of the veteran pilots could whip the Japanese, but in a mass battle, outnumbered by superior planes, they didn't stand a chance. So they ran.

Even the strikes against the Japanese left much to be desired. "The Chinese bombardiers," recalls Tommy Walker with disdain, "couldn't hit the roof of a barn from a dozen feet." Chennault asked Tommy to fly as a pilot or as lead bombardier on missions with Martin 139W (B-10) bombers imported from the United States. On low-level raids with the Martins or in single-engine Vultee attack bombers when the weather was poor, Tommy led the other planes in right on the deck to dump their bombs from four hundred feet. The Chinese and the other crewmen screamed that it was suicide, for their own bomb explosions riddled them with jagged fragments of steel. Tommy ignored the protests and kept on with his low-level strikes.

It was a wild, haphazard and thoroughly disorganized war. For the most part the flying was dangerous and ragged. Discipline in the air was a hollow joke. Except on rare occasions pilots flew where they pleased, and it was virtually impossible to entrust your life in battle to the Chinese air crews.

Tommy wasn't always on the end that dished out the punishment, for the air war went largely the way the Japanese called the shots. In the Nanking area one day with three other Hawks, ten Mitsubishis streaked out of the sun in a classic bounce of their formation. It was a slaughter. One of the boys got a Mitsubishi, but two Hawks went down immediately with dead pilots. His own plane a shattered wreck,

Tommy managed to stay in the air, fighting, until his engine exploded in flames. He stood the fire as long as he could. Over the Chinese lines he bailed out, delaying opening his chute in order to avoid giving the Japanese pilots free target practice, until he was five hundred feet above the ground. His stunt jumping had saved his life before and once again it saved him; he was on the ground and running like a madman into thick brush before the Japanese could gun him down. That made him a two-time member of the Caterpillar Club.

Tommy gained notoriety of a welcome sort on New Year's Eve that closed out 1937. In a running Pier Six brawl that became one of Chennault's favorite stories, Tommy took on with his fists and feet the elite of German hoodlums in the Far East. They were Nazis decked out in fancy uniforms, all fair-haired and husky. The Germans made no secret of their close working association with the Japanese, but diplomatically they enjoyed full freedom.

In a Hankow cabaret Tommy ran into eight of the blond Aryans. The woman proprietor begged Tommy to leave, warning him that the Germans were mean and looking for trouble. Tommy shrugged and left. But as he went out the door a hulking form strode immediately behind him, mouthing curses, and then spitting out "yellow *Amerikaner*" and several other choice phrases.

Tommy went berserk. The big Kraut weighted in at about 250 pounds, eighty more than Tommy at the time. But he didn't care. He was a hell of a lot faster, could hit harder, and knew how and where to hit. He threw himself at the German, almost clawing his way right up the fancy Nazi shirt. Before the startled German knew what had happened, Tommy hit him flush in the face a dozen times, hammering in his blows with twisting knuckles that slashed open his opponent's face and splashed blood freely. The Kraut went down, out cold, like a poled ox.

Two more Germans came down the street, arm in arm, swaggering as they shoved the Chinese aside. They gaped at the scene of their bloodied comrade collapsing to the street, but before they could get their arms unlinked Tommy tore into both men, fists swinging expertly. The fight lasted less than two minutes as Tommy called on all his ring savvy, his street brawls, and his speed and strength. When it ended one man lay unconscious and the second was doubled up, vomiting blood from a wicked smash into his stomach.

By now Tommy was covered with blood, all of it German. He was also acting like a madman. Hundreds of Chinese followed him, cheering and clapping, as he ran down the street, yelling for Germans to come out and fight. The Chinese shouted with glee as the berserk American stormed into the Del Monte Cafe, and emerged moments later dragging a stunned Nazi by the collar. This one cringed, hands before his face, refusing to fight. Tommy spat in his face. Suddenly the German cursed and rushed forward, swinging wildly. Laughing, Tommy sidestepped deftly, jabbed him rapidly in the face with a piston-like right hand, doubled him over with a left to the stomach, and followed with a whistling right cross that laid open the man's cheek. The German screamed and fell to the ground. As Tommy stepped back the coolies rushed forward to kick and bludgeon the shuddering form senseless. Tommy grinned.

Chennault got all the details the morning following, and ordered Tommy to report at once to the Anlee House. There Tommy received a withering reaming out by the Old Man. "Just what the hell are you doing, Tommy?" Chennault roared. "The whole town is talking about the scrap last night! Ain't I keeping you busy enough, damn it?" They laughed together.

Ten months after he started fighting in China, Tommy returned to Nanking in a Vultee shot to ribbons from Japanese ground fire. One gunner was dead, the other wounded. Streaking down the runway, the bomber's gear collapsed. The ship careened wildly, flipped over once in a wild somersault, and came to rest as jumbled, burning wreckage. The Chinese hauled Tommy out of the blazing mess, his right knee torn open and bleeding. He was in the hospital for more than a month, and came out on crutches.

He never again flew in China. During his hospital stay, the critical shortage of planes, the storm of training accidents, and a devastating Japanese raid that smashed dozens of planes on the ground forced Chennault to disband the International Squadron. Tommy Walker had done an outstanding job— seventy missions in Hawk fighters, twelve raids in the Martins, and thirty-five missions in the Vultees. With two kills to his credit and an earned reputation as a deadly killer on strafing attacks, Tommy could look back with satisfaction on his flying in China.

His knee healed perfectly, and with a fat wallet Tommy left China in the summer of 1938 on the opening leg of what he

Hawk III

hoped would be a leisurely, luxurious barnstorming-dream flight around the world. He never made it. In Singapore he was contacted by an agent of the Royal Air Force, and invited to contribute his knowledge of Japanese air operations in China to British Intelligence. The next morning Walker was sworn into the Royal Air Force as a Flight Lieutenant!

For six weeks he was a special guest, in uniform, of the R.A.F. They gave him a Gloster Gladiator (at long last) to play with. When he wasn't answering questions or writing reports, Tommy went into the blue to wring out the highly responsive British fighter.

Finally, his work completed, he "resigned" his commission, and with the grateful thanks of the British, returned again to civilian status. He had several thousand dollars free and clear and he decided to enjoy life for a while. He rented a De Havilland biplane and took off for an air tour of the Dutch East Indies. A long stopover at Bali proved to Tommy the truth of rumors about Balinese women, and with a cock-eyed grin on his face he sailed through the air to new pastures. For the next several months, with enough money to fly wherever he wanted and whenever he pleased, Tommy Walker lived what can only be described as an idyllic life and a barnstormer's paradise.

In 1941 he returned to his first love, the air show. A telegram to Dutch Wendt brought his old friend out to the West Coast, where the two men formed a stunt team.

It was with Dutch that he performed his first double jump. Gripping each other tightly they tumbled out of a plane at five thousand feet. Dutch was to open his chute first. Then Tommy would fall away into space, jerking his ripcord just above the crowd. Fortunately for Dutch he was scheduled to begin the act. At four thousand feet he jerked the ripcord—but the chute failed to open.

He screamed to Tommy: "Hold on to me, hold on tight, damn you!"

Grasping his friend with a death grip, Tommy plummeted with Dutch, climbing around to his back in an attempt to pull the chute free. Nothing happened, except that the earth rushed upward with terrifying speed.

"Hang onto the straps!" Tommy shouted. "I'm going to open my chute!"

Dutch gripped him tightly as Tommy's hand jerked on the ring. Their double weight nearly proved their end. There was a tremendous smacking noise as the silk inflated, and then a booming *craaaccck!* as several panels ripped open. The brutal shock knocked Dutch unconscious, and as his body was slammed away from Tommy a suspension line raked open his ear, slicing it deeply. Blood streaming down the side of his face, Tommy stared in horror as the unconscious Dutch plunged toward his death. And then, miraculously—*silk!* The wind had pulled the silk from the pack! Dutch was still out cold when he tumbled onto the ground on the bank of the Duwamish River. Tommy landed smack in the center of the river and was rescued by a couple fishing from a motorboat. Blood was all over him and still streaming from his ear, but he was grinning like an idiot. Who wouldn't, after *that* close call!

Walker had tried every crazy stunt a parachutist can attempt. Whenever Tommy watches films of paratroopers filing out of transports and sees their special jump boots, helmets with chin straps, and other equipment, he clutches his sides and roars with laughter. For Tommy Walker has jumped from ten thousand feet, consistently, wearing nothing more than a pair of swimming trunks and his parachute—and has blown a bugle all the way down to a thousand feet before jerking the ripcord.

He has held thousands of people spellbound—and horrified—by falling out of a parachute harness, and blowing madly on that bugle as he fell in a final gesture of bravado before being killed—only to jerk open a second chute barely three hundred feet above the ground.

He is the only man known ever to make a parachute jump while stark naked. And for a special bonus of a thousand dollars, paid him by a sheriff's convention! He sailed in a stiff breeze over the grandstands, waving and smirking at the crowd below. They say you could hear the screams of the wives for miles around. As soon as he hit the ground the lawmen bundled him up in a blanket, hustled him into a car, and roared off in a cloud of dust.

Then, suddenly, came Pearl Harbor—and Tommy signed up at once as an air cadet. He had the kind of qualifications that raised eyebrows to the ceiling at the recruiting office: more than two thousand hours' flying time; 117 combat missions in China; two confirmed air kills; past commissions as a captain in the Chinese Air Force and as a Flight Lieutenant in the Royal Air Force; he was a skilled parachutist and stunt man.

And he was ordered to report for basic training as an Air Corps cadet. He found it almost impossible to wipe from his face the grin that drove his officers mad . . .

No cadet, however, ever had the paradise that Tommy enjoyed. When he reached primary training he discovered that several instructors were the very same pilots with whom he had performed at barnstorming air shows many years back. His own "instructor" had jumped with Tommy as a chutist in West Coast air shows. His flying routine as a cadet was a lark. He slept through his classrooms, and his flight instructors read comic books or went to sleep as Tommy flew the prescribed training courses better than they could have flown the airplanes. From advanced training in the "hot" Curtiss AT-9's (a clod compared to the Hawk III of China days) Tommy went into Lockheed P-38's, the big twin-boomed Lightnings with nearly three thousand horsepower—a dream under his skilled hands.

He drove his new instructors wild. He couldn't be held down to a standard procedure, for the P-38 was like a drug. When other pilots flew standard traffic patterns, Tommy was

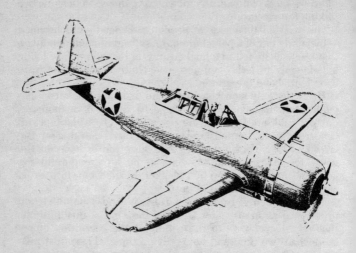

Lockheed P-38 "Lightning"

bored. Instead of peeling off and following the others he slow-rolled the P-38 as he dropped toward the ground. Everyone on the field shuddered and his C.O. screamed.

"Hell," Tommy says with a grin, "I spent more time in a brace, explaining what I was supposed to be doing, than I did in a cockpit."

The fact that he led other pilots to insubordination in the air didn't help matters any. "We used to have fun diving the P-38's across our own parade grounds at treetop level," he drawls, "rolling over and then flying the field inverted, across the entire grounds, while the troops were on review. They threatened to shoot me if I didn't cut that out . . ."

In the summer of 1943 he was a lieutenant assigned to the 360th Fighter Group in California. To his immense relief he was soon transferred. Maintenance with the 360th was the worst he had ever seen, and a series of broken oil lines, short circuits and other mechanical failures brought him to earth eight times in forced landings. He was lucky. A dozen pilots were killed.

Reassigned to the 330th Fighter Squadron, 329th Fighter Group, in San Diego, he flew coastal patrol missions with long hours of bombing, gunnery, and combat-tactics practice, all duck soup to him. Repeated attempts to go overseas were denied. The 330th was the first outfit to try dive bombing at night with P-38's, and the AAF said the men would go overseas only as a unit.

Combat, explains Tommy, would have been an immense relief against that night dive bombing. The first time they tried it they peeled off singly and plunged for earth. The signal for each plane to dive was the flash of an exploding bomb from the preceding plane. But after the first pass of each plane, no one knew where anyone else was, and they milled about blindly in the sky. He hated the missions because skill was forcibly replaced with luck in averting collisions.

In October of 1943 Tommy climbed into the cockpit of a P-38H at North Island, San Diego. He took off loaded to the brim with fuel, ammunition and bombs. In a seething downpour, he hauled the big fighter off the deck at 110 mph and started a turn to the left. Three hundred feet up the left engine exploded.

Immediately the heavily loaded fighter plunged at a steep angle for the ground. Tommy pulled frantically at the yoke trying to get the nose up, but the Lightning wouldn't respond. At the last instant he slapped a wing down, striking the runway in a steep bank.

At 120 mph the big fighter smashed with a booming roar against the ground. The fuel tanks exploded with a fiery scream to envelop the careening airplane in flames. For more than a thousand feet the blazing wreck skidded wildly down the runway. Inside the cockpit Tommy was beating desperately at his burning clothes. Flames burst up through the shattered cockpit floor, searing his face and hands. The ship was still sliding wildly when Tommy threw back the canopy and dove out through the blaze.

Lady Luck stayed around for company. Tommy was suffering from shock, severe bruises, and spot burns. Sixteen days later he slapped a nurse's bottom and checked out of the hospital, ready again for the air. The AAF assigned him to instructing new pilots. Despite repeated and bitter protests they refused to send him overseas.

He vented his wrath by "borrowing" a Curtiss SNC trainer at Alameda Naval Air Station, and taking along a Navy enlisted man, the tower operator on duty, for the ride. The Navy boy said he would like some aerobatics . . .

"So," says Tommy, with a straight face, "we wound up the aerobatic ride by looping over the Golden Gate Bridge and flying under the bridge at the bottom of the pullout. When we came out the other side, I barrel-assed out of there, hugging the water, heading up toward Hamilton Field. For a long time there was silence from the back seat. Then the enlisted man said: 'Lieutenant, you-all shore stoppin' traffic. Nothing was movin' on that bridge when we left.'"

In October of 1945 Tommy returned to his beloved air shows, stunting, wing-walking, and leaping into space, still blasting away on his bugle. He hungered for something new to try and found it when a friend, Jack Hardwick, introduced him to the gentle art of deliberately crashing airplanes!

In May of 1946 Tommy climbed into an old Aeronca C-2, and rumbled over the ground at ten feet and sixty-five miles per hour. Ahead of him waited a wall of boards and plaster, erected between two telephone poles. Tommy smashed directly into the wall. He was amazed. The Aeronca fell apart with ridiculous ease. The airplane was totally demolished but there hadn't been any body shock to him. No sweat!

They handed Tommy a check for one thousand dollars. "This is the life for me!" he exulted. "Hell, that was the easiest thing I ever did!"

He flew to Willow Run to crash a Stearman biplane for another air show. It wasn't quite so easy this time. He was to plunge into a barn doing eighty-five miles an hour. Tommy came down the field expertly, bracing himself as the ship tore into and through the first wall. Debris exploded outward as he burst into fourteen-inch thick telephone poles that stripped back the wings. He ripped through the second wall with a screeching roar, wreckage flying in all directions. The Stearman twisted wildly and started to cartwheel. A tremendous jolt shook Tommy as the remains of the biplane smashed into the ground on its nose and started to whirl. Finally it hung up on its nose, the fuselage standing askew. The crash shook up Tommy and left his ears ringing—but he didn't have a scratch on him.

A week later at another barnstorming show he smashed into a barn wall with an old Commandaire, a ship so ancient and battered that it was literally held together with wires and tape. The airplane was a total derelict. Its rusty engine couldn't deliver full power, and it staggered and lurched like a drunk through the air.

Just before he smashed into the barn wall the old engine collapsed. The water cap erupted from the radiator and clouds of scalding steam exploded outward, the wind hurling the searing mist directly back against Tommy. The next instant the Commandaire burst through the barn wall and exploded with a deafening blast. As the steam scalded his face and hands he was sure he was burning alive. Then the engine came back four and a half feet and ended up in his lap.

He didn't break any bones, but he was badly bruised. He was grateful that there wasn't any fire, for he felt he was pinned securely in the wreckage. On looking down, however, he noticed that his seat belt was still fastened. He released the belt and climbed out under his own power to grin and wave at the shrieking, cheering crowd.

For the next ten years Tommy Walker lived his full and happy life in the air. He barnstormed around the country, running through his daring wing-walking acts. He became famous for his breathtaking aerobatics, for his drunk acts in which he scraped wing tips wildly along the ground, and for his zany stunting with his parachute and bugle. He added a "little excitement" for the crowd by snap-rolling over a barn on the deck just before coming around for a second run to smash into the building.

He has been bruised, hurt, cut, chewed, scalded, slammed around, burned—but never enough to keep him out of the air for long. He ran his leaps into space to more than 360 stunt and demonstration jumps plus the several dives into space to save his life—including ripping the tail off one plane as a test pilot. He has crashed deliberately twenty-three times and never with anything more than a football helmet in the way of special protection. His crashes were executed with superb precision, most of them within 150 feet of gaping onlookers.

He flew again for the Air Force as a flight instructor, and graduated with the highest grades ever scored in his class at the pilot instructor school. He taught precision flying and aerobatics and a dozen other fine arts of flight. For four years he flew crop dusters through the south and the midwest, often beneath power lines, a wild and hazardous job that has claimed many a life. He flew DC-3 and C-46 transports for Meteor Air Transport. He flew for European airlines as a commercial airliner pilot. He's been a civilian instructor,

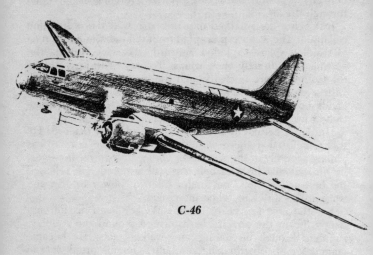

C-46

charter pilot, bush flier, test pilot. He took to the heady speeds of flying jet fighters—as a guest of the U.S. Navy—with a wild exhilaration. He has qualified to fly everything in the book that includes four-engine seaplanes, autogiros, gliders and anything else with wings or rotors on it.

The air show of today isn't the air show of yesteryear. There are plenty of air shows still going, but they're crisp and efficient and they aren't like the old days of wild and impossible stunts in the blue. Tommy has long wanted to perform a really spectacular scene: a deliberate head-on crash of two planes only fifty feet off the ground. The Government says it's suicide and they won't permit it. What Tommy Walker says about the Government isn't fit for print.

Where is he now? Still flying, still irrepressible.

I received a letter from Tommy Walker early in December of 1964. It was posted in Benghazi. He wrote in part:

> I barely have time to think. They've been flying my butt off every day. Maybe that's good. It keeps me from thinking about what it's really like here. And if you've never

made this part of the world, offer "thanks" and don't come. It's the bottom of the barrel.

Y'know what I do? Every day they point in a different direction and say, in essence: "Go down yonder, about three hundred and fifty nautical miles into the desert. There you will find, in the middle of all that sand—no checkpoints, no radio facilities—one lousy oil derrick. There's a soft sand strip about two thousand feet long where you will land. Get rid of the load you're carrying and bring back whatever it is that they will load into your airplane. Oh yes, there may be a sandstorm today. Well, have a good trip!"

Man, I'm learning to do things with a DC-3 that I never believed were possible . . .

And for a guy named Tommy Walker, that is saying a hell of a lot.

The Man Who Flew
Like a Bat

In all the history of barnstorming, air shows and special air circuses, there have been only seventy-six *batmen*—and R. W. "Red" Grant, diminutive in stature but a giant in courage and skill, is the last of the breed. The batman is perhaps the most unusual of all the men who leap through the air. He tumbles out of an airplane three miles high and quickly becomes a human projectile that swoops, darts, turns, spirals, dives and glides—until his arms almost begin to pop out of their sockets from the hammering pressure of the air against his special bat wings.

Clem Sohn, one of the veteran barnstormers in business before World War II, started the dangerous stunt back in 1935. Sohn was already famous for his long delay drops from airplanes, and when he rigged up a set of homebuilt wings and sails to attach to his body, hurtling through the air like a huge bat or an aerial manta ray, he proved to be an immediate crowd sensation. The proof was in the gate; dollar income soared wherever he appeared. In 1937 he took his wings to France. Parachuting in Europe before World War II was already a sport of great enthusiasm, and the Continentals had the habit of looking down their noses at parachuting in the United States. But the batwinged Sohn proved an immediate smash hit. In a way he reached the peak of his career in France . . .

He bailed out one afternoon before a packed crowd of several thousand Frenchmen. They went through the appropriate gasps and clutching of breasts in fright as Sohn started his batwinged glide toward the earth. Sohn jerked the ripcord of his main chute, and the crowd sat up straight and started rising to their feet when the silk streamered instead of cracking open into the full canopy. They were all on their feet and screaming when he deployed his reserve pack and that one streamered also. Both chutes fluttering behind him like two useless rags, Clem Sohn smashed into the ground at ninety miles per hour. The first spectators to run to the scene found a red pulp instead of a man; Sohn was very dead.

It was ten years later that Red Grant had occasion to think clearly of Clem Sohn. At that moment Grant, who said the vision of Sohn came to him like a flash, was plummeting toward the earth. And like Sohn, he also had trailing behind him two long, whistling, and very useless ribbons of silk. With some frantic maneuvering and handling of the shroud lines Grant managed to get a canopy open before he plunged into the earth to this death. Muses Red Grant:

It's a miracle I'm still alive. Only a damn fool would have gotten into this business in the first place—a business I got into by accident.

As most of you remember, the fall of 1945 was a crazy, mixed-up period. What was left of my outfit, the 507th Parachute Infantry, came back from the ETO to get paid off. I changed into civvies after seven years in the Regular Army and immediately got into trouble.

I went up to Denver to see a chick I had been more or less engaged to during the war. Killing time, I went into a typical soldier trap to have a beer. There was an argument going on at the bar. Some Services-of-Supply soldier was mouthing off at a B-girl, then he hit her. All five-feet-seven of me got up from the table and I went over and clipped that bird twice. He slumped out of sight. A low growl came behind me—I had committed the cardinal sin of hitting a *soldier*. Some more rear-echelon commandos came from nowhere and I hightailed it out of there and went flying up the street. I caromed off three guys who grabbed me and yelled, "Whoa there, little man!" I looked up at three bruisers wearing the patch of the 82nd Airborne on their shoulders. I knew them all, so we went back and cleaned out the bar. Afterwards we went up to my hotel room and toasted Fightin' Slim Jim Gavin with three fifths of Old Joyful.

Next day, I cleaned up and went to see my fiancée. She was downright cool, and I didn't get the drift until I saw her flicking her eyes back and forth from me to the picture on the mantel. It was taken in London, and I looked like a Mexican general: white silk scarf, fruit salad down to there, the *fourragère*—the works. When she told me she couldn't possibly introduce me to her friends until I put on my uniform, boots and ribbons, I walked out the door and haven't seen her since.

I had no job, no fiancée, no prospects. Soldiering was all I knew. I was used to living under pressure, never knowing from one day to the next whether I would get killed or be doing the killing. Most of the guys who came out of the greatest adventure of them all settled down; a few of us weren't ready to face the same desk day after day. For me, there was always that next hill to climb . . .

It was the end of the first world war all over again. Then Red Grant, through dating another chick, ended up at a meeting of the Civil Air Patrol in Denver. He fidgeted while the meeting went on; the CAP was getting together an air show. Grant's ears perked up a bit when he heard the words "parachute jumper," and the next moment everyone heard from his date that Red Grant *was* a jumper. He agreed to their request to make a jump at the air show. Red's girl would provide the transportation herself; she would fly a beat-up old PT-23 trainer. With something interesting happening for the first time since he came back stateside, he went out and rented a full jumper's rig.

"It wasn't until I was alone in my hotel room that night," admits Red, "that I realized I didn't know a damn thing about free fall; all my combat jumps had been static-line drops from C-47's. I worried about it all night.

"There was nothing to it. Alice got the PT-23 up to three thousand feet and I stepped out on the narrow wing and went off into space, keeping my left hand over my head to act as a rudder. The landing strip rushed up to meet me, I pulled the D-ring, my bones were wrenched by the shock of the chute opening, then I landed on the runway standing up. The crowd roared—and I had just made fifty bucks."

Red jumped again that afternoon; this time, however, he pulled the D-ring just a bit too late, missed his target, and

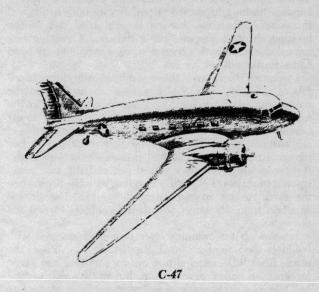

C-47

almost plowed into the grandstand. He was gathering up the folds of the parachute when a woman approached him.

"How many free falls have you made?" she asked.

"You just saw the first two," Red admitted candidly.

"Well, you stupid so and so," she said easily, "if you live a year jumping like that you'll be lucky. But if you do live, you'll be one of the best."

Red stared open-mouthed at her. That was his introduction to Fay Cox, whom he calls "America's greatest female parachutist."

At the end of the day, Red Grant had made one hundred dollars and decided he had just started a new career. He began to jump for different air shows throughout the United States and in Canada. He went through one minor disaster after another, but always avoided major injury. He stresses with candor:

I knew cold fear. In Valley City, North Dakota, on Labor Day of 1948, I went out of a Super Cub at eight thousand feet in a freshening wind. I fell through space until I could smell the earth, then I pulled the ripcord handle. Nothing happened. I pulled with both hands and the handle came off, leaving the rip cord still in the housing. It can't happen, but it did, and I was hurtling toward the earth with a useless ripcord handle in my hand and a stupid look on my face.

I went for the reserve chute and frantically threw handfuls of silk away from me. I was on my back when the chute popped and it felt like I had kicked myself in the back of my head with my heels. I looked up and saw to my horror that I had a double Mae West—four small pulls of silk instead of one big one—and that three panels had blown. I tried to work the fouled lines off the tops of the reserve canopy, but they stayed fast and the silk began ripping to shreds. I was still struggling with the lines when the earth rushed up and slammed into me. The air was smashed from my lungs and then somebody turned out the lights.

I woke up ten minutes later in a field covered with boulders the size of my head. Ripped silk was all over the place. That little angel sitting on my shoulder had saved my life. No bones were broken, but by late that night I had turned a sickly shade of yellow-green from my neck to my ankles. When I heard the taped playback of the radio announcer's hysterical description of my fall and probable death, the reaction hit me and my legs gave way—it was the nearest I ever came to fainting.

Undaunted by his brushes with death, Red Grant added new gimmicks to his act. He was a natural crowd-pleaser, the kind of man who forms one of the major elements of any air circus. He leaped from airplanes—or rather, just fell out of them—with open bags of flour beneath each arm. It is an extremely difficult way to sustain a long free fall, since the jumper has no opportunity and lacks the means of stabilizing his plunge. Notwithstanding the kind of problem that would give a sky diver the screaming horrors, Red plunged from on high with the flour streaming from the two sacks, with his "twin flour contrails" weaving a pattern through the sky. By changing body position and the angle of his legs he actually achieved a controlled descent. Finally he tossed aside the bags, which fluttered behind him like falling moths, and jerked open his chute.

Red was much more than a stunt jumper. Like other stunt men he rode the top wing of a powerful Stearman, especially rigged for air show work, secured to "that bucking bronco only by straps on my feet and thin cables kept taut by locking my knees together." Like Frank Clarke, Tommy Walker and many of the great barnstormers, he stood up in a convertible and leaped aboard a rope ladder dangling from an airplane that passed overhead. Despite the variety of "gimmicks" he added to his routine, he kept inching toward what he wanted most of all—jumping the batwings.

It was in Jackson, Mississippi, that the crowd—the "pack of jackals"—finally drank its blood, and Red Grant got his batwings. As he recalls the day:

I went on early in the show, jumped and free-fell a long way while three ships weaved around my flight path, wrapping me in great white swaths of smoke. I touched down gently and sat on the grass to watch Billy Fisher wring out his little Ross Parakeet. . . . Billy taxied out, swung into the wind and shoved the throttle forward. The burst of power shot the Parakeet into the air like a rocket. He rolled, half-rolled and snap-rolled just off the deck. Then Billy pushed the nose up and got up to 1,200 feet and leveled off. The nose dropped straight down and the shriek of his engine tore apart the sky. At eight hundred feet the sound of the engine changed key and a puff of smoke erupted from the cowling. The nose came up sharply in a high g-load maneuver and the engine ripped loose from the mounts and hurtled backwards through the cabane struts. Parts of the upper left wing tore off and fluttered away in the slipstream. I was on my feet yelling to Billy to get out. I saw him stand up in the cockpit, then settle back in the bucket. The plane did a crazy kind of flat turn and skidded drunkenly away from the thousands of people in the stands below. The Parakeet half-rolled and went in inverted. Fisher was killed instantly.

The M.C. stayed on the mike and kept the crowd from smashing through the barriers to get at the wreckage and a few bloody souvenirs. Then he asked me to ride the top wing of the Stearman to get the crowd's mind off the tragedy. I secured the cables, the pilot revved up the engine and we took off. It was the most horrible moment of my life when we climbed out over the wreckage of

Billy's plane. I looked down past my feet at the pilot and saw unashamed tears streaming under the rubber rims of his goggles.

After four years of working air shows I finally got my batwings . . . our regular batman came up to me and said, "Red, I've had it. The equipment is all yours." Then he walked away. I stood there wondering if that was the way I would wind up—defeated by too many women and too much booze before I was thirty-two.

I looked at the equipment I had inherited with two feelings: pride and fear. There was a lot of tradition behind those wings, and there was a lot of built-in danger.

You get in the wings like pulling on a pair of pants, except the pants are like webbing, stretched between the legs. The wings start at the ankle and go out at an angle almost to shoulder height. The wings are supported at the top by heavy round wooden poles, which are gripped with each hand halfway down the length so you can control the flight attitude. The whole rig is permanently attached and can't be ditched in flight if something goes haywire. The

"Bat Man"

wings go on over the regular jump suit, along with the main chute and the reserve, which hangs halfway down in front. An altimeter is attached to the reserve pack.

Including the boots and buffet hat and oversized goggles, the whole rig weighs 180 pounds. Bear in mind that I'm a little guy, tipping the scales at 140. Once I'm clear of the ship I am a human airfoil, prey to the laws of flight. But there is no engine for power, and only sheer endurance keeps the wings taut and at the proper attitude.

Red made his first batwing jump in August of 1949. He was scheduled to go into his act immediately after the comedy routine performed by Gloria Lynch. Gloria at twenty-four years of age was only four feet six inches tall, as pert and cute as a new button. She dressed in a pinafore and wore her hair in pigtails and looked exactly like a little girl—instead of one of the best female pilots in the flying business. Her act called for her to skip up to the announcer and beg for a ride in an airplane. Finally, with a carefully worked-out routine, she won the sympathy of the crowd and the announcer "gave in." He summoned a pilot, and Gloria went out to a biplane where she was strapped into the front seat. As the pilot started to the rear seat Gloria slapped home the throttle. She staggered into the air with a chorus of shrieks and horrified screams from the audience who were convinced that they were about to see the little girl killed. On his first day as a batman, Red was circling high over the field, waiting for Gloria Lynch to finish her act before he jumped.

He watched the little biplane far below him, dragging the field and roller-coasting in its mock landing attempts. Then something went wrong. An updraft snatched at the airplane, whisked away its lift and left it helpless in the air. The ship plunged into the field. Red's pilot side-slipped out of the sky like a bomb as he banged down to a landing. The two men ran from their ship to the crumpled wreckage just as rescuers were pulling Gloria from the cockpit.

She was a lot shorter now. Both feet had been torn off at the ankles.

Red's debut was postponed; the tragedy to Gloria overshadowed any "the show must go on" routine. Nobody wanted to fly any more that day.

Finally he jumped the wings. Wisely he paid strict attention to everything that happened and swiftly gained great skill with his bat gear. "Then," he explains, as confidence began to override natural caution, "I became confident enough to think I could pull off one of the biggest damnfool stunts ever dreamed up in aerial show business. Nobody had ever made an international batwing flight, and I elected myself to be the first man to try."

Red planned to make the big attempt when the circus made its showing in Houlton, Maine. The idea was for him to bail out with enough altitude to cross the border into Canada, glide to a safe landing area, crack his chute, and land. He picked his possible touchdown sites carefully, the newspapers played it up big, and the gate grew in leaps and bounds. The promoters were delighted.

The day before the jump Red decided to rest easy and went off to Presque Isle to loaf. He missed two boys who had hustled to the field to get the batman's autograph. The kids asked Rod Joclyn, one of the circus pilots, where the batman could be found. Rod told them that Grant had flown off, but would be back later. He told the kids to wait by the corner of the hangar.

"Now, he'll be flying high and fast when he comes," Rod explained carefully, "so you'll have to listen close to hear the birdlike noises he makes in flight." The kids waited till sundown gazing up into the sky with their hands cupped by their ears.

Despite the hullabaloo raised about Red Grant's international bat flight, show business demanded a lot of work before he would go into his climax. First he did his long free fall, with two smoke planes writhing earthward about him. What happened on his next act nearly canceled out the ballyhooed stunt. He was to go through the bit of standing on the wing while the pilot jostled the airplane about. Red explained:

We were going to do this one in an Argo, a biplane built in late 1918. They had wisely manufactured no more than nineteen of these beasts. I climbed up on the top wing, secured the thin cables and got ready for the takeoff. The pilot was feeling frisky as hell and turned that old biplane every way but loose. It's cold, windy and lonesome up there on the wing, and when the pilot starts violent aerobatics, the world goes insane: sky, earth and horizon whirl crazily, blending together in a mash of colors. The blast of wind from the prop wash threatens to tear me loose from my slender moorings and fling me backward into space.

The pilot decided to give us all a little extra thrill; he stalled out at the top of a loop and the plane fell off into a vicious spin. We did about five turns before he leveled off and dragged the field. My knees were weak when we landed, and when one of the cables holding me to the wing snapped, I fell straight back and wedged my butt in the windscreen. I was stuck fast, my legs dangling on either side of the fuselage. Somebody came out with tools and cut the windscreen apart so I could get free. Somehow, I had lost all confidence in that pilot. . . .

Fifteen minutes later Red was bundled and strapped into his cumbersome gear, jammed into the seat beside the pilot of a Piper Tri-Pacer, and climbing steeply for his X in the sky where he would shove himself out of the airplane and begin his long glide to Canada. But first there was that climb to altitude, and of all the things a jumper dislikes the most, it's waiting while the airplane sticks its nose into the sky and drags itself away from the earth. The jumper has nothing to do but sit. And when you're bundled into your gear and jammed into an airplane, that sitting means thinking, and a swift train of thoughts rumbles through your mind. It's not clear thinking; the man with the chutes on his back sweats out the climb by trying hard to concentrate on his procedure for the bailout. There are mental pictures of falling away from the airplane, of body movements, then a swift scan of the landing area, not seen in static position, but expanding steadily and rapidly. On his way to altitude, Red offered himself silent congratulations on not having eaten before taking off.

"I figure that if I get clobbered," he explains, "the time the docs save in pumping out my stomach can be put to better use saving my neck."

By the time the Tri-Pacer has leveled off, Red has noticed:

My hands are getting cold. In a few minutes they are like lumps of ice. I look at the altimeter, we are at 14,600 feet and I am not wearing gloves. It's easier to feel the ripcord with my bare hands, but nearly three miles up it's freezing cold. Then I see the signal far below—a car circling slowly on the runway. It's time to go.

I look down and pick out the clump of trees I have

selected as my jump point. The right wheel blocks the trees from sight and I reach over and hit the pilot on the shoulder and scream, "Chop it!" The pilot cuts back the throttle and I place my hand on either side of the door and propel myself backward, clearing the struts. The Tri-Pacer shoots forward away from me, the sound of its engine is quickly lost in the rush of air past my head. I am on my back, staring up at the sky, my wings extended. My arms quiver with the strain and I am chilled clear through.

Snap! I half-roll out automatically with a sharp wrench and am now flat and stable—a true winged projectile hurtling steeply and swiftly through the sky. There is no sound except the whistling of the wind and the popping of loose fabric on my jump suit. My eyes search the earth, seeking the swatch cut through the woods that marks the border. I see it a little to the left, and raise my right arm slightly to bank in that direction. I cross the border at eight thousand feet and—for the benefit of the crowd behind me at the airport—bank steeply and execute a 360-degree turn to let them know I made it.

I am down to five thousand feet, peering ahead to spot the cleared areas chosen the day before. I see one, then another and another. But five thousand is too high to pull, and I keep going. My arms are beginning to feel the strain of the long glide. Approaching the next cleared area I realize I can't hold out much longer and start a series of ever-steepening spirals that will get me down quickly. A thousand feet over the deck I pull the ripcord. My body is wrenched violently and I see champagne bubbles rising up before my eyes. Thank God there is no crosswind, for I am too exhausted to fool around with the shroud lines. The ground rushes up and I land with a bone-jarring thump.

Too beat to rise, I lie on the ground letting the cool breeze wash over my eyes. I stay flat on my back for ten minutes, waiting for the recovery team. Then I hear a jeep coming through the woods in low-low gear.

Newsmen inveigled the customs officials of Canada and the United States to grab Red from the Canadian and the American sides of his anatomy, his legs straddling the border, and pretend to be fighting over him. Red went along with the publicity tug-of-war over his body and made the front pages throughout the entire area. Back at the airport from where he took off, twenty-five thousand people gave him a standing ovation.

Later, pilots estimated that Red Grant had flown the wings over a ground distance of four miles, while dropping less than three miles—a new record for the world.

Red was immensely pleased with his jump from the United States into Canada, but a short time later he was reminded once again—in the most ominous fashion possible—that every jump is a new leap straight into the jagged maw of unpredictable danger. He went out of a Cessna L-19 flown by a Kentucky Air National Guard pilot. Red always faced the problem of never knowing from what type of plane he would bail out, and the L-19 chilled him to the quick. Its door was narrow and confined and it seemed nothing but trouble in respect to making an exit with all his gear in a high wind. But the show was on, no other planes were available, and Red clambered into his seat. Then the pilot, a young lieutenant, strapped himself into the front seat, and secured his body with a new type of shoulder harness. The harness was secured with a cable that ran inside the cockpit from the belly of the ship and was linked to an inertial system that provided limited freedom of movement. The L-19 dashed down the runway into the wind for no more than seventy feet and leaped into the air, hanging on its prop and scrabbling for the sky. At ten thousand feet the lieutenant leveled off and eased back on the throttle. Then Red got ready—

They signaled from the ground to *go!* and I unbuckled the seat belt and strained to heave myself up in a semi-upright position so I could get out of the door. I felt like a Labrador retriever trying to get out of a sardine can. I couldn't make it facing the door, so I worked myself around so my back could go out first. I gave the pilot the signal to chop the throttle, then heaved myself out into the blast of the slipstream.

I was brought up short with a wrenching jolt. Oh, my God! *I had fouled my gear on something!* I dangled underneath the belly of the airplane, unable to move. My first thought was, can the pilot keep the airplane stable? He *had* to—my job was to free myself from whatever it was that locked me to the airplane.

I looked up and saw that the handgrip on my right wing

was caught on the cable that ran underneath the belly of the ship. The lieutenant had told me the cable was stressed for 2,500 pounds, so breaking the cable was out of the question.

I reached for the cable, but missed it by inches; the terrific buffeting from the wind was bounding me around like a wet rag. I tried for the landing gear, but the wind pressure blew me backwards. I flapped there under the belly of the ship, completely helpless.

It was getting harder to draw air into my lungs, and I remembered that a trooper at Fort Bragg the year before had got hung up like I was and had died before they could untangle his harness. I beat on the belly of the plane to let the pilot know I was still there. Then to my horror I began to oscillate back and forth under the landing gear. I saw that each swing brought me closer to the wheels. I made countless grabs for the wheels, missing each time. With each miss, I felt panic rising inside me. I fought it down. After an eternity, I managed to grab one of the rubber tires and hung on, fighting the blast from the prop.

I heaved myself up a few inches and looked straight into the anxious face of the pilot. He cut back the throttle and yelled: "Can you pull yourself back into the plane?"

"Negative! Negative!"

The pilot unbuckled his harness and reached across the right-hand seat, stretching his right arm outward while keeping his left hand on the control column. That scared me as much as anything. I could just see him grabbing my hand and me pulling him out there with me—a great act, with both of us hanging from the landing gear, but what would we do for an encore?

"It won't work!" I screamed. "Try to pull me up there!" But he couldn't hear me. I groped upward, trying to reach the door, but the hurricane of wind whipped me back. I felt real despair and was sure we were both going to die.

What was he doing now? A strap whipped out from the door and almost hit me in the face. I reached for it and missed. I tried again. Failure. Once more, and I had it. I pulled myself painfully upward and shifted my weight, hoping to lessen the pressure that locked me to the cable. Up, up, up.

Suddenly I was free.

I fell away from the plane and fought down an instinct to

pull the ripcord. I kept falling through space until I caught a flash of sunlight glinting from a pond. The thought passed through my mind; *if I don't pull, I'm going to get wet!* I yanked the ripcord.

The shock of the opening jerked me upright in the harness, and the sight of that orange-and-white canopy billowing above my head was the most beautiful thing I had ever seen.

I owe my life to the coolness of that pilot. He could have panicked and gone over the side with his chute, leaving me to my fate in the sky. But he didn't; he stuck it out and I was allowed to live.

Red Grant didn't learn until later just how much he really did owe to that young lieutenant in the front seat. When Red's weight snagged on the cable, the officer was slammed back in his seat and immobilized. He zipped open his flight suit and shrugged it off his shoulders.

Red stared at two deep, bleeding groves where the cables had sawed back and forth through the pilot's flesh when Grant had started to oscillate. The lieutenant, who was in agony during Red's own torment, would carry those scars the rest of his life.

Red Grant isn't anxious to be the *best* jumper in the business. But those who know him, who have flown with him, who have watched him sail out of the sky in his tremendous batwing flights, say that there isn't any question but that Red *is* the best.

And what does this jumper want?

To be the *oldest* jumper in the business.

The Big Show

No one will ever tell the full story of the men who blazed their aviation trail through American history, because whatever the barnstormers had going for them, it didn't include enough historians and photographers. Much of the greatest era of flight in this country went unrecorded either in words or on film. Many of the men who participated in flying that defied safety, sanity, reason and credulity are no longer with us. But we have some vignettes to round out the flash of wings in the sun against a background of thunder made by the voices of thousands of people . . .

One hot summer day in 1927, some months before Charles A. Lindbergh was to stand the world on its ear with his first solo crossing of the Atlantic, Dr. Hodge Smith of Washington, Pennsylvania, had a visitor. The young man who approached him asserted that he was a professional daredevil and wing-walker. Would the good doctor take him aloft in Smith's Jenny, so that the daredevil might perform in the air for the purpose of attracting paying passengers to the local airport? Smith, a flying physician, took the man at his word and agreed that such a stunt might well prove to be a good drawing card.

The stranger withdrew a bulky rope ladder from his car and attached one end to the airplane cockpit. The Jenny was more of a beloved creature than one that was airworthy, but Smith managed to coax it into the air and sustain a gentle climb to a thousand feet. This seemed, thought the doctor, a rather high altitude for a man to practice dangling from a rope ladder. But you never could tell and . . . ah, *there* he was! The daredevil ventured from his seat, gingerly climbed onto the wing and performed a strange half-shuffle along its surface. He crept about for a while, the doctor's eyes growing wider at this weird performance, while his arm steadily grew more tired. It is not the easiest task in flying to keep a Jenny straight and level with weight and drag concentrated on one wing. With a sigh of relief, for he did not wish to prove an intemperate host by shouting at the man to hurry things along, Doctor Smith watched the self-claimed hero start to descend along the rope ladder. And that's where the fun began . . .

The stranger was no daredevil. He had never walked a wing in his life, and that ladder he dragged from his car had never before been affixed to an airplane. All this the doctor-pilot learned quickly, a conclusion assisted by a look of stark terror on the face of the "daredevil" as he slowly slid from view. No sooner did he get a good grip upon the ladder when he clutched it mightily in what proved to be a steel-hard death grip. The man froze solid with fear and ceased all rational thinking.

Doctor Smith groaned. Only with the greatest difficulty could he see the man dangling from his airplane, gibbering terror painted across his face and in his wide, white eyes. For perhaps fifteen minutes the doctor cruised about in a wide gentle circle, giving the man time to come to his senses and snake his way back into the cockpit. Nothing happened except that he burned gas and the poor fellow below hung on for dear life. Smith chopped power, leaned over his cockpit, waving furiously and shouting for the man to climb back into the airplane.

The reaction to his pleas did not come. If the frightened rope-clutcher heard his pilot, he gave no sign that his hearing was effective or that he was capable of moving even a finger. As the minutes passed Doctor Smith took stock of his situation which was, he thought moodily, worsening by the minute. He was running low on fuel. He had to land, but he couldn't land with that silly, terrorized bumpkin dangling from below.

The doctor did his best to help his frightened ex-passenger. He descended to a low height, slowed down the airplane, flew into the wind and dragged the surface of a lake. If the man had any presence of mind left he could release his grip and fall safely into the water. Nothing. The "daredevil" hung on with claws of steel to his precious rope ladder.

Smith looked about desperately. There, directly beyond the lake: a huge pile of hay drying in the sun. He banked gently and headed for the hay. Maybe the poor man was frightened of water. Maybe he couldn't swim. Well, he couldn't drown in the hay! He passed low over the hay, and he still had a passenger when he flew beyond the haystack. Smith groaned and headed back for the lake. Nothing doing. That passenger just wasn't quitting that ladder.

Smith had only one choice left: to fly around until he exhausted his fuel. As the tank went lower and lower, the man held fast. Finally the fuel was near the bottom; the Jenny would cough and sputter at any moment. Smith turned from the lake in a glide to bring him back to the field.

As he neared the grass strip, the Jenny suddenly ballooned. It lifted rapidly in a soaring motion as if freed of a heavy weight. Smith looked below and saw the rope ladder— empty.

The daredevil had made his first and his last performance. His crumpled body lay still on the earth far below.

There were some men who could never avoid trouble as long as they kept flying. And since they would rather be dead than grounded for the remainder of their lives, they accepted the trouble that unerringly came their way. They shrugged off their woes and ignored trouble as an old friend who could stay around if he wanted, or shove it and disappear. It just didn't matter.

One of those men was Aaron F. "Duke" Krantz. "Duke," recalls veteran flier and barnstormer Russ Brinkley, "was the first person we know of to stand upright on the top wing of a Hisso Standard while such great pilots as Clyde Pangborn and Bill Brooks of the Gates Flying Circus executed loops, wingovers and other maneuvers of the day. That started in the 1920's after a number of lesser known daredevils helped potentate Ivan Gates to attract passengers and sightseers to just about every pea patch in the nation. Duke was a triple-threat man. He did parachute jumping, wing-walking, and helped keep the rolling stock rolling—the toughest job of all."

Those were the days, all right, and the Gates Flying Circus knew some that no other group did. Such as the day when a

Hisso engine fell out of a Standard one Monday morning while flying over the coal-mining country of Pennsylvania. The engine screeched horribly through the air as it fell, narrowly missed a woman standing in her back yard and hanging up her wash, and it buried most of the wash a long way beneath the ground—*under* the engine, of course.

And what about that airplane with its center of gravity gone all to hell? Some of those boys could think *fast*. Without the engine where it belonged the nose pitched up violently and the airplane began a flip-flopping death waltz to the ground. But not for long. A passenger in the back seat threw aside his belt clambered atop the fuselage, and scrambled forward past the pilot up onto the engine mount. He crawled into the bracing bars, locked his arms and legs in position and grinned at the pilot, who grinned back with a mixture of amazement and delight. With the passenger acting as dead weight to retrim the airplane, the pilot landed smoothly on the side of a nearby hill!

He bought the passenger all he wanted to drink for the next month . . .

The man who preceded Duke Krantz with the Gates Flying Circus died at the game. His specialty was to do a breakaway from an airplane, to be caught short at the end of a rope, where he dangled and waved gaily to one and all below. But one day, as the rope jerked him short after simulating his "death fall," it rebounded. It swung back and forth with its human cargo transformed suddenly into a pendulum. That wasn't too bad, except that the rope was too long.

On one forward swing the stunt man went far into the propeller. He fell to earth in little pieces and a fine crimson spray from the dismembered chunks of his body. But—that was the game.

"Duke is one of the few survivors of the old Gates Flying Circus," adds Russ Brinkley, "and the stories circulating about him are enough in number to fill a dozen books. It was his daring which gained nationwide fame for Gates, whose airplanes carried Texaco signs. And Duke made sure those airplanes stayed in the air, even when faced with the biggest obstacle of all—spanking-new government agencies that overnight tried to regulate everything in sight, things that had gotten where they were without any regulations at all. Duke and the government had some beautiful head-on clashes . . ."

The truth was that the Gate's airplanes in many cases

simply weren't safe. They weren't even airworthy, and only madmen would willingly take them into the sky. But Duke was surrounded by madmen who were competent and skilled and always ready to do their job. Duke said to fly; they flew. Life was that simple.

Then the Department of Commerce decided to license all pilots and all airplanes. Parker Cramer was one of the first inspectors for the Department of Commerce. This made other pilots and operators scream with a blue fury, because Cramer also was in the flying business and his own airplanes were notorious for their decrepit condition. With Cramer wielding government authority he could nail much of the opposition to the nearest hangar wall, while ignoring the condition of his own machines.

Duke's reputation was nationwide. The Department ordered Cramer to catch up with the Gates Flying Circus and enforce the regulations that Gates's airplanes conform to the new government standards. Duke learned only on sight of the approaching Cramer that this was the man who would enforce the law. This was the man who was wielding the knife to cut open fabric wings so as to inspect the wood spars. Duke blew up. *"Never!"* he roared to Cramer.

Cramer invoked authority. He told Duke that the planes were unsafe, unairworthy, and had to be grounded for repairs. What Duke told Cramer could not be printed.

Cramer smiled and called in the United States Marshal. That worthy backed up Cramer at the point of a gun and under the reflection of a bright federal star on his shirt. The planes were grounded, the new regulations went into effect, and the spice of barnstorming lost some of its tang. The boys called it the real beginning of the end of the greatest flying era ever known . . .

And then there was safe and sane Bill Smith, who came from a town with the unlikely name of Punxsutawney, Pennsylvania. There'a a great irony in his name. "Bill carried me for my first attempt at wing-walking at Brookville, Pennsylvania, in August of 1924," recalls Russ Brinkley, "and I knew him as well as any, I think. He became famous for his saying of what he would do if a student ever froze on the controls of his Canuck. Bill said he would, and we all believed him, lay on solid with a fire extinguisher. We call him Safe and Sane Smith because he disdained many of the foolish flying things that others did for kicks. Bill sneered at them; he just didn't buy the kicks routine. But for money? Ah! *That* was a matter of a different viewpoint. For money, Safe and Sane Bill Smith would do just about anything that his Canuck could do . . ."

At the time that Smith was active in flying, the Ku Klux Klan was also active in its own way. Smith reasoned that wherever the KKK went into its routine on the ground there were bound to be emotional fireworks of all kinds, and where that went on there usually would be a niche for an enterprising pilot and his airplane. Since there were emotional fireworks, he reasoned, why not add the real thing to the conclaves of the KKK? With the prospect in sight of some extra dollars, he fitted out his airplane with a battery and bright lights. At the next meeting of the KKK he flew over unannounced, circling the gathering as a brilliant but slow and circling meteoric display in the sky. This attracted so much attention that KKK officials came to see him to purchase his special services.

Elated with proof of his convictions, Smith decided to extend his nocturnal pyrotechnics, and rigged up the airplane so as to drop lighted flares during his night flights. He mounted a big sandpaper board on the fuselage outside the rear cockpit. While he flew, a companion was to sit in the back seat, reach out and scrape a flare against the board, igniting it in the manner of some monstrous kitchen match. With the flare lit the man was to fling it away and it would then burst into its brilliant form and blaze all the way down to the ground.

Bill made the mistake of assuming that his first helper was cognizant of the characteristics of the crude flares then in use. He took off at night with his cargo of ignorant assistant and highly inflammable flares. That night, as the Klan gathered in a sprawling ball park, he appeared overhead in his Canuck.

For several minutes, while the airplane was well illuminated by spotlights mounted on the struts and shining against the fuselage and the wings, he put on some in-the-night-sky aerobatics, looping and sailing up and over in neatly executed wing-overs. Whenever he cut back on the throttle in his gyrations he could hear clearly the roaring approval of the crowd below.

Then came that moment of providing the extra thrill; Safe and Sane Smith signaled his helper to get ready for the big event. He was convinced that his assistant knew the routine: scrape the flare and then drop it—*quickly!*—whether or not it seemed to be lit. Unlit flares after scraping sometimes blew up to ignite an entire airplane and give a crowd the kind of thrill they never bargained for.

Whatever was his reasoning, Smith's assistant reached out, scraped his flare, and then moved about strangely in the rear seat. Bill Smith twisted around to look and nearly died of instant strangulation. His widened eyes stared at the helper who held the flare in both hands, directly in the center of his cockpit, studying it with a mixture of adoration and fascination. For what was probably the only time in his life that Bill Smith was known to raise his voice above his normal speaking tone, he bellowed forth a thunderous "DROP IT!" The bull-ish crescendo was so loud and so unexpected that the helper reacted by flinging away the flare as though it were trying to bite him. And not a second too soon; it cleared the man's hand, erupted into brilliant red flames; and whooshed past the tail section with only inches to spare. The KKK from that moment on, decided Smith, would have to settle for spot-lights and loops, and that would be enough.

And the irony of Safe and Sane Smith? Well, one day he

Waco

did get a student who froze in fear on the controls of his trainer, on this occasion a Waco. And on this same day Safe and Sane Smith didn't have that fire extinguisher with him with which he had threatened to brain a frozen student.

The Waco went on going straight down and disappeared in a great *whooomp!* as the tanks exploded. . . .

Sure, and next we have the likes of Smiles O'Timmons, who was last heard of when he was at Portsmouth, Ohio. There were parachute jumpers who were good, and there were parachute jumpers who, like Tommy Walker and Red Grant and Jim Greenwood and many others, were great. Well, Smiles O'Timmons was not only good, he was great, and he was not only great, but there was never another one like him and likely there never will be.

Who else do you know who was a parachute jumper and a wild stunt man who had only one eye, one arm, and one leg?

That was Smiles O'Timmons. Before he went into the parachute jumping game as an endeavor of relative sobriety and safety, Smiles was a circus high diver. Unfortunately his aim left something to be desired, and one fine day on the way down he smashed into the side of a blazing water tank and ripped away assorted bits, pieces, and chunks of his body. When he dragged from the hospital what was left of his torso, embellished with a clanking, creaking assemblage of artificial parts, he kissed good-bye to the high dive and leaped, literally, into the air.

When Smiles went out of an airplane, he had to take himself apart. Prosthetic limbs were far in the future, and he had a wooden leg that seemed to weigh a ton. So he removed it before going out of an airplane! Once, and only once, he disdained this particular precaution, and he tumbled away from his jump ship with the limb still attached. It was a grand mistake that made Smiles famous in his own particular way.

When the silk streamed out and the canopy blossomed full, it was with a powerful jerking motion. Smiles came to a stop in the air, but not his heavy wooden limb. The shock of the parachute opening snapped the heavy leather strap that connected Smiles and his artificial leg. Along with the *snap!* came a sharp whistling sound. The latter was caused by the wooden limb knifing earthward with tremendous speed. The limb picked up velocity like a streamlined bomb and it hit with a blasting force. In an automobile parked at the airport were two young people. Fine folks they were too, she lovely and he handsome and the both of them sitting close to one another doing whatever young lovers do in the front seat of a car. They were rudely interrupted, in a way long to be remembered.

Who else could claim to have a lover's clinch separated with the smashing impact of a wooden leg falling out of the sky, hitting their automobile, and barreling right through the metal top as if it were so much cheesecloth?

Unlike other troopers who dropped blithely through thin air and then arrowed down to precision landings before a crowd, Smiles was unable to control his descent. It must be remembered that he had only one arm. Because he ended up at the mercy of the winds as he fell, he became a human missile—at parachute speed—sailing unexpectedly out of the sky. He landed in the middle of streets, frightening motorists, causing near-riots, and sometimes narrowly escaping being run over. As he plowed with a rousing thump on one leg (which is a brutal way to hit the earth!), he collapsed in a heap. Encumbered with his harness, reserve pack and shroud lines, he would either be helped to his feet and propped up, would bend and leap like a fish onto his one leg, or would perform in a unique thrashing fashion. He was an incredible sight to behold as he landed, grinning broadly, in the midst of heavy traffic!

He landed in many other places. Sometimes, if the wind were right, and he proved lucky, he would thump to a crash landing right on the airport in front of the crowd. And they would scream and cheer and shout their approval as Smiles rose to his precarious balancing perch and grinned at them, hoping to stay up long enough for help to rush to him with his artificial limb, so that he wouldn't fall down.

He sure did learn what the world looked like from the top, middle, sides, and underhangs of trees. He plunged into trees with a persistency that would have made other jumpers weep in frustration. He crashed to a jarring halt on rooftops. One might imagine the reaction of a housewife who thinks a bull steer had landed on her roof, what with the lights swaying and plaster falling, and rushes outside to find a one-legged parachute jumper with an artificial arm and a glass eye smiling at her!

Smiles also brought special attention to the church. He did this in the most difficult fashion one might imagine—plunging out of the sky to crash onto church steeples, where he held on with a steel grip until he could be extricated. It's difficult to undo yourself, with one arm and one leg, from such a precarious perch.

Once—far, far from any body of water—he nearly drowned. Who else but Smiles O'Timmons would land in a *swimming pool?*

Because of his particular infirmities, Smiles wasn't able to pack his own parachute, a chore that no jumper would ever entrust to anyone else. But Smiles had no choice in the matter. So he accepted the job of instructor and director of anyone around who was willing to repack the silk and the shroud lines in their proper manner back into their pack. Now, it should be understood that good intentions and enthusiasm will never replace skill and experience in the matter of getting all that bulk neatly into a small pack so that it will all come out in the proper fashion when it is supposed to do so: as a man plunges for the earth. Volunteers from gas stations packed Smiles's chutes. Men in a poker game, or sagging in the nearest bar, or simply driving by, were one and all impressed into packing service by Smiles. He had young boys and old waitresses, policemen and traveling salesmen, pilots and other jumpers, anyone who proved to be within reach of his grin and his voice.

Where were his chutes packed? Not in special rigging rooms. Oh, no. They were packed in hotel corridors, on fields filled with sharp rocks and enthusiastic grasshoppers, on sidewalks, on runways, on hangar floors and even—once, and perhaps appropriately—on the floor of a hospital hall. Smiles never did suffer an opening failure when he jumped, but there were some very *long* hesitations before the whole assembly finally extricated itself from its amateur stuffings.

Smiles was a true showman. Russ Brinkley was running a show that ran into a serious problem when their scheduled wing-walker failed to show for his act. They had promised the crowd wing-walking and the crowd, no two ways about it, wanted their admissions' worth. It was none other than Smiles O'Timmons who volunteered to carry on for the air circus by doubling in brass, before his scheduled jump, as the wing-walker. There were misgivings about the whole thing, but out there waited that sea of faces . . . It was a hot August afternoon and the Lincoln Highway traffic, because of the show, was backed up for miles and miles.

Bob Clohecy, famed as the flying coal miner and a smash hit in the Pennsylvania country, climbed into the cockpit after Smiles dragged his own way into his seat. Because of the heat it took a long time to reach 1,200 feet, with Smiles leaning out of his seat and waving merrily to the mob. Finally they were in position and the Canuck started to drift back across the field.

High above the earth, Smiles, his peg leg strapped securely to his body, climbed out on the lower wing. Balancing himself with that monstrosity of weight below his body, and with one good arm, was a tremendous feat in itself. But he leaned into the wind and worked his way through the wires and the struts. The pilot said later Smiles had a murderous job just to get out there, but he fought his way out to the first strut bay. And then things seemed to be going just a bit wrong.

The airplane circled for several minutes, just going around and around in wide turns with nothing happening. Smiles could be seen clearly well out on the wing, but he remained where he was, and this mystified the crowd as well as Brinkley and the other barnstormers. What the hell was O'Timmons acting like a statute out there for? With each passing minute it became more and more difficult for Clohecy to hold up the wing. The Canuck wanted to drop one wing and start sliding out of the sky from all that extra weight and drag on one side. Clohecy signaled for Smiles to climb back into his seat. On the ground someone ventured that Smiles seemed to be frozen with fear, and received for his pains a loud snarl from the nearest pilot.

Now the plane was starting to lose altitude; it couldn't stay in the air with all that out-of-balance force on the wing. Clohecy wanted to come in to land while Smiles stayed out there, if necessary, but he didn't dare enter into any tight turns. If he steepened the bank just a bit too much the Canuck could easily whip into a spin, and coming out of it with a man on the wing was asking too much of the airplane. Brinkley adds:

Then only Clohecy knew what was wrong. The crowd couldn't figure it out, and a buzzing rose from them as if they were a giant swarm of bees. I was at the microphone and trying to keep them patient. After several more minutes of those wide sweeping turns I began to worry myself. Something sure as hell was wrong. The Canuck glided in its turns down to about seven hundred feet as it came back across the field and I could see that Clohecy was really busy. For another five minutes that enigmatic circling went on while the airplane kept losing altitude in the steady bank. The Canuck drifted off in the distance, turned, and came back across the field. People were on their feet when they noticed that Smiles was gone—no one was out on that wing. There were some screams from the audience and curses from the barnstormers. It sure as hell looked as if Smiles had fallen off the wing and tumbled to his death.

We stared at the Canuck. There was something sticking up from the lower wing. We couldn't figure out anything by now and when Clohecy landed we all rushed over to find out what the hell was going on. When we saw what was stabbed into the wing, we broke up. There were wide-eyed gasps and then low chuckles and roars of laughter and pretty soon we were howling with tears running down our cheeks. . . .

The object sticking up from the wing was Smiles's wooden leg.

When Smiles ventured out onto the wing, he had to plant his feet firmly to keep from being blown away from the airplane. Unfortunately the fabric on the lower wing was pretty rotten. The heel of Smiles's peg leg tore through the fabric and wedged between two nose ribs in the wing. Smiles couldn't do a thing—he was trapped! He was snared just as effectively as if he were in a bear trap, only he was 1,200 feet straight up and without a parachute.

For half an hour Smiles struggled to get free. Then, wedging himself in the strut bay, he used his artificial arm for a lever and by sheer, incredible strength, managed to break the heavy shoulder strap that kept his wooden leg attached to his body!

But that wasn't all . . .

During the desperate operation to break free of his wooden leg so he could drag himself, one-legged, back into the cockpit, Smiles lost his pants. He was so busy trying to save his life that he never realized what had happened. And when the crowd swarmed around the airplane, Smiles stood up on his one leg to show everybody that he was all right.

At that moment he realized what was causing the shocked and startled looks around him.

Did you ever see a one-legged man stand up on the seat of an airplane cockpit without his breeches? They said the laughter could be heard clear over into the next county.

Russ Brinkley tells of one of the most unusual days in the highly unique history of barnstorming—

On the same day that Smiles O'Timmons lost his pants, we staged what was probably the only air show in history that featured barnstorming by the entire rolling stock of a well-known 1927 airline. To spread good will, Dewey Noyes and Merle Moltrup brought the airlines' only airplanes, two Waco Nines, over to us from Pittsburgh. They certainly added some real thrills to the show.

As long as Noyes and Moltrup lived and worked together, they were friendly competitors and they tried to outdo the other in whatever flying might be going on. Both men were really topnotch pilots, and they gained the kind of experience that counts when they flew the first airmail from Pittsburgh to Cleveland.

During the air show both Noyes and Moltrup participated in the race of the day, a wild free-for-all that was enough to scare the wits out of any human being, including their boss—whose bankroll and prestige were tied up in the two airplanes. That was the kind of race where anything could, and often did, happen, including people locking wings and smashing into the ground.

Then came the big blowoff. The two men took to the air at the same time to see which one could outfly the other. They went wild in the air and they were both breathtaking and frightening in what they did. They looped and they spun, recovering from their spins only a few feet from the ground when survival seemed impossible. They played the hairiest follow-the-leader you ever saw, with the man behind expected to outdo the one who introduced each new maneuver. There were terrifying misses-by-inches in near head-on collisions as they went through their 1927 version of chicken.

Whatever a Waco Nine could do, those boys did and the crowd went absolutely mad with the whole thing. Along the Lincoln Highway drivers just abandoned their cars as they climbed out to watch the show. State Highway patrolmen on motorcycles tore out their hair trying to untangle that mess on the road, and finally they gave up and watched the show themselves. Refreshment stands didn't sell a hot dog for a half-hour as those pilots cavorted no higher than the trees that surrounded the airfield. Finally, as a grand finale, the planes flying almost wing-tip-to-wing-tip, they pulled up beautifully into vertical turns, stalled high at the top, and kicked off in opposite directions in tight spins.

They had little altitude to begin with. The owner of the airplanes watched his entire airline shrieking down toward the earth in those spins and he turned his head and squeezed tight his eyes. No one else did. They couldn't; they were hypnotized. I was at the microphone and, with all my experience talking to the crowds, I was struck dumb. I was speechless.

There was one turn, then another, and the Wacos recovered—incredibly, unbelievably, again wing-tip-to-wing-tip! When they came out their wheels were only a few inches from the ground. The two pilots landed and you never saw so many thousands and thousands of people on their feet, screaming and shouting and beating their hands raw. Even the other pilots were whooping it up and applauding. It was the most incredible exhibition of its kind ever seen.

Not since that day—and never will it happen in the future, I'm sure—would an airline take part, a thrilling part, in any barnstorming air show. The next day, Noyes and Moltrup were back flying the airmail, respectable citizens looking for new ways in which to outdo each other. . . .

It has been said that the main difference between the barnstormer and the tramp was that the barnstormer didn't have to walk. It's high time that this nonsense was answered once and for all, and I believe that in these pages we have put the truth to the story of the barnstormer—the men who lived legends that were real.

There could be no denial (and there isn't) that the barnstormers affected aviation and the nation at large in many ways. There's the unhappy truth that after several years many of the airplanes which began the barnstorming troupes were falling apart, and that their pilots, desperately seeking the payoff in a successful air show, lacked the finances to keep their planes in good shape or, much wiser, to purchase new machinery.

The danger in performing aerobatics before large crowds increased in proportion to the age and poor maintenance of the airplanes. What could rumble safely from one town to another in the air simply couldn't withstand the punishing loads and forces of maneuvers. And so the planes began to fall apart in the air, and sometimes the pieces and the pilot's body fell into the grandstands directly into the crowds. The big show at times looked like a charnel house as flaming wreckage spewed forth among helpless observers, who had come, possibly, to see death and now were contributing to its presence. City and state officials became less than enchanted with the arrival in their areas of winged death, and not even the prospect of a dazzling air show could drown out the memory of children smashed and maimed by an out-of-control machine whistling into an audience.

The lawmakers got their dander up, and different communities struck back at the barnstormers by legislation. They forbade aerobatics in their locales, and very suddenly the barnstormers found legal barriers erected before their flight path, which had always been a will-of-the-wisp adventure.

Barnstorming as it had always been was clearly in its decline. The death knell had been sounded. What lack of funds could not do, what casualties among their own ranks could not accomplish, the legislators were doing. If enough laws continued to be passed, political control would strangle the aerial gypsies.

And then, unexpectedly, aviation itself stood by the barnstormers. But this was no misty-eyed rescue effort; it all happened strictly by accident. Aerodynamics blossomed in ninety directions at once; airplanes became the product of science instead of by gosh and by guess, and the new god was speed. Speed for vicious little stub-winged flying bombs with flashing propellers and hardly enough room for the pilot to scream in tight turns around the pylon markers of air racing corridors. The air races! That was the crowd pleaser now, watching the razor-airfoil shapes howling their way in snarling packs along the marked courses. The checkered flags and buzz-saw whine and big prizes all drew the crowds.

And the crashes, the tumbling, flipping, blazing, disintegrating crashes that maimed and killed with an appalling regularity and number. Oh, yes, there were the crashes. Racing rid the country of what had been barnstorming, and public outcry that once had laid its hand upon the barnstormers began to lift against the racers. But where the barnstormers were gypsy caravans and circuses, the air racers were supported by big business—by huge industrial concerns, by newspapers, by money. The aviation industry was leaping higher and higher every year in its growth; building the best racers often meant getting the biggest contracts and so millions of dollars financed the tight-course hell of the racing pilots.

There were some great names among them: Jimmy Doolittle, Roscoe Turner, Tony Levier, Fish Salmon, Paul Mantz, and many others. They scrambled and fought with slashing propellers for the Bendix, the Thompson, the Harmon and other trophies.

But because the races were backed by big money, and because big money is respectable, barnstorming knew its savior. The crowds came to the races for the same reason that Beachey had called them "a pack of jackals." They thirsted for excitement and they lusted for blood. The races couldn't supply all that. No, but a good air circus, with aerobatics and stunt men, with wing-walkers and parachute jumpers, with comedy routines, and with clowns and popcorn and soda and beautiful girls—hey! What we need at the big air races in this country are the barnstormers!

And so barnstorming, changed and modified and really not what it once was (and can never be again), came back to life. In its resurrection barnstorming also grew respectable. The unshaven heroes who drifted from town to town, from state to state, were fading ghosts of yesteryear. The airplanes hadn't any resemblance to the sagging Jennies and Standards and Canucks. The new ships were beautifully made and unbelievably strong, their engines screamed power, and they were polished and shined and hell, but they *were* beautiful. And so were the women who flew in them and, if you could judge by the screams of the teen-agers in the crowds, so were the pilots.

Aerobatics were better than ever, because the new airplanes could do things the old-timers never saw. And the jumpers still had their crazy routines. Maybe they didn't have one leg and one arm and one eye like Smiles O'Timmons, but the shows had Tommy Walker and Red Grant and men of their caliber.

The barnstorming acts became part-and-parcel of the big scene around the national air races, notably the tremendous

Cleveland Air Races—which drew as many as four hundred thousand spectators! And the strange thing about it was that some of the new acts were like nothing ever seen before— which, when you think about it, isn't at all unusual. There were new engines and new planes and there were also new ideas.

No one ever matched a man named Harold Johnson, who earned himself the title of King of the Tin Goose. Johnson's *Goose* was a hefty Ford tri-motor airlines transport, and in that hulking piece of machinery he made history. He brought massed crowds to their feet by taking the six-ton machine through unbelievable aerobatics that ran the gamut of vicious hammerhead stalls to Cuban eights, and whirling spins that he started at a thousand feet.

Harold Johnson had even the old-timers staring wide-eyed when he came across a field at 350 feet to start his grand finale. He went through two consecutive snap rolls (which are mean in almost any airplane), came out of the second roll at only twenty-five feet off the ground to rip upward into a wide and clawing loop. But he didn't just loop, he did three in a row without a break, and snapped out of the last one to sideslip in to a perfect landing.

After a classic performance at Dearborn, Michigan, where the airplane was built (it was a stock airplane without any modifications), Henry Ford, Sr., handed Johnson his own check for ten thousand dollars in appreciation for his proving just what the old *Tin Goose* really had in her.

No aerobatics star has ever been paid more money than Beverly E. Howard. Bevo is regarded by old-timers in aviation as perhaps the greatest precision aerobatics pilot ever to fly in the United States. In this instance the writer is an old friend of Bevo Howard, and stands firm in supporting that regard. Unlike many of his predecessors who were flamboyant and hell-raising, Bevo Howard is a prime model of a family and business man, and just about the "nicest guy" ever to hit aviation.

He began with an airplane he bought for a hundred dollars, the money earned selling newspapers. As he gained skill, he immediately was recognized as a standout. Bevo was seen at virtually every air meet, show and race in the nation— commanding as much as one thousand dollars for a dazzling exhibition of precision flying that lasted exactly a quarter of an hour. In 1938, still in his early twenties, Bevo became the first man in the world to whirl through an outside loop, a feat long considered impossible. He did it in a Piper Cub.

Paul Mantz proved just how "impossible" was the outside loop by doing forty-six such loops, one after the other. But then, Paul Mantz, like Bevo Howard, had an unfair advantage. He could fly in a manner that would turn an angel green with envy!

Bevo's stunts included screaming down the airfield at minimum altitude while inverted, and his head and shoulders, and his arms, dangling *beneath* the airplane! He could do this and snatch up ribbons and handkerchiefs from poles, and perform the whole works with greater precision than the average experienced pilot can fly from A to B in dead-calm air. But Bevo is always anxious to pass on the credit, and he regards his special airplane as deserving of that credit.

"Professional exhibition fliers," he explains, "regard this little brute as the most maneuverable aerobatic plane ever built. It is a Buecker-Jungmeister, manufactured in Germany in 1936. It was ostensibly designed as a sport plane, but this model actually was used to train fighter pilots for the Luftwaffe. A Rumanian aerobatic ace brought it to the United States aboard the German dirigible, *von Hindenburg*. Mike Murphy . . . who was a pretty hot pilot in the late 1930's, got hold of it before I did. It took me five years to get it away from him. It can perform the most complex maneuver with comparative ease. It has been a consistent winner in international competition around the world."

In 1960, after the writer flew with Bevo in dazzling aerobatics, we spent the dinner hours discussing flying. Bevo explained all aerobatics are variations of three basic maneuvers. The slow roll comes in five variations, there are seven variations to the loop, and the snap roll (with multiple aileron control) can be adapted in fourteen different ways. In his agile Jungmeister Bevo brought these maneuvers to such perfection that before he retired from active competition he had racked up six world championships for precision flying.

Today men look about them and are dazzled by their new world. Other men sealed within a complex and small capsule are flung in a mysterious balance between gravity and centrifugal force around the entire planet with a speed of three hundred miles per minute. Intricate machines with electronic senses plumb the depths of space and snuffle gingerly at the moon and distant worlds. Behind all that goes on each day is

Buecker-Jungmeister

the monstrous shadow of the thermonuclear cloud. Even within the realm of flight the old world seems lost forever as black machines wing their path through the naked air many miles above the earth at more than two thousand miles per hour.

But that world isn't all lost. There's a saying that history always repeats itself, but in different ways. The gypsy troupers are gone forever; there's a new world about us and the old must give way. Where once there was the traveling air circus, now there is the modern air show. The razzle-dazzle is still there, all right, and in some ways it's flashier and just as much fun, but without the maverick touch to it, and the kids sure have a swell time. There are many of these new shows, such as the one held June 28, 1964, for the dedication of the Bridgeport Municipal Airport in Connecticut.

They did it up in a big way, and sixty-four thousand people came out to cheer and drink pop and eat hot dogs and buy balloons and ooh and aah at what went on in the sky. They were just as wide-eyed as people were many years ago. The little boys screamed with delight as men plummeted from airplanes in long free falls and friends cavorted in parachutes. Other men stood atop the wings of biplanes and waved to the crowd in skillful showmanship as the airplanes, trailing smoke, weaved through their maneuvers. There were superb aerobatics and all manner of precision flying, fun acts and, as a backdrop for today's air show, screaming Air Force jets that cut in their afterburners and rocked the crowd below with the frightening smash of all that jet thunder.

That's something else we have today: the miracle of precision formation and solo flight in the modern sweptwing jet fighter. Nothing they ever had in the old days could compare to the wonder of flight of the Air Force Thunderbirds or the Navy's Blue Angels. This is flying of a wholly new horizon, and it is spectacular and, more than that, it is beautiful precision and the magic of flight.

We're going through a resurgence of the air show. And strange to say, it's getting better than it has been for a long time. At special air events throughout the country that last for several days, a crowd of a quarter-million people no longer is unusual. That speaks for itself . . .

North American P-51 "Mustang"

And then there are pilots like Harold Krier, who brings even the old-time professionals to their feet in roaring applause for his exquisitely precise aerobatics. There isn't a single major award for precision flying that doesn't rest on the mantelpiece of Krier's office. It isn't just that he is spectacular (which he is) or that he is precise (which he is), he has brought to demonstration flying a professionalism and competence that leaves no question as to the intensive effort that stands behind his seemingly effortless performances. A major show by Krier means the flawless execution of forty-three maneuvers, each a showcase of how aerobatics should be flown. He caps off his routine with the crowd standing on its feet in awe as he enters and performs the *Lomcevak*. It's a maneuver best described by the remark, "I see it but I still don't believe it!" Krier enters the *Lomcevak* (which means "headache") from an inverted position and then sends his airplane *tumbling end-over-end through the air*.

Nor is there anyone else known who can quite match the man considered the greatest deadstick artist of all time in the flying business, Charles Hillard. At twenty-five years of age, Hillard has gained a very special kind of fame by performing sensational aerobatics with his engine off and the propeller stopped dead. He flies a beauty of a monoplane that is tiny and superbly balanced at the controls and that permits this brilliant pilot to perform stunts that, like those of Krier, must be seen to be believed, and even then there is much disbelief and shaking of the head! Without power Hillard plunges straight down from the sky in a precision tailspin for more than five thousand feet. And then, well above the ground, he wrenches out of the spin and plunges into double snap rolls, hesitation rolls held at four points, Texas 8's, and wild barberpole rolls, from which he emerges at ground level to slice onto the runway on one wheel, holding that position as he hurtles by.

And then there's the man called Bob Hoover, who takes up a North American P-51 Mustang fighter and stuns even the best of the veteran fighter pilots in maneuvers that, any hard-eyed instructor will tell you flatly and unequivocally, are impossible.

If we were to sit back and take stock of all that's going on in aviation today, and we had to select the one person or flying team that's doing the most to keep alive the bridge between the past and the present, the choice is swift indeed; without competition or argument, the prize goes to the team of Frank Tallman and Paul Mantz. These two veterans of flight through many decades have earned the eternal gratitude of all those who have been in flying and have helped to make of flight the wonder which so many of us can now share.

Both men are not only skilled pilots, they are superb in their handling of controls. For decades Paul Mantz has carried the accolade of "Mr. Aviation," through his spectacular flying as a barnstormer, racing pilot, stunt man, and movie pilot. This doesn't call for just flamboyancy in the sky. Remember the first cinemascope films of the United States and then other parts of the world from the air? Remember those breathtaking scenes of beauty and majestic vistas, of flight from on high and on the deck? At the controls of that special B-25 bomber was none other than Paul Mantz, who was called on for rock-steady precision flying that, in its own way, is more demanding than swirling aerobatics.

Frank Tallman is perhaps the greatest stuntman of our time in the air. He is as adept in Spads and Fokkers as he is in a

B-25

Bonanza or a Comanche. He can fly the old World War I fighters, the Jennies and the Standards, the Wacos and the Fleets, with a mastery that is a marvel to behold. When he steps into a rickety Curtiss Pusher or a Nieuport 28 it is almost as if the clock were turning backward in a blur and we were stepping with him into yesteryear.

Mantz and Tallman some years ago pooled their very special talents in a living testimonial called Tallmantz, Inc. They made no bones about their intentions: to portray the antique aircraft of our past as they can only be properly portrayed—in the air. They have nearly one hundred airplanes of a bewildering variety of types, superbly maintained, and each in its own way a misty-eyed remembrance of times past. At their Movieland of the Air at Orange County Airport, Santa Ana, California, hundreds of thousands of people visit their world's greatest collection of historical and military aircraft. More than two million dollars worth of famous planes of yesteryear are carefully preserved in a display that covers an outside area and a special, air-conditioned hangar for the older and more delicate machines.

It is more than a museum. Wisely the two men have set aside several airplanes, old and new, for the kids to climb all over and about and through. Every day, weather permitting, some of the old machines lift into the sky for a page out of barnstorming history. In an old Waco open-cockpit biplane, the barnstorming practice of taking up passengers for three cents per passenger-pound is maintained, and it's often a struggle to see if a boy or his dad gets the first ride!

Reality also must be faced in this endeavor, and those of us long in aviation have the greatest appreciation of and respect for the task fulfilled by Mantz and Tallman.

"No one realizes the amount of time and money it takes to keep this many airplanes flying," explains Tallman. "Sometimes we go for months without any movie work, yet the planes have to be kept up so that we're ready to roll on short notice. Movie companies can't afford delays, but they don't want to have to pay the cost of keeping a Lockheed Vega licensed for five years in order for it to fly in one movie scene.

"You have to love these old beasts, or go in some other business. No one wants to subsidize aviation history, so it's up to people like us to do it. Luckily we somehow managed

Lockheed Vega

to keep everyone satisfied, including the full time army of mechanics who want a pay check every week."

So it is there for one and all to see, five miles south of Santa Ana in southern California.

If ever you would like to step out of today and into yesteryear, that's the place to go.

Down there . . . barnstorming is still very much alive.

MARTIN CAIDIN

The author of over fifty books and more than a thousand magazine articles, MARTIN CAIDIN is one of the outstanding aeronautics and aviation authorities in the world. The National War College, the Air Force's Air University, and several other institutions use his books as doctrine and strategy guides, historical references, and textbooks. He has twice won the Aviation/Space Writers Association award as the outstanding author in the field of aviation: in 1958 for his *Air Force: A Pictorial History of American Airpower*, and in 1961 for THUNDERBIRDS!

Mr. Caidin flies his own plane throughout the United States. He has also flown private planes to various countries, and bombers to Europe. He is rated for both landplanes and seaplanes, single-engine and multi-engine. For six weeks in 1960 he flew aerobatics in an F-100F Super Sabre with the famed Air Force Thunderbirds. He has also ridden in centrifuges, dived vertically at 1,100 mph, undergone explosive decompression in an altitude chamber, witnessed the firing of literally hundreds of missiles, rockets, and space vehicles, and toured military, research, and industrial installations throughout the United States.

A Note About The Bantam Air & Space Series

This is the era of flight—the century which has seen man soar, not only into the skies of Earth but beyond the gravity of his home planet and out into the blank void of space. An incredible accomplishment achieved in an incredibly short time.

How did it happen?

The AIR & SPACE series is dedicated to the men and women who brought this fantastic accomplishment about, often at the cost of their lives—a library of books which will tell the grand story of man's indomitable determination to seek the new, to explore the farthest frontier.

The driving theme of the series is the skill of *piloting*, for without this, not even the first step would have been possible. Like the Wright Brothers and those who, for some 35 years, followed in their erratic flight path, the early flyers had to be designer, engineer and inventor. Of necessity, they were the pilots of the crazy machines they dreamt up and strung together.

Even when the technology became slightly more sophisticated, and piloting became a separate skill, the quality of a flyer's ability remained rooted in a sound working knowledge of his machine. World War I, with its spurt of development in aircraft, made little change in the role of the flyer who remained, basically, pilot-navigator-engineer.

Various individuals, like Charles Lindbergh, risked their lives and made high drama of the new dimension they were carving in the air. But still, until 1939, flying was a romantic, devil-may-care wonder, confined to a relative handful of hardy individuals. Commercial flight on a large scale was a mere gleam in the eye of men like Howard Hughes.

It took a second major conflict, World War II, from 1939 to 1945, to provoke the imperative that required new concepts from the designers—and created the arena where hundreds of young men and women would learn the expertise demanded by high-speed, high-tech aircraft.

From the start of flight, death has taken its toll. Flying has always been a high-risk adventure. Never, since men first launched themselves into the air, has the new element given up its sacrifice of stolen lives, just as men have never given up the driving urge to go farther, higher, faster. Despite only a fifty-fifty chance of any mission succeeding, *still* the dream draws many more men and women to spaceflight than any program can accommodate. And still, in 1969, when Mike Collins, Buzz Aldrin and Neil Armstrong first took man to the Moon, the skill of piloting, sheer flying ability, was what actually landed the "Eagle" on the Moon's surface. And still, despite technological sophistication undreamed of 30 or 40 years earlier, despite demands on any flyer for levels of performance and competence and the new understanding of computer science not necessary in early aircraft, it is piloting, *human* control of the aircraft—sometimes, indeed, inspired control—that remains the major factor in getting there and back safely.

From this rugged breed of individuals come the bush pilots of today, men who even now fly their little planes above the vast, icy expanse of the Arctic, landing in small open stretches, on wheels, skis, or pontoons, carrying with them all the spare parts they need to repair their own craft. The first of the AIR & SPACE series is about one such pilot—*The Last of the Bush Pilots*, by Harmon Helmericks.

The horrors of World War II bred and trained literally hundreds of pilots. Here the expertise of piloting in life and death situations began to teach the designers. *Fork-Tailed Devil: The P38*, by Martin Caidin, was a fighter plane whose deficiencies cost lives until its pilots used their combat experience to correct its faults. On the other hand, there was the unbelievable strength of the War's greatest bomber, the Flying Fort. Pilots called it the airplane you could trust. It, too, saw improvement both in design and effectiveness that was a direct result of battle, and the Fort brought its bomber crews home when the problem lay not so much in flying the monster as in landing an aircraft that was half shot away. . . . *Flying Forts: The B-17 in World War II* by Martin Caidin, tells the magnificent, edge-of-the-seat story of this fantastic aircraft.

The War also saw the start of a new kind of flying machine—one without propellers—for jet propulsion was born at this time. And very secretly, right after the close of hostilities, Chuck Yeager was busy testing the X-1 and breaking the sound barrier. This was just the beginning. Even the early test pilots of the U.S. Air Force carried the speed of piloted jet aircraft to 1,900 miles an hour—nearly three times the speed of sound. Frank Everest flew his X-2 at these incredible speeds, and as high as 60-odd miles. John Guenther, noted aviation writer, tells the story of Frank Everest in *The Fastest Man Alive*.

After America first landed men on the Moon, the Russian space program pushed ahead with plans for eventually creating a permanent space station where men could live. And in 1982 they sent up two men—Valentine Lebedev and Anatoly Berezovoy—to live on Solyut-7 for seven months. This extraordinary feat has been recorded in the diaries of pilot Lebedev, *Diary of a Cosmonaut: 211 Days in Space* by Valentin Lebedev.

The Bantam AIR & SPACE series will include several titles by or about flyers from all over the world—and about the planes they flew, including World War II, the postwar era of barnstorming and into the jet age, plus the personal histories of many of the world's greatest pilots. Man is still the most important element in flying.

Here is a preview of the next book
in the Bantam Air and Space Series:

THE ELECTRA STORY

by Robert Serling

Prologue

It all began on a warm, humid night—September 29, 1959.
A farmer named Richard E. White, too sleepy to watch
the eleven o'clock news on television, turned off the set
and yawned his way to the bedroom. His wife already was
asleep.

Their forty-nine-acre farm was only a few miles from the
tiny town of Buffalo, Texas (population 1200). Their children,
grown-up, lived and worked in Dallas. The Whites themselves had moved from Dallas to find more quiet. Their lives
were peaceful, content, and prosaic—until the precise moment of 11:08 P.M., when White, his eyes heavy with drowsi-
ness, jolted to attention.

He didn't see the garish, blinding, weird yellow light that
filled the sky outside. But he heard the sound. Metallic,
snarling, tortured, vibrating in his eardrums.

The startled White jumped out of bed and ran outside
without bothering with his shoes. The entire sky seemed on
fire, then suddenly faded as if a monstrous Roman candle had

spent itself. White's wife had just run out to join him when a clap like thunder shook the earth. White put his arm around her in a gesture of futile protection and stared into the night, wondering and waiting.

Out of the black sky came a new sound—shrill, deafening whistles pitched to different keys. Next a roar—faint at first, then mushrooming into the approach of a thousand freight trains. Like two helpless, frightened children, the Whites huddled close together.

Heavy metal objects began crashing about them. The clamor ceased and the night was still again.

"It's raining," said Mrs. White incredulously.

"It couldn't be," her husband muttered. "Look at the stars."

But it apparently *was* raining. Gently, but most perceptibly. White sniffed the air suspiciously.

"That's not rain," he said. "It's—it's like coal oil."

In his bare feet he ran toward his vegetable patch, where most of the objects had fallen. It was littered with pieces of torn aluminum and strips of yellow insulating material. White turned his horrified eyes toward a tree close to his pigpen a few yards away.

There, resting in the branches, white and gleaming, was the huge rudder of an aircraft. On it were some red letters. It suddenly dawned on farmer White what had fallen from the skies.

"FLY BRANIFF," the letters said.

The "rain" White thought smelled like coal oil was kerosene. Fuel for jet-powered engines. And the rudder in the tree by his pigpen belonged to Braniff International Airways Flight 542, an L-188.

Otherwise known as the Lockheed Electra.

1

The Electra Is Born

Go back three decades—to another warm fall night in the year 1932, to an aircraft plant in Burbank, California.

A young Lockheed aeronautical engineer named Hall L. Hibbard looked up from his blueprints and was surprised to find his attractive wife, Irene, standing there.

"Hi," she said. "I knew you'd be working late again so I thought I'd come down and keep you company."

Hibbard smiled and went back to his blueprints. Irene Hibbard watched for a while, sipped some coffee, curled up on a big unused drawing board, and went to sleep.

Just behind her, sleek and shining under the bright lights, an airplane was taking shape. Soon it would travel the skies as one of the world's first all-metal, twin-engine, low-wing transport planes. It bore the technical name of Lockheed Model 10. But, like virtually every plane Lockheed had built since the mid-twenties and early thirties, it also carried the name of a star. There had been the Orion, Vega, Sirius, Altair.

This one would be called the Electra. And on her rested the entire hopes of the fledgling company, reorganized only a few months after its parent company, Detroit Aircraft, had sunk into bankruptcy.

Lockheed itself had been organized only six years before, by pilot-aeronautical engineer Allan Lockheed. Despite the fast-growing reputation of his planes, he ran into tough financial sledding. In 1929 he merged Lockheed with Detroit Aircraft, actually a holding company, and stepped out.

The little Burbank factory tried valiantly to operate under the twin handicaps of absentee ownership and the worldwide depression. But Detroit Aircraft itself folded, and the Lockheed Aircraft Corporation followed it into bankruptcy.

On June 6, 1932, thirty-five-year-old Robert Ellsworth Gross walked into the U.S. District Court in Los Angeles and offered $40,000 for the assets of the bankrupt Burbank company. Gross, who had worked for other aircraft firms but wanted one of his own, raised the money with six other adventuresome men, including a Lockheed executive named Carl Squier.

Squier had been running Lockheed until it went broke through no fault of his own. The preceding Christmas Eve, as the disheartened employees filed out of the plant, Squier had been at the gate to wish them a Merry Christmas—and hand each of the one hundred and twenty workers a ten-dollar bill. The money was the last of his own personal savings.

The following January he had to mortgage his car and home to meet the payroll. When Lockheed went into bankruptcy a few months later, Squier's final payroll consisted of three persons—a secretary, an accountant, and a stockroom clerk who also doubled as night watchman.

At the moment Gross walked into the courtroom to enter his $40,000 bid, the name Lockheed already was a proud one in America's infant aircraft industry. Its traditional "Winged Star" emblazoned ships that from 1928 through 1931 broke virtually every speed and distance record on the books. The names of pilots flying Lockheed equipment were household words. Frank Hawks. Ruth Nichols. Roscoe Turner. Charles Lindbergh. And a former Lockheed test pilot named Wiley Post who flew a Vega christened *Winnie Mae* around the world in only eight days.

In effect, Gross and his six associates were purchasing a reputation and nothing else. The bankruptcy inventory added up to less than $130,000, most of it consisting of a few spare parts, machine tools, furniture, and a pencil sharpener listed at fifty cents. There also was a one-hundred-and-seventy-one-dollar safe, with nothing inside it.

There were no competing bids, although Gross had an anxious moment when he spotted Allan Lockheed in the courtroom. The founder, however, had been unable to raise enough funds to buy back his company and the judge approved the sale with the wry comment:

"I hope you know what you're doing."

It was Gross who hired Hibbard, regarded as one of the best designers in the business even though the young engineer never learned to fly himself. Hibbard's first assignment was to create a single-engine, all-metal passenger plane carrying ten persons. But Gross got another idea.

He was eating breakfast one morning at the old Union Air Terminal in Burbank when he spotted three planes parked outside. One was a Lockheed Orion, the second a Ford trimotor, and the third Boeing's new twin-engine transport, the 247. Gross thought to himself, "Which plane would I choose if I were going to fly to San Francisco?" He gulped down his coffee, drove over to the two-story former ranch house that was Lockheed's executive building, and stuck his head into Hibbard's office.

"Let's junk what we're doing and put two engines on it," he told his chief designer.

When it came time to name the new project, Gross went to the Burbank public library and pored through astronomy books. He wanted to retain Lockheed's system for naming its planes after stars. He finally settled on Electra, the so-called "lost" star of the Pleiades, named after the mythological Greek goddess who became a comet and wandered eternally through the heavens.

Development costs on the new transport mounted alarmingly. At one point the new firm's credit standing was so shaky that packages addressed to Lockheed were delivered C.O.D.

No romantic thoughts about past history were in Hall Hibbard's mind as he struggled over the blueprints. Of more import was the fact that the Electra was Lockheed's first venture into the multiengine transport field and its most important single project. If the Model 10 flopped, so would Lockheed.

Hibbard looked at his sleeping wife for a moment and shook his head in a gesture of pride mingled with guilt. Then he resumed his work.

"I still think we may have trouble with that rudder setup," he said to a colleague. "Now suppose we . . ."

It took Hibbard and eleven other men a year to design the first Electra. Only one year elapsed between the original blueprint and the initial test flight. Twenty-five years later, the Electra of the jet age was the product of nearly one thousand engineers and two years of work between blueprint and test-flight stages.

In 1932 Hibbard required only one drawing to detail the entire electrical system of the old Electra. The plane that flew twenty-five years later needed one thousand separate drawings for its electrical innards. For the first Electra, one man did all the stress analysis—determining what key structural parts will do under various strains and loads of flight. A typical structural test involved somebody pushing a foot against a piece of tubing to see if it would hold. The Electra of a quarter century later had more than 300 engineers and equipment costing millions of dollars assigned to this one phase of testing.

When the 1932 Electra made her first flight, Hibbard waited anxiously on the ground for the verdict of a single person—test pilot Marshall Headle. Headle landed and broke Hibbard's heart.

"She's nice, but the rudder forces are lousy," he reported bluntly.

Hibbard went back to work redesigning the Electra's twin rudders. Thirty years later, he recalled the incident as another reminder of how aviation has progressed.

"We used to depend solely on the word of the test pilot," he said. "He told us 'she flies good' or 'she flies bad.' His reaction was all we had to go on. Now the pilot is just one cog in the test program. Every time he moves his hands or feet in a new airplane, the results are recorded on machines and graphs. We're interested in a pilot's reactions, of course, but we wouldn't dare evaluate a plane's performance on what one man feels through the seat of his pants."

Despite that relatively primitive method of determining whether "she flies good or bad," however, the Model 10 was an almost immediate success. The first Electra carried a price tag of $50,000, which wouldn't pay for one of her successor's Allison engines. United States airlines ordered nearly 150, and the Electra was the first American-built transport to find a large market among foreign carriers.

Before the orders began rolling in, the Electra gave its then-youthful designer a few final moments of concern. Headle had just finished putting the plane through its final Civil Aeronautics Authority certification tests and radioed Hibbard he was coming in.

"We'll have a celebration tonight," Headle announced gleefully as he banked the trim transport over the Burbank airport and swung into his approach.

But as the ship came in, Hibbard's heart went into his mouth. One wheel still was retracted, and in 1932 engineers had yet to come up with a device to lower a stuck gear manually. Hibbard knew a crash was inevitable and that there was nothing anyone could do. It also happened to be the only Electra built and the plane Lockheed was going to use for sale demonstrations. In about thirty seconds there wasn't going to be any Electra.

Headle did a beautiful job of landing on one wheel, but eventually a wing had to touch ground and that was it. Luckily damage was not too severe, the plane was repaired, and Carl Squier, now a key sales executive in the reorganized company, started selling the nation's newest transport aircraft.

One thing should be remembered about the early sales efforts and the original Electra itself. In those days Lockheed and other manufacturers literally told the airlines what they wanted and needed. Twenty-five years later they had found they could not sell an airliner merely by building it first and then hoping someone would like it well enough to buy it.

Lockheed's second Electra project dates back to 1953 when Capital Airlines approached the Burbank firm on the possibility of designing a turboprop (jet engines hitched to conventional propellers) airliner. Capital, however, primarily was interested in a short-haul plane and Lockheed's engineers were not too enthusiastic about the prospects. They were thinking of a bigger, more versatile aircraft and in 1954 American Airlines laid down the specifications for a new type of commercial transport along those lines. Eastern also expressed interest, although at first glance what they wanted literally was an aeronautical moon.

Give us, said American's hard-bitten president C. R. Smith, a turboprop ship that can:

—Cruise easily at speeds of more than 400 miles per hour,

—Operate profitably on flights as short as 100 miles and as long as 2700 miles,

—Carry at least sixty-five passengers,

—Take off fast enough and land slowly enough to serve any of the nation's 100 major airports, large and small—particularly fields that never would be able to handle the forthcoming pure jets.

What American and Eastern were seeking was the most versatile airliner ever designed. There was nothing like it flying or, for that matter, on any drawing board. American said literally:

"This is what we want. Can anyone build it?"

Britain proposed a streched-out version of the popular Viscount and a couple of new designs. American also was offered U.S. piston-engine planes converted to turboprop engines. Douglas, as ever Lockheed's chief competitor, even then was busy on the DC-8 jetliner but still managed to come up with a new prop-jet transport proposal.

Lockheed jumped into the competition with a technical ace in the hole. It already had flown the C-130 Hercules, a muscular cargo plane designed for the Air Force and equipped with four 3750 horsepower Allison turboprop engines. The Burbank engineers designed an airframe for use with those well-tested power plants. American's equipment experts looked over all entries and picked the Lockheed color-bearer. So did Eastern.

Officially the new plane was assigned the unromantic sobriquet of L-188, L for Lockheed and the 188 standing for the project number. But Lockheed still had a penchant for naming its aircraft after stars.

"What do we call it?" a Lockheed official asked board chairman Robert Gross.

Gross, who for more than twenty years had nursed nostalgic sentiment for the trim little airliner that had saved his company from financial ruin, didn't hesitate one second.

"We'll call it the Electra," he said.

"It is," said Bob Gross to his engineers, "going to be the most thoroughly tested airliner in aviation history."

The engineers took him at his word. The Electra "flew" on drawing boards. In wind tunnels. On electronic computers.

In laboratories. And in some of the most grueling flight tests ever to torture a commercial airliner.

They built three full-scale mock-ups, one structurally complete fuselage section, layouts of complete systems, test rigs, engine stands, and a special sound chamber.

They constructed a full-sized wooden model to provide dimensional studies of passenger and flight-crew compartments, interior styling, and equipment location.

They fashioned a mock-up of metal for checking structual tolerance, fabricated parts, and actual operation of the complicated control systems.

They took a remote-controlled, stainless-steel ax and hacked away at a fuselage pressurized far beyond normal needs and subjected in advance to the simulated but violent turbulence of an approximate tornado—to determine if damage, once inflicted, could spread.

They slashed into window frames, windshield posts, skins and frames, door corners and fuselage-to-wing attachments.

They tore a six-foot gash in the fuselage and still couldn't make the wound spread.

"Fail-safe" structure was the aeronautical engineer's term. The providing of reserve stength so that if a major structural part failed, damage would remain localized and would not affect other key components.

They built a forty-foot unit that represented a regular Electra fuselage to check, test, and improve the heating and cooling system. It looked like a giant sausage because of its thick layers of insulating material placed around the tubing. But it manufactured weather on the ground and at 30,000 feet, and it made certain that the real airplane would remain comfortable at any level in any temperature.

They put twelve-inch samples of floor-covering material in the lobby of Lockheed's research laboratory. After 100,000 persons had walked over the samples, they picked the best.

They put a $48,000, one-sixteenth-scale model Electra through 60,000 wind-tunnel tests at speeds of more than 400 MPH.

They built two more scale models plus a reproduction of the engine nacelles and flew each 100,000 miles to determine the Electra's aerodynamic characteristics.

They put the main landing gear through 270,000 simulated

flights involving every load from an empty plane to one carrying ninety-five passengers plus full cargo and baggage bins and maximum fuel capacity.

They also put the gear through free-fall drop tests that duplicated the Electra's maximum sink speed of ten feet per second with a gross weight of 96,650 pounds. Then they pushed the weight up to 125,000 pounds—six tons heavier than the plane's greatest allowable take-off weight—and dropped the gear a few thousand more times.

They took four-pound carcasses of electrocuted chickens and blasted them out of a compressed-air cannon against cockpit windshields at 450 MPH. The chickens couldn't hurt the five-ply combination of glass and plastic, so they tried artificial hailstones and even steel pellets. Then they deliberately broke the outer glass and fired chickens, hailstones, and pellets at the inner vinyl panel to see if it was strong enough to withstand any impact on its own.

They put the integrated staircase through 5000 cycles to see if it would break down or develop any bugs.

They loaded the wings down with sandbags, adding tons of weight gradually until they were sure they could withstand anything from an abrupt pull-out from a 400-MPH dive to the worst thunderstorm the heavens could create.

They put the wings on giant racks and subjected them to countless strains, twists, gusts, and violent maneuvers.

Allison technicians hurled frozen ice balls—make-believe hailstones—into engine air-intake ducts at speeds up to 415 MPH. They aimed a high-pressure stream of water into the engines to simulate the worst rainstorm any plane could encounter—the equivalent of 41.5 inches an hour, more than any recorded rainfall in history.

Lockheed already had accumulated 250,000 flight hours' experience with the Allison engines on the C-130s. But the engineers weren't satisfied. They mounted four of the big power plants on a Super Constellation and flew it for another 3370 hours.

In another Allison-equipped military transport, they conducted "Operation Hourglass"—twelve hours of flight daily over an airline type of schedule until the engines accumulated another 2000 hours.

When the Electra prototype finally was built, its various

flight tests added 4200 more engine hours by the time the Electra was certificated.

As soon as the full-scale Electra mock-up was finished, complete to cockpit layout with full instrumentation, Lockheed invited aviation's severest critics to look it over—an evaluation committee from the Air Line Pilots Association, representing the flight crews of the several airlines that had ordered the plane by now.

The committee looked over the cockpit, the various systems, and the blueprints. It suggested sixty-three modifications, ranging from better fire-warning arrangements to the location of the cockpit ash trays. Lockheed accepted thirty-nine recommendations, partially agreed to eighteen, and rejected only eight as impractical or unnecessary. It was the highest batting average for proposals accepted ever recorded by a pilot evaluation committee.

Later, committee members flew the actual plane. Two incidents of note occurred during the test program. One involved an accidental landing at a greater speed and with more forceful impact than encountered by a carrier-based fighter. There was only minor damage.

The ALPA evaluation report commented:

"The ability of the Electra to survive such an impact . . . is remarkable and represents the best possible testimonial to its structural integrity."

In the second incident the test crew inadvertently kept the landing gear down for several minutes after taking off. The ALPA representatives were not even aware the gear was still down, becausee the Electra continued to climb without breathing hard.

Eighteen of the nation's best airline pilots were members of the committee. Their final report included these comments on the Electra's performance:

Landing—"the airplane had good control characteristics and no difficulty was experienced in making consistently good landings."

Emergency power during an aborted take-off—"members were very much impressed with the rapid power application possible and with the immediate airplane response in climb performance. It definitely exceeded the balked landing and pull-out of any propeller-driven airplane which we have ever flown."

Stalling—"the stall characteristics of this airplane, in all configurations, were exceptionally good. There was no fall-off on one wing or any other adverse tendencies. In fact, the stall characteristics were very similar to a 'Cub' with ample warning indication and no violent change of attitude."

Handling in the event of multiple engine failure—"the airplane is definitely flyable and controllable."

Stability—"high-speed stability is good . . . good control response at touchdown speeds . . . responded well to the flare-out on landing . . . cross-wind take-off and landing characteristics seemed to be most normal. . . ."

Cockpit visibility—"contrast between the visibility from the cockpit of the Electra and from previous Lockheed transports is tremendous. Visibility . . . is excellent and Lockheed is to be commended for the special effort that has been put into producing this cockpit."

Bad-weather landings—"in making ILS (Instrument Landing System) approaches, the airplane was found to be very easy to control on the glide slope . . . quite maneuverable and responsive and was considered by the pilots to be equal to or better than present-day transports in its handling characteristics."

The report concluded with about the most glowing praise ever offered in the traditionally conservative ALPA evaluation documents.

"This committee is more than reasonably confident," it declared, "that the manufacturers, the operators, the pilots and the public will be satisfied with the record of safety, efficiency and economy which will be achieved."

Typically, the ALPA evaluation report tempered praise with a sober note of caution.

"As has been true of all transports," it concluded, "the real evaluation of the Lockheed Electra will begin the day the first Electra airplane goes into scheduled airline operation and will continue until the last airplane of the final modification of the basic airplane has been retired."

That note of caution, however—that traditional touch of cynicism that is as much a part of the airline pilot as his uniform—was just an uneasy whisper amid loud acclaim for an airliner that seemed to have been conceived out of pilot dreams and desires. From the moment the first Electra snarled into the sky, it became the mistress, sweetheart, or wife of virtually every man who flew it. It was a ship that fulfilled the pilot's prerequisites for a transport better than any other plane in history. It had enormous reserve power. It handled smoothly, docilely, responsively. It was fast, versatile, uncomplaining and even—for such a huge aircraft—forgiving of mistakes. In brief, it was a pilot's airplane.

The Electra's comparatively short, stubby wings bothered some pilots the first time they saw the plane. Captain Art Weidman, one of the first check pilots assigned to American's Electra training program, went out to the Burbank plant for his introduction to the new plane. Lockheed rolled out an Electra and Weidman's first question was:

"Where the hell is the wing?"

It was a natural question, for the wings do appear abnormally short. Actually the wing span is only five and a half feet shorter than the fuselage. Weidman was fooled by the size of the huge engines, with large exhaust nozzles extending to the trailing edge and literally hiding much of the wing area. The monster propellers also create the illusion of a "too-small" wing. But Weidman and other pilots quickly learned that Lockheed had built into the Electra a completely new airfoil.

American and Eastern had demanded a plane equally adept at short- and long-haul operations. This was achieved mostly by the thirteen-and-a-half-foot props, which swept their mighty air stream over all but nine feet of the wing area. The Electra was meant to manufacture her own lift in greater quantities than any plane ever built.

Demonstration flights proved to all doubting pilots that the engine-prop-wing combination resulted in fantastic performance. Weidman recalls one of those flights. Lockheed test pilot Herman "Fish" Salmon brought an Electra in for a landing, flaps partially extended, wheels down and locked. In every plane this is a moment of tension, for the pilot is committed to the touchdown. He can only wait for his aircraft to settle, then hit the brakes, reverse props, and come to a stop.

Salmon let the Electra's wheels touch the runway. Then, with an almost imperceptible throb of power, he suddenly began climbing again.

"I had never seen this done with any other aircraft in the years I had flown," Weidman marveled. "If I hadn't seen it with my own eyes, I wouldn't have believed it possible. This was the 'wave-off' characteristic that pilots had dreamed about but never enjoyed. An airplane that never really was committed to a landing. An airplane in which you could make as many passes at a field as you desired without any worry about emergency climb power."

Slim Cockes, a crusty and capable Eastern veteran, didn't believe what he heard about the Electra's effortless power until he took one off on a test hop at Miami's International Airport.

"When we passed over the runway threshold, we already were touching 3000 feet altitude," Cockes said. "The bird climbed like a damned fighter plane."

Lockheed spent 50,000 man-hours trying out more than one hundred flight-deck configurations. Of special interest and affection to pilots was the "panic button" for engine fires. All a pilot had to do was pull a single fire-control lever. That one action automatically feathered the prop, shut off the fuel and oil supply, armed the chemical fire extinguisher and set it off. Emergency action time: one second. On a conventional plane the four separate procedures would take as long as ten seconds—which seem like an eternity in an engine-fire situation.

The Electra's de-icing and anti-icing system works on the same single-motion principle. One push of a button and hot air is pumped from one of the engine's compressor stages. It flows instantly through stainless-steel ducts to the leading edges of the wings and stabilizers. It not only keeps ice from forming, but melts it in seconds. It is so efficient that it is possible to fry an egg on a wing edge being de-iced.

Lockheed extended much of the soundproofing in the cabin to the cockpit. The result was a flight-deck noise level that is about fifty percent quieter than a piston-engine cockpit and almost as quiet as the pure jets.

Even mechanics found they had been considered in the Electra's design. The plane squats relatively close to the ground, which means that many fuselage inspection plates can be opened without the necessity of a stepladder.

The anti-collision rotating light on most planes is on the top of the tail, requiring a crane or portable platform for changing. On the Electra there are two beacons located at the top and bottom of the fuselage. To replace the former, a mechanic needs only to unscrew it from inside the cabin. To change the bottom light, he just stands underneath the fuselage and reaches up.

Lockheed cut the overhaul time for props and engines by twenty hours, simply by using self-locking nuts and self-threaded inserts instead of the usual safety wire and cotter pins. Cabin-interior panels are pretrimmed and snap quickly in and out of place. A soiled or scratched panel can be replaced in a few moments.

The Electra also incorporated the hydraulically operated cabin stairs first introduced on the Convair 240. This was a design decision that appealed to the airlines, because an outside boarding ramp costs more than $3000.

Customer plaudits were not enough for Lockheed. The prototype Electra was sent on a round-the-world flight—the first such test program ever conducted for a commercial transport. It was no pleasure trip either. The test pilots deliberately went looking for rough weather. They slammed into thunderheads without slowing down. They landed on fields with runways about as smooth as a 4000-foot stretch of railroad ties. They flew in temperatues ranging from 40 below to 110 in the shade.

Before the Civil Aeronautics Administration (later to become the Federal Aviation Agency) certificated the plane as safe for carrying passengers, Lockheed subjected the Electra to tests the CAA didn't even require—abrupt pull-ups after deliberate high-speed dives. One such test was unexpected. The crew had a false fire warning and went into an emergency dive at a speed 100 MPH faster than any airline would ever fly the plane. When the fire-warning light suddenly flickered out, they pulled out of the dive—exerting a force on the wings greater than any CAA structural test.

Construction of the prototype began in December, 1955, with two firm orders on the books—thirty-five Electras for American and forty for Eastern. Later, a total of fourteen airlines ordered nearly 180 of the big planes. The first test flight came just two years later, on December 6, 1957, beating the Boeing 707's initial hop by two weeks and leaving the other two U.S. jet-age entries—Douglas and Convair—trailing by many months.

Behind that first flight were four years of research, a conservative fifty million dollars in development costs, and the firm conviction of Lockheed that it had designed, tested, and built the finest airplane in its long and honorable history.

Unfortunately, nowhere in the Electra blueprints—which, laid end to end, would stretch forty miles—nowhere in the reports in 20,000 separate design studies or 7000 pages of mathematical calculations—was there any mention of a scientific phenomenon known as "whirl mode."

THE ELECTRA STORY by Robert Serling, will be available in January 1991 wherever Bantam Books are sold.